The NBA
From Top to Bottom

The NBA From Top to Bottom

A History of the NBA, From the No. 1 Team Through No. 1,153

Kyle Wright

iUniverse, Inc.
New York Lincoln Shanghai

The NBA From Top to Bottom
A History of the NBA, From the No. 1 Team Through No. 1,153

Copyright © 2007 by Kyle Jayson Wright

All rights reserved. No part of this book may be used or reproduced by any means, graphic, electronic, or mechanical, including photocopying, recording, taping or by any information storage retrieval system without the written permission of the publisher except in the case of brief quotations embodied in critical articles and reviews.

iUniverse books may be ordered through booksellers or by contacting:

iUniverse
2021 Pine Lake Road, Suite 100
Lincoln, NE 68512
www.iuniverse.com
1-800-Authors (1-800-288-4677)

Because of the dynamic nature of the Internet, any Web addresses or links contained in this book may have changed since publication and may no longer be valid.

The views expressed in this work are solely those of the author and do not necessarily reflect the views of the publisher, and the publisher hereby disclaims any responsibility for them.

ISBN: 978-0-595-45959-9 (pbk)
ISBN: 978-0-595-69796-0 (cloth)
ISBN: 978-0-595-90259-0 (ebk)

Printed in the United States of America

Contents

Introduction ....*vii*
    Defining dominance: The POST formula

I. The Top of the Class *1*
    The 10 most dominant teams in NBA history
II. The Heartbreakers *39*
    The five most dominant teams not to win an NBA title
III. The Right Place at the Right Time *56*
    The five least dominant teams to win an NBA title
IV. The Bottom of the Barrel *73*
    The 10 least dominant teams in NBA history
V. Team by Team *107*
    The good, the bad, and the interesting from every NBA franchise
VI. The NBA From Top to Bottom *173*

Conclusion *265*
    Discussing dominance: The POST formula's results
Selected bibliography *269*

Introduction

Defining dominance: The POST formula

dominant (dam-a-nant) *adj.*—ruling; prevailing.

A fine definition, but one that applies to so many teams in NBA history.

The Boston Celtics of the 1960s ruled as NBA champions 11 times in 13 years during the Bill Russell era.

The 1995-1996 Chicago Bulls and Michael Jordan prevailed 72 times in 82 games en route to the NBA title.

The Minneapolis Lakers of the 1950s ruled as NBA champions five times in six years during George Mikan's career.

The 1971-1972 Los Angeles Lakers, led by Jerry West and Wilt Chamberlain, prevailed in 33 consecutive games on their way to an NBA championship.

Another Los Angeles Lakers team, led by Magic Johnson and Kareem Abdul-Jabbar, ruled the 1980s with five championships.

How does one designate just one of those teams as the "most dominant" in NBA history? Comparing teams across generations seems an impossible task. Could the Boston Celtics of the 1960s match up with the taller, more athletic players of the 1990s? Did the Chicago Bulls of the 1990s charge through a league watered down by expansion?

Fans have debated such questions since the advent of the 24-second clock.

Fans do seem to agree on one thing: Average is average, regardless of the year.

Most would agree the 1946-1947 Cleveland Rebels, who finished with a 30-30 record during the inaugural season for the league that would evolve into the NBA, achieved just as much as the 2003-2004 Milwaukee Bucks, who also finished with a break-even mark at 41-41.

Few would disagree that the 1951-1952 Philadelphia Warriors, who finished 33-33, "dominated" their opponents just as much as the 1999-2000 Orlando Magic, who finished 41-41.

If one uses such "standard" teams as a baseline, then comparison between all other teams becomes possible.

Let the arguments begin.

The POST formula

Introducing the POST formula: **P**oints **O**ver or under a **S**tandard **T**eam.

The POST formula assigns a rating to a team based on how it would perform against a "standard" team in a given season.

A "standard" team is defined as a team with an equal number of wins and losses, and an equal number of points scored and points allowed.

The No. 100 team in the all-time NBA POST ratings—the 1994-1995 San Antonio Spurs—achieved a POST rating of +5.811. This means San Antonio would have beaten a "standard" team from the 1994-1995 season by 5.811 points.

The No. 1,000 team in the all-time NBA POST ratings—the 2001-2002 Golden State Warriors—achieved a POST rating of -4.876. This means Golden State would have lost to a "standard" team from the 2001-2002 season by 4.876 points.

The author developed the POST formula in the 1990s and refined it during his time as a journalism and applied statistics student at Valparaiso (Ind.) University.

The POST formula has identified 56 percent of the NBA's champions correctly (34 of 61). By comparison, the team with the NBA's best regular season record has gone on to win the title just 48 percent of the time (29 of 61).

The following pages provide the complete POST rankings for every team in NBA history, from No. 1 to No. 1,153.

You'll find detailed analysis of the 10 most dominant teams and least dominant teams of all time, with surprising choices for No. 1 and No. 1,153.

The analyses include reasons people might argue with the selections and the reasons those people are wrong!

You'll meet the five most dominant teams that did not win a title and the five least dominant teams that did.

You'll also learn about the most dominant, least dominant, and other notable teams for all 30 current NBA clubs and the 15 defunct franchises.

Important definitions

Dominance: The 2004-2005 Atlanta Hawks, who finished 13-69, probably possessed more raw talent than the 1946-1947 Washington Capitols, who finished 49-11. Different teams, different eras. The 1946-1947 Capitols (No. 7 all-time) rank far better than the 2004-2005 Hawks (No. 1,139 all-time) because the POST formula does not evaluate raw talent. It ranks teams relative to the "standard" teams of their respective seasons. The 1946-1947 Capitols clearly had a season more "dominant" than that of the 2004-2005 Hawks. The POST formula ranks the teams accordingly.

Expected wins: *The NBA From Top to Bottom* includes occasional comments about how teams with a certain average point differential should win a certain number of games. The expected win totals are determined using a formula based on the Pythagorean theorem. Several sources provide such calculations. *The NBA From Top to Bottom* uses the Pythagorean projections on the basketball-reference.com Web site.

Where's my team?

Rules for inclusion: Only one team per franchise per era qualified for the list of the 10 most dominant teams. Otherwise, the title of this book would be *Michael Jordan's Chicago Bulls and NBA Champions of the Early 1970s: An Appreciation.*

Only NBA champions qualified for the list of the 10 most dominant teams, for obvious reasons.

Only teams that *never* won NBA titles with a given nucleus qualified for the list of the five most dominant teams not to win championships. The 1971-1972 Milwaukee Bucks technically rank as the most dominant team not to win a championship. They don't qualify for the list since they did claim the 1970-1971 title with a virtually identical roster.

NBA only: The NBA recognizes the 1946-1947 BAA season as its inaugural campaign. The NBA recognizes the 1946-1947 BAA champion Philadelphia Warriors as its first title winner. For consistency's sake, *The NBA From Top to Bottom* does the same.

The author acknowledges that NBL teams from 1946-1948 almost certainly were superior to BAA teams. The author also acknowledges that ABA teams, particularly by the mid-1970s, almost certainly played on the same level as NBA teams.

One cannot, however, positively establish a way to evaluate NBL and ABA teams relative to "standard" NBA teams of the same seasons. Therefore, the NBL and ABA teams are not included in *The NBA From Top to Bottom*.

I. The Top of the Class

The 10 most dominant teams in NBA history

1. The 1970-1971 Milwaukee Bucks
Record: 66-16
Overall ranking: 1st, 11.817 points above average.
Other dominant Milwaukee Buck teams of the era: 1971-1972 (4th overall, 10.646 points above average); 1972-1973 (27th overall, 7.762 points above average); 1973-1974 (32nd overall, 7.555 points above average).

The key players

Kareem Abdul-Jabbar, 7-foot-2 center—Abdul-Jabbar was known as Lew Alcindor during the 1970-1971 season. He was one of the greatest centers in basketball history, by any name. He still holds the NBA record for career points with 38,387. The 1970-1971 season was his second in the NBA.

Oscar Robertson, 6-foot-5 point guard—Robertson came to the Bucks from the Cincinnati Royals in a trade on April 21, 1970. Robertson averaged a triple-double for the season in 1961-1962. He would retire as the NBA's leader in career assists. He still ranked as one of the league's top point guards in 1970-1971.

Why they're ranked here

The combination of Abdul-Jabbar and Robertson clicked immediately. The Bucks powered to a league-best 66-16 record and won the Midwest Division by 17 games.

Abdul-Jabbar led the league in scoring with 31.7 points per game. He also won the first of his six Most Valuable Player honors.

Robertson produced 19.4 points and 8.3 assists per outing.

Milwaukee's season included winning streaks of 17 and 20 games. The latter set an NBA record at the time. The Bucks' season totals for field goal percentage, total field goals, and total assists also established league records at the time.

Milwaukee ran roughshod over a competitive Western Conference that included the Los Angeles Lakers and Chicago Bulls, two other early-1970s teams that would earn impressive POST ratings. All four teams in Milwaukee's Midwest Division (the Bucks, Bulls, Phoenix Suns, and Detroit Pistons) won at least 55 percent of their games during the 1970-1971 season.

The Bucks posted a regular season average point differential of +12.2 points per game, a full seven points better than any other team in the league and the third-best margin ever.

Milwaukee cemented its place in history with an impressive playoff run.

The Bucks beat the San Francisco Warriors and Los Angeles Lakers by 4-1 series scores to win the Western Conference. Milwaukee capped its season with a four-game sweep against the Baltimore Bullets in the NBA Finals. The Bucks won their playoff games by an average of 14.5 points, the best margin in league history. Milwaukee's postseason wins all came by at least eight points.

Why a bunch of people will argue and why they're wrong

Argument: "The Milwaukee Bucks?!?"

Counter argument: For whatever reason, most of the dominant teams in NBA history played in "big markets."

The Chicago Bulls. The Los Angeles Lakers. The Boston Celtics. The Philadelphia 76ers. Most subjective listings of the NBA's greatest teams focus on those franchises.

It seems safe to assume the 1970-71 Milwaukee Bucks, with credentials every bit as impressive as the easily recognizable great teams in league history, get overshadowed because of where they played their home games.

They shouldn't. Put a 66-16 NBA champion with a Hall of Fame center and a Hall of Fame point guard in New York and that team would enjoy instant immortality. The 1970-1971 Bucks merit the same recognition.

Argument: "The Bucks should have a worse ranking because lots of teams won more than 66 games."

Counter argument: Milwaukee's 66-win season barely ranks in the top ten on the all-time list for single-season victories. The Bucks get a caveat here. Milwaukee rested its top players after clinching home court advantage for the playoffs. The Bucks went 1-5 down the stretch. They almost certainly could have won more of those games had they desired.

Argument: "If this team was so good, why didn't it win another title with Kareem Abdul-Jabbar and Oscar Robertson in the lineup?"

Counter argument: One could ask the same question about the 1971-1972 Los Angeles Lakers with Wilt Chamberlain and Jerry West. Yet few people hesitate to include that one-time champion on a short list of the league's best teams.

The 1971-1972 Lakers seem to get a free pass on such criticism because of the franchise's overall history of greatness. The 1970-1971 Milwaukee Bucks apparently do not enjoy the same luxury.

Argument: "Kareem Abdul-Jabbar had yet to enter the prime years of his career and Oscar Robertson had passed his prime, so both players surely led more-dominant teams."

Counter argument: Several teams on this top 10 list feature Hall of Fame players in the early years of their careers and/or past their primes. Those players just happened to play on dominant teams during some of their less-dominant individual seasons.

Abdul-Jabbar and Robertson did not produce their best individual statistics during the 1970-1971 season. Their efforts did result in the most dominant team of both players' careers.

Look at another team featuring Kareem Abdul-Jabbar as an example. Magic Johnson and Abdul-Jabbar never played together during the prime years of their respective careers. Yet few people would leave the Los Angeles Lakers of the 1980s off of a list of the NBA's most dominant teams.

Another example: Michael Jordan enjoyed perhaps his best individual season during the 1989-1990 campaign, when he averaged 32.5 points, 8.0 rebounds, and 8.0 assists. Yet no sane basketball fan would point to the 1989-1990 Chicago Bulls as the most dominant Chicago team of the Jordan era.

Argument: "No one can name one person on this team besides Kareem Abdul-Jabbar and Oscar Robertson, so how can it be the best ever?"

Counter argument: Here are five more names: Jon McGlocklin, Bob Boozer, Greg Smith, Bob Dandridge, and Lucius Allen.

McGlocklin, a perimeter shooter, somehow finished fourth in the league in field goal percentage during the 1970-1971 season.

Dandridge averaged 18.4 points and 8.0 rebounds in 1970-1971. He eventually would play in four All-Star games.

Smith rounded out the starting lineup. He contributed 11.7 points and 7.2 rebounds per game.

Milwaukee acquired Boozer and Allen via a preseason trade. Boozer, a center, had played in an All-Star game. Allen, a guard and Abdul-Jabbar's teammate at UCLA, would average 19.1 points per game in 1974-1975. They gave the Bucks support in reserve roles during the 1970-1971 season.

A bunch of Hall of Famers? No. A bunch of stiffs? Hardly. Certainly comparable to, say, Luc Longley and Ron Harper of the 1995-1996 Chicago Bulls. Certainly good enough to form the supporting cast on the most dominant team ever.

Postscript

Milwaukee followed up its 1970-1971 championship season with a 63-19 mark in 1971-1972. Hardly shabby, but lost in the wake of the Los Angeles

Lakers' record-setting 69-13 season. The Bucks fell against the Lakers in six games in the Western Conference finals. Abdul-Jabbar averaged a career-best 34.8 points per game and repeated as the NBA's Most Valuable Player.

Milwaukee went 60-22 during the 1972-1973 campaign and became the first NBA team to post three consecutive 60-win seasons. The milestone year ended with a surprising six-game loss against the Golden State Warriors in the first round of the playoffs.

The Bucks finally returned to the NBA Finals in 1974. Milwaukee engaged in a back-and-forth series against the Boston Celtics. The teams traded wins six consecutive times before Boston prevailed 102-87 in Game 7.

The 1974 Finals loss signaled the end of the Robertson-Abdul-Jabbar era in Milwaukee.

Robertson showed signs of age during the 1973-1974 campaign. He would retire after the season.

Abdul-Jabbar long had expressed a desire to complete his career somewhere other than Milwaukee. Abdul-Jabbar turned that desire into a trade demand after a frustrating 1974-1975 season. Abdul-Jabbar missed the first 16 games of the year with a hand injury sustained when he slapped a backboard during an exhibition game. Milwaukee started slowly without Abdul-Jabbar and missed the playoffs with a 38-44 record.

The Bucks accommodated their star center's wishes following the 1974-1975 season. Milwaukee closed the most dominant chapter in its history by trading Abdul-Jabbar to the Los Angeles Lakers.

1970-1971 Milwaukee Bucks final statistics

Name	G	PPG	FG%	FT%	RPG	APG
Kareem Abdul-Jabbar	82	31.7	.577	.690	16.0	3.3
Oscar Robertson	81	19.4	.496	.850	5.7	8.2
Bob Dandridge	79	18.4	.509	.702	8.0	3.5
Jon McGlocklin	82	15.8	.535	.862	2.7	3.7
Greg Smith	82	11.7	.512	.662	7.2	2.8
Bob Boozer	80	9.1	.450	.818	5.4	1.6
Lucius Allen	61	7.1	.447	.700	2.5	2.6
Mccoy McLemore	28	4.7	.368	.829	3.8	1.1
Gary Freeman	41	3.7	.508	.737	2.4	0.8
Marv Winkler	3	2.7	.300	1.000	1.3	0.7
Dick Cunningham	76	2.6	.415	.661	3.4	0.6
Bob Greacen	2	2.5	.083	.429	3.0	6.5
Jeff Webb	29	2.2	.346	.733	0.8	0.7

Bill Zopf	53	2.2	.363	.556	0.9	1.4
Team	82	118.4	.509	.742	53.0	27.4
Opponents	82	106.2	.424	.744	48.8	23.5

2. The 1995-1996 Chicago Bulls

Record: 72-10

Overall ranking: 2nd, 11.767 points above average.

Other dominant Chicago Bull teams of the era: 1996-1997 (5th overall, 10.570 points above average); 1991-1992 (6th overall, 10.023 points above average); 1990-1991 (10th overall, 8.572 points above average); 1997-1998 (46th overall, 7.105 points above average); 1992-1993 (86th overall, 6.131 points above average).

The key players

Michael Jordan, 6-foot-6 shooting guard—Jordan would retire for good in 2003 as the NBA's career leader in points per game. Jordan had retired in 1993 after leading Chicago to three consecutive NBA titles. He returned late in the 1994-1995 season. The 1995-1996 season marked the first full season in his comeback.

Scottie Pippen, 6-foot-7 small forward—The perfect complement to Jordan. Pippen initiated much of the Bulls' offense, scored enough to keep defenses from swarming around Jordan, and terrorized opponents on defense.

Dennis Rodman, 6-8 power forward—Chicago traded for "The Worm" during the summer of 1995. The Bulls frequently battled with Rodman when the latter played for the Detroit Pistons, but Chicago needed a physical presence at power forward after Horace Grant left the franchise in 1994. Rodman, who won seven consecutive rebounding titles from 1992 to 1998, could provide that presence.

Why they're ranked here

Michael Jordan played the end of the 1994-1995 season wearing the No. 45 jersey. The murder of Jordan's father, James, in the summer of 1993, partly prompted Jordan's first retirement. When Jordan returned, he said his father had seen the last game for No. 23 and he wanted to keep it that way.

Jordan started the 1995-1996 season back in his old No. 23 jersey. He also brought his old game back to NBA arenas. He averaged 30.4 points to reclaim the league scoring crown and the Most Valuable Player award.

Pippen had established himself as a legitimate All-Star player during Jordan's absence. He continued to play at a high level during the 1995-1996 season. He contributed 19.4 points and led the team in assists.

Rodman showed up in Chicago with the Bulls' logo dyed in his hair. He proceeded to lead the league in rebounds (14.9 per game), tattoos, and hair designs.

The Bulls stampeded through the 1995-1996 season. Chicago showed it meant business with a 5-0 start. The Bulls won 18 consecutive games midway through the season, including a perfect month of January.

Chicago finished the regular season 39-2 at home. The squad set a league record with 33 road victories.

The Bulls beat Milwaukee 86-80 on April 16, 1996, to become the first team in NBA history to win 70 games. Chicago completed the season with a 72-10 mark, still the NBA record for wins in a season. The Bulls posted an average margin of victory of +12.2 points per game, the second-best margin ever.

Chicago lost just one game during its run through the Eastern Conference playoffs. The one defeat came in overtime against the New York Knicks.

The Bulls returned to the NBA Finals with a sweep of the Orlando Magic in the Eastern Conference finals. Orlando eliminated Chicago from the playoffs in 1995, but the Bulls gained revenge one year later. Chicago rallied from an 18-point deficit to win Game 2, the series' pivotal contest.

The Bulls won the first three games of the NBA Finals against the Seattle Supersonics. Chicago clinched the championship with an 87-75 home victory in Game 6 on Father's Day.

Jordan collapsed in an emotionally spent heap in the Bulls' locker room after the game. Jordan spent the 1995-1996 campaign overwhelming the NBA. The memorable season and the Father's Day memories of James Jordan combined to overwhelm him.

Why a bunch of people will argue and why they're wrong

Argument: "The Bulls should rank No. 1 because no other team won 72 games."

Counter argument: Michael Jordan made a powerful argument when he summed up the 1995-1996 Chicago Bulls' place in history thusly: "Anyone else win 72 games?"

The 1970-1971 Milwaukee Bucks didn't win 72 games. They did post a virtually identical average point differential and they did it against tougher competition.

Milwaukee played the majority of its games in a Western Conference that boasted an aggregate winning percentage of .550. Chicago played the majority of its games in an Eastern Conference with an aggregate winning percentage of just .503.

Put simply: On a representative night, the 1995-1996 Chicago Bulls would win by 12.2 points against a team that would finish with a 41-41 record. On a representative night, the 1970-1971 Milwaukee Bucks would win by 12.2 points against a team that would finish with a 45-37 record.

The strength of schedule factor allows the Bucks' 66 wins to trump the Bulls' 72 victories.

Argument: "The Bulls should rank No. 1 because of the presence of Michael Jordan."

Counter argument: This Chicago team might have boasted the most dominant player of all time, but that doesn't mean the Bulls had the most dominant team.

Furthermore, if one uses the "presence of Michael Jordan" argument, shouldn't the Chicago team with the most dominant version of Jordan jump to the top of the list?

Go back to Jordan's brilliant 1989-1990 season. Jordan produced 32.5 points per game, 8.0 rebounds, and 8.0 assists. Yet one won't hear many people clamoring to include the 1989-1990 Bulls on the list of the all-time great teams.

Argument: "The Bulls should have a worse ranking because expansion diluted their competition."

Counter argument: The two-team expansion to Toronto and Vancouver for the 1995-1996 probably did dilute Chicago's competition to some degree.

Yet a look through dominant teams' POST rankings during the NBA's expansion seasons shows mixed effects. A four-team expansion in the late 1980s coincided with a *decline* in dominance by the top teams. A gradual expansion in the late 1960s had a negligible effect on the top teams' rankings.

The 1995-1996 Bulls played six games against Toronto and Vancouver. They went 5-1 in those games. Had the NBA not expanded for the 1995-1996 season, Chicago would have played six additional games against a variety of Eastern Conference teams, with three of those games at home. The Bulls would have needed a 3-3 record in those games to achieve a 70-win season.

One would think these Bulls could have handled that challenge.

Argument: "The 1995-1996 Bulls should have a worse ranking because they weren't even the best team of the Chicago dynasty."

Counter argument: Many educated observers say the 1991-1992 Chicago Bulls would have beaten the 1995-1996 version in a head-to-head meeting.

The 1991-1992 team better? Perhaps. More dominant? Absolutely not.

The 1995-1996 Chicago Bulls produced more victories and a more impressive point differential against better competition. The 1995-1996 Bulls won 72 games playing in an Eastern Conference with a 60-win team (the Orlando Magic) and seven teams with 46 victories or more.

The 1991-1992 Chicago Bulls won "just" 67 games playing in an Eastern Conference where just five teams finished with winning records.

Furthermore, the 1991-1992 Bulls had some trouble getting through the playoffs. The New York Knicks pushed Chicago to seven games during the conference semifinals. The Cleveland Cavaliers pushed the Bulls to six tough games during the Eastern Conference finals. The Portland Trail Blazers came within a few minutes of forcing a Game 7 during the NBA Finals, but Pippen and a brigade of Chicago reserves led a memorable comeback in the decisive Game 6.

The 1995-1996 Chicago team had no such difficulties.

Postscript

The Chicago Bulls went on to a "repeat three-peat." Chicago edged the Utah Jazz in six-game NBA Finals in both 1997 and 1998. The titles gave the franchise a trophy haul of six championships in eight years.

The Bulls' run ended suddenly.

Chicago owner Jerry Reinsdorf and general manager Jerry Krause long had expressed a desire to begin building the foundation for a post-Jordan championship team.

The Jerrys got their chance after the 1997-1998 season.

The contracts of Jordan, Pippen, Rodman, and coach Phil Jackson all expired after the 1998 playoffs.

Jackson either did not seek or did not receive a contract extension. He proclaimed the end of the Bulls' dynasty during the team's public championship celebration in mid-June. He left Chicago for good a few days later, riding off into the sunset on his motorcycle.

All of the Bulls' other key dominoes tumbled in Jackson's wake.

Jordan elected to "retire." Chicago sent Pippen to the Houston Rockets in one of the NBA's first sign-and-trade deals. The Bulls did not ask Rodman to return.

Chicago then embarked on a lengthy rebuilding process. The Bulls would not return to the postseason until 2005.

1995-1996 Chicago Bulls final statistics

Name	G	PPG	FG%	FT%	RPG	APG
Michael Jordan	82	30.4	.495	.834	6.6	4.3
Scottie Pippen	77	19.4	.463	.679	6.4	5.9
Toni Kukoc	81	13.1	.490	.772	4.0	3.5
Luc Longley	62	9.1	.482	.777	5.1	1.9
Steve Kerr	82	8.4	.506	.929	1.3	2.3
Ron Harper	80	7.4	.467	.705	2.7	2.6
Dennis Rodman	64	5.5	.480	.528	14.9	2.5
Bill Wennington	71	5.3	.493	.860	2.5	0.6
Jack Haley	1	5.0	.333	.500	2.0	0.0
Jud Buechler	74	3.8	.463	.636	1.5	0.8

Dickey Simpkins	60	3.6	.481	.629	2.6	0.6
James Edwards	28	3.5	.373	.615	1.4	0.4
Jason Caffey	57	3.2	.438	.588	1.9	0.4
Randy Brown	68	2.7	.406	.609	1.0	1.1
John Salley	17	2.1	.343	.600	2.5	0.9
Team	82	105.2	.478	.746	44.6	24.8
Opponents	82	92.9	.448	.717	38.0	19.4

3. The 1971-1972 Los Angeles Lakers
Record: 69-13
Overall ranking: 3rd, 11.581 points above average
Other dominant Los Angeles Laker teams of the era: 1972-1973 (18th overall, 8.110 points above average)

The key players

Jerry West, 6-3 point guard—"Mr. Clutch" earned his reputation with years of sharp shooting, particularly in the playoffs. West turned 33 before the start of the 1971-1972 season, but still could score with the best.

Wilt Chamberlain, 7-1 center—Chamberlain would retire after the 1973 playoffs as the NBA's leader in career points, scoring average, and rebounds. He served as a defensive stopper as a 35-year-old on the 1971-1972 Lakers. He still could score when called upon.

Why they're ranked here

Los Angeles' 1971-1972 season started on a gloomy note. Elgin Baylor, a Laker staple since 1958, retired nine games into the season after years of struggles with knee injuries. Baylor retired one spot behind Chamberlain on the league's career scoring average list.

Los Angeles defeated Baltimore on November 5, the same day Baylor announced his retirement. The Lakers would not lose again until January 9. Los Angeles reeled off 33 consecutive wins in between, a record for North American professional sports.

The Lakers won 10 of their last 11 regular season games to finish with a 69-13 ledger. Los Angeles established a then-NBA record for victories in a single season, topping the 1966-1967 Philadelphia 76ers by one win. The Lakers set then-league records for single-season wins at home (38) and on the road (31). Los Angeles set another then-record by scoring at least 100 points in 81 of its 82 games.

The Lakers still hold league records for consecutive wins (33) and average point differential (+12.3 points per game).

West and Chamberlain remained the Lakers' biggest names. Both delivered big seasons. West averaged 25.8 points per game and led the league with 9.7 assists per outing. Chamberlain led the NBA in rebounds (19.2 per game) and field goal percentage (.649), and also scored 14.8 points per game.

The Los Angeles supporting actors turned in Oscar-worthy performances around the two Laker stars.

Sweet-shooting guard Gail Goodrich led Los Angeles in scoring at 25.9 points per game. Jim McMillian contributed 18.8 points from a forward position. Harold "Happy" Hairston, the other forward, averaged exactly 13.1 points and 13.1 rebounds. Chamberlain and Hairston became the first teammates to total 1,000 rebounds during the same season.

The Lakers achieved their records in a Western Conference that included two other dominant teams (the Chicago Bulls and the Milwaukee Bucks). Los Angeles swept Chicago in the opening round of the playoffs. The Lakers then dethroned defending champion Milwaukee in the Western Conference finals. The Bucks, playing without injured Oscar Robertson, outscored Los Angeles over the course of the series. Yet the Lakers found a way to prevail.

The Lakers wrapped up the franchise's first title since its 1960 move to Los Angeles with a 4-1 series victory against the New York Knicks in the NBA Finals. The Knicks defeated the Lakers in the Finals in 1970 and caused some worries in Tinseltown when they won Game 1 in 1972. Los Angeles regrouped quickly. The Lakers swept through the next four games to put their footprints in the NBA version of the Walk of Fame.

Why a bunch of people will argue and why they're wrong

Argument: "The Lakers should have a better ranking because no other team has matched their 33-game winning streak."

Counter argument: The streak stands as perhaps the most impressive accomplishment in NBA history, but not sole grounds for declaring a team the most dominant of all time.

Look at other sports. The 1916 New York Giants set the major league baseball record for consecutive wins with 26, but finished third in the National League. The 1972 Miami Dolphins set the National Football League standard with a 17-0 season, but don't get many votes as the best in league history.

In the final analysis, Los Angeles slips to third place on this list because the Laker schedule included six division games against an 18-win Portland Trail Blazers squad.

Argument: "The Lakers should have a worse ranking because their most famous players had passed their primes."

Counter argument: Jerry West and Wilt Chamberlain indeed had passed their best individual years, but they had underrated teammates surrounding them. West had perhaps the best supporting cast he ever enjoyed

Take West and Chamberlain out of the lineup. The 1971-1972 Lakers still had a 25-point scorer (Gail Goodrich), a 19-point scorer (Jim McMillian), and a dominant rebounder (Happy Hairston).

The discussion here centers on dominant teams, not dominant individuals. West and Chamberlain never played on a team that dominated opponents like the 1971-1972 Lakers. Their teammates haven't received nearly as much credit as they deserve.

Postscript

The Los Angeles Lakers returned to the NBA Finals in 1973. The Lakers appeared poised to defend their title when they defeated the New York Knicks in Game 1.

The Knicks' defense clamped down the rest of the way. New York limited Los Angeles to less than 100 points in four consecutive games. The Knicks won all four games to complete a 4-1 series triumph.

Chamberlain surprisingly ended his NBA career after the series. He signed a contract to coach and play for the San Diego Conquistadors of the American Basketball Association. Courts ruled Chamberlain could not play for the Conquistadors, but Chamberlain nonetheless left the Lakers to coach the San Diego squad. He would not return to the NBA.

West played one more NBA campaign. He retired after averaging 20.3 points in 30 games during the 1973-1974 season.

The Lakers won just 30 games during the 1974-1975 season. They began building a new dynasty when they acquired center Kareem Abdul-Jabbar from the Milwaukee Bucks prior to the 1975-1976 season.

1971-1972 Los Angeles Lakers final statistics

Name	G	PPG	FG%	FT%	RPG	APG
Gail Goodrich	82	25.9	.487	.850	3.6	4.5
Jerry West	77	25.8	.477	.814	4.2	9.7
Jim McMillian	80	18.8	.482	.791	6.5	2.6
Wilt Chamberlain	82	14.8	.649	.422	19.2	4.0
Happy Hairston	80	13.1	.461	.779	13.1	2.4
Elgin Baylor	9	11.8	.433	.815	6.3	2.0
Flynn Robinson	64	9.9	.490	.860	1.8	2.2
Pat Riley	67	6.7	.447	.743	1.9	1.1

Keith Erickson	15	5.7	.482	.857	2.6	2.3
John Trapp	58	5.7	.443	.699	3.1	0.7
Leroy Ellis	74	4.6	.460	.695	4.2	0.6
Jim Cleamons	38	2.6	.350	.778	1.0	0.9
Team	82	121.0	.490	.734	56.4	27.2
Opponents	82	108.7	.432	.768	52.3	24.3

4. The 1985-1986 Boston Celtics

Record: 67-15

Overall ranking: 8th, 8.842 points above average

Other dominant Boston Celtic teams of the era: 1979-1980 (42nd overall, 7.284 points above average); 1986-1987 (73rd overall, 6.398 points above average); 1983-1984 (75th overall, 6.306 points above average); 1984-1985 (77th overall, 6.297 points above average); 1981-1982 (83rd overall, 6.218 points above average); 1987-1988 (96th overall, 5.886 points above average).

The key players

Larry Bird, 6-foot-9 small forward—"Larry Legend" led Boston to three NBA titles during the 1980s. He led his Celtic teams in scoring. His court sense helped him produce more than his share of rebounds and assists. Bird and the other starters in the Boston frontcourt were in the primes of their careers during the 1985-1986 season.

Kevin McHale, 6-foot-10 power forward—The "other" forward in Boston's lineup was a Hall of Famer in his own right. McHale provided the Celtics with inside muscle and defense.

Robert Parish, 7-foot-1 center—The center in perhaps the best frontcourt ever. Parish's numbers mirrored McHale's. "The Chief" also anchored the Celtics' defense.

Dennis Johnson, 6-foot-4 point guard—Yet another All-Star in the Boston lineup. Johnson was second on the team in assists behind Bird. He also was named to the NBA's All-Defense team.

Bill Walton, 7-0 center—The big redhead led Portland to an NBA title in 1977, but foot injuries derailed his career. Walton came to Boston via trade prior to the 1985-1986 season. Walton backed up Parish and gave the Celtics yet another Hall of Famer in the frontcourt.

Why they're ranked here

Larry Bird's Boston Celtics and Magic Johnson's Los Angeles Lakers pushed each other and the game of basketball to great heights in the 1980s.

Bird's Celtics climbed the highest the fastest. Boston responded to a loss against Los Angeles in the 1985 NBA Finals—the first time the Lakers defeated the Celtics in the championship series—with one of the greatest seasons ever.

Basketball fans remember the 1985-1986 Celtics for this mark: 40-1. Boston suffered just one loss in 41 home games, the best home record in NBA history. The lone home defeat came December 6, 1985, a 121-103 setback against the Portland Trail Blazers.

Boston certainly could win on the road, where it went 27-14. The Celtics posted an average point differential of +9.4 points per game, the best margin in the franchise's storied history.

Bird shrugged off back pains during the early part of the season and finished among the league leaders in scoring (25.8 points per game), rebounding (9.8 per game), and steals (2.02 per game). He won his third consecutive Most Valuable Player award.

McHale (21.3 points per game, 8.1 rebounds per game), Parish (16.1 points per game, 9.5 rebounds per game), and Johnson (15.6 points per game, 5.8 assists per game) all enjoyed strong seasons. Walton managed to play 80 games despite his aching feet. He contributed 7.6 points and 6.8 rebounds per game and won the NBA's Sixth Man award.

Boston won 15 of its 18 playoffs games en route to its 16th NBA title.

The Celtics swept the Chicago Bulls in the first round of the postseason, surviving a 63-point explosion from Michael Jordan in the second game of the series.

Boston beat Atlanta 4-1 in Round 2. The Celtics then swept a very good Milwaukee Bucks team in the Eastern Conference finals.

The Houston Rockets provided the surprise opposition in the NBA Finals. The Rockets had stunned the defending champion Los Angeles Lakers in the Western Conference finals.

Houston put up a tough fight—figuratively *and* literally at some points—but the Celtics controlled the series from the outset. Boston put the finishing touches on the franchise's most dominant season with a 4-2 NBA Finals triumph.

Why a bunch of people will argue and why they're wrong

Argument: "The 1985-1986 Celtics should have a better ranking because they had more great players in the prime years of their careers."

Counter argument: Who knows? The 1985-1986 Boston Celtics might have waxed the parquet floor with any of the three teams ranked ahead of them. Yet they did not dominate their contemporaries to the same degree. Boston's average point differential lags almost three points behind the average point differential of the teams in the top three. The Celtics won far fewer games than the 1995-1996

Chicago Bulls and the 1971-1972 Los Angeles Lakers. Boston's strength of schedule lags far behind that of the 1970-1971 Milwaukee Bucks.

Argument: "The Celtics should have a better ranking because expansion watered down the competition for teams like the 1995-1996 Bulls."

Counter argument: First, one must explain the following logic:

The NBA's gradual growth from nine teams to 23 between 1966 and 1980 did not water down the competition for the great teams of the 1980s. Yet the addition of six more teams between 1988 and 1996—a slower rater of expansion—somehow made the league dramatically weaker in the 1990s?

If anything, the numbers indicate the 1985-1986 Boston Celtics benefited from expansion more than the 1995-1996 Chicago Bulls.

Argument: "The Celtics should have a worse ranking because they didn't have the best team of the 1980s."

Counter argument: Many basketball observers regard the Los Angeles Lakers as the "Team of the '80s." Los Angeles won five championships during the decade. Boston won three.

The Lakers did dominate for a longer period. Yet by most measures, the 1985-1986 Celtics enjoyed the most dominant season of the decade. Boston's 1985-1986 squad posted the best average point differential of any team in the 1980s. The Celtics did so against a schedule far tougher than the typical Los Angeles schedule of the 1980s.

Postscript

This proud Boston Celtics team endured a long, painful decline.

Boston returned to the NBA Finals in 1987, but lost in six games against the Los Angeles Lakers.

The Celtics made the Eastern Conference finals in 1988, but lost in six games against the up-and-coming Detroit Pistons.

Bird played just six games during the 1988-1989 season because of a foot injury. Boston snuck into the playoffs with a 42-40 record, but the eventual champion Pistons eliminated the Celtics in the first round.

Bird returned from his injury and led Boston to three more 50-win seasons, but the Celtics of the Bird era never again threatened to win a championship.

Bird retired after the 1992 Olympics. McHale played one more season before he called it quits. Parish stayed with the Celtics through the 1993-1994 season before leaving to join the Charlotte Hornets.

The tragic deaths of promising Boston prospects like Len Bias and Reggie Lewis left the Celtics bereft of up-and-coming talent to replace its legendary frontcourt players. Bias, the No. 2 overall pick in the 1986 draft, died of cocaine poisoning a few days after the draft. Lewis, the Celtics' leading scorer during the 1992-1993 season, died of a heart ailment during the summer of 1993.

Boston regrouped briefly and made the playoffs as a No. 8 seed during the 1994-1995 season. The Celtics then missed the next six postseasons.

1985-1986 Boston Celtics final statistics

Name	G	PPG	FG%	FT%	RPG	APG
Larry Bird	82	25.8	.496	.896	9.8	6.8
Kevin McHale	68	21.3	.574	.776	8.1	2.7
Robert Parish	81	16.1	.549	.731	9.5	1.8
Dennis Johnson	78	15.6	.455	.818	3.4	5.8
Danny Ainge	80	10.7	.504	.904	2.9	5.1
Scott Wedman	79	8.0	.473	.662	2.4	1.1
Bill Walton	80	7.6	.562	.713	6.8	2.1
Jerry Sichting	82	6.5	.57	.924	1.3	2.3
David Thirdkill	49	3.3	.491	.625	1.4	0.3
Sam Vincent	57	3.2	.364	.929	0.8	1.2
Sly Williams	6	2.8	.238	.583	2.5	0.3
Rick Carlisle	77	2.6	.487	.652	1.0	1.4
Greg Kite	64	1.3	.374	.385	2.0	0.3
Team	82	114.1	.508	.794	46.4	29.1
Opponents	82	104.7	.461	.748	41.5	23.5

5. The 1986-1987 Los Angeles Lakers
Record: 65-17
Overall ranking: 13th, 8.409 points above average
Other dominant Los Angeles Laker teams of the era: 1985-1986 (56th overall, 6.940 points above average); 1984-1985 (64th overall, 6.558 points above average); 1988-1989 (67th overall, 6.507 points above average).

The key players

Earvin "Magic" Johnson, 6-foot-9 point guard—The catalyst for Los Angeles' dominant teams of the 1980s. Johnson entered the league in 1979 as the first player of his height to play the point guard position. He led the league in assists throughout the decade. He boosted his scoring when his team needed points.

Kareem Abdul-Jabbar, 7-foot-2 center—Abdul-Jabbar turned 40 just before the 1987 playoffs, but the old Kareem still produced like the Kareem of old. He still made over half of his shots, relying on his signature skyhook.

James Worthy, 6-foot-9 power forward—Most highlight reels from the Lakers' "Showtime" era have multiple clips of Worthy taking a pass from Johnson on the fast break and going in for a slam dunk. "Big Game James" also elevated his performances in the postseason.

Why they're ranked here

The Los Angeles Lakers' "Showtime" team put on its finest performance during the 1986-1987 season.

As noted earlier, Los Angeles and Boston took turns pushing each other to greater heights throughout the 1980s. The Lakers reached their peak in 1986-1987.

This Los Angeles team had four overall No. 1 draft picks on its roster: Magic Johnson, Kareem Abdul-Jabbar, James Worthy and reserve center Mychal Thompson.

Johnson directed the Los Angeles offense starting with his rookie year in 1980. Johnson also shouldered the majority of the Lakers' scoring load in 1986-1987. Johnson averaged a career best 23.9 points per game. He also led the league in assists with 12.2 per game. He earned his first Most Valuable Player award.

Abdul-Jabbar accepted a reduced role in the Los Angeles offense. He still made 56.4 percent of his shots and averaged 17.5 points per game.

Worthy ran the floor for 19.7 points and 5.0 rebounds per game. Shooting guard Byron Scott made 43.6 percent of his three-point attempts and averaged 17.0 points per game. Michael Cooper rounded out the starting lineup. He averaged 10.5 points and also won the league's Defensive Player of the Year award.

Los Angeles completed the regular season with a 65-17 record, now the third-best mark in franchise history. The Lakers posted an average point differential of +9.3 points per game, the second-best mark in franchise history.

Los Angeles won its sixth Western Conference title in eight years, losing just one game in its first three postseason three series.

The Lakers got a matchup against the defending champion Boston Celtics in the NBA Finals.

Los Angeles ran away with the first two games on its home floor. The Lakers took command of the series when Johnson scored in the lane in the final seconds of Game 4 to lift Los Angeles to a 107-106 victory. Johnson's "junior skyhook"—named in honor of Abdul-Jabbar's signature move—gave Los Angeles a 3-1 series lead. The Lakers clinched the championship five days later in Los Angeles.

Why a bunch of people will argue and why they're wrong

Argument: "The 1986-1987 Lakers should have a better ranking because they eventually won five championships and dominated the 1980s."

Counter argument: Los Angeles dominated the Western Conference throughout the 1980s. Yet the Lakers didn't necessarily dominate the NBA. The Lakers achieved the league's most dominant POST rating only twice during the 1980s (in 1987 and 1985).

Los Angeles benefited from playing in the less-than-dominant Western Conference. Eastern Conference teams like Boston, Milwaukee and Philadelphia all fielded championship-caliber teams throughout the 1980s. Detroit eventually surpassed them all late in the decade. Those four teams all had to knock heads against each other just to reach the NBA Finals. Fifteen Eastern Conference teams from the 1980s cracked the top 100 in the all-time POST rankings.

Los Angeles faced no such obstacles in the Western Conference.

The second-most dominant Western Conference team during the Lakers' "Showtime" era? The 1986-1987 Dallas Mavericks, who come in 109th on the all-time list and couldn't even win a playoff series.

Put Los Angeles in the Eastern Conference during the 1980s and the distribution of NBA titles might have changed greatly.

Argument: "The 1986-1987 Lakers should have a worse ranking because other teams achieved greater single-season success."

Counter argument: Basketball fans easily identify certain numbers with teams like the 1966-1967 Philadelphia 76ers and the Boston Celtics squads of the 1960s. The 76ers had a 68-13 record. The Celtics won 11 titles in 13 years.

The less-obvious numbers favor the 1986-1987 Los Angeles Lakers.

This Los Angeles team produced an average point differential just as impressive as the great Philadelphia and Boston teams of the 1960s. The Lakers played in the relatively weak Western Conference, but still faced statistically tougher competition than those Philadelphia and Boston teams. The 1986-1987 Dallas Mavericks mentioned above to demonstrate the weakness of the Western Conference during the 1980s still rank ahead of all non-Celtic teams from the early 1960s.

Postscript

Los Angeles Lakers coach Pat Riley "guaranteed" a repeat title during the locker room celebration immediately following the 1986-1987 championship.

The Lakers fulfilled their coach's pledge. They won three consecutive seven-game playoff series to claim the 1987-1988 title. Los Angeles rallied from a 3-2 deficit to defeat the Detroit Pistons in the 1988 NBA Finals.

The Lakers returned to the NBA Finals in 1989 seeking a "three-peat" in Abdul-Jabbar's final season, but Los Angeles' title hopes ended when Magic Johnson injured his hamstring during Game 2 against Detroit. Johnson would miss the rest of the Finals. The Pistons won the series in a sweep.

Johnson led the Lakers to the NBA's best record during the 1989-1990 season, but Los Angeles' season came to a surprising end in a Western Conference semifinal loss against the Phoenix Suns. Riley resigned after the postseason.

Johnson willed the Lakers to an NBA Finals appearance in 1991, but Los Angeles proved no match for the Chicago Bulls in the "Michael vs. Magic" Finals. Chicago bulled to victories in the last four games of the series to win its first championship.

Johnson's career halted abruptly on November 7, 1991. Johnson announced he had contracted HIV, the AIDS virus. He announced his immediate retirement, bringing the curtain down on the "Showtime" era.

1986-1987 Los Angeles Lakers final statistics

Name	G	PPG	FG%	FT%	RPG	APG
Magic Johnson	80	23.9	.522	.848	6.3	12.2
James Worthy	82	19.4	.539	.751	5.7	2.8
Kareem Abdul-Jabbar	78	17.5	.564	.714	6.7	2.6
Byron Scott	82	17.0	.489	.892	3.5	3.4
A.C. Green	79	10.8	.538	.780	7.8	1.1
Michael Cooper	82	10.5	.438	.851	3.1	4.5
Mychal Thompson	33	10.1	.480	.743	4.1	0.8
Kurt Rambis	78	5.7	.521	.764	5.8	0.8
Billy Thompson	59	5.6	.544	.649	2.9	1.0
Adrian Branch	32	4.3	.500	.778	1.7	0.5
Wes Matthews	50	4.2	.476	.806	0.9	2.0
Frank Brickowski	37	3.9	.564	.678	2.6	0.3
Mike Smrek	35	2.2	0.5	.640	1.1	0.1
Team	82	117.8	.516	.789	44.4	29.6
Opponents	82	108.5	.467	.764	42.1	27.0

6. The 1966-1967 Philadelphia 76ers

Record: 68-13

Overall ranking: 14th, 8.395 points above average

Other dominant Philadelphia 76er team of the era: 1967-1968 (22nd overall, 7.896 points above average).

The key players

Wilt Chamberlain, 7-foot-1 center—Chamberlain joined the 76ers via trade during the 1964-1965 season. He started the 1966-1967 campaign as the league's seven-time defending scoring champion.

Hal Greer, 6-foot-2 shooting guard—Greer was in the prime of his Hall of Fame career in 1966-1967. He served as the team's top perimeter scorer and could handle the ball like a point guard.

Chet Walker, 6-foot-7 power forward—Walker emerged as the team's No. 2 interior scorer and rebounder behind Chamberlain.

Billy Cunningham, 6-6 small forward—"The Kangaroo Kid" jumped into games in a reserve role to provide the 76ers with an instant spark. Cunningham was in the second year of his Hall of Fame career.

Why they're ranked here

The Philadelphia 76ers summoned a historic effort to end the Boston Celtics' eight-year reign as NBA champions.

The 76ers traded for Wilt Chamberlain during the 1965 All-Star break. Philadelphia and Chamberlain pushed Boston to a seventh game during the 1965 Eastern Conference finals, but lost when John Havlicek "stole the ball!" to preserve a 110-109 Boston win.

The 76ers put together the NBA's best regular season record during the 1965-1966 season, but again failed to defeat the Celtics during the playoffs.

Philadelphia brought in veteran coach Alex Hannum before the 1966-1967 season. Hannum coached the St. Louis Hawks to the NBA title in 1958. Boston had won every league championship since.

Hannum convinced Chamberlain to sacrifice some scoring for the greater good of the team. Chamberlain responded favorably. He averaged "only" 24.1 points per game and failed to win the scoring title for the first time in his career.

Chamberlain's individual sacrifice produced a better team. Chamberlain still led the league in rebounding (24.2 per game) and field goal percentage (68.3 percent), and finished third in the league in assists with 7.8 per outing. He won the league's Most Valuable Player award for the third time.

Hal Greer led the supporting cast with 22.1 points and 3.8 assists per game.

Chet Walker and Luke Jackson formed an imposing front line. Walker upped his scoring to 19.3 points per game, and also grabbed 8.1 rebounds per game. Jackson contributed 12.0 points and 8.9 rebounds per night.

Wali Jones rounded out the lineup. He contributed 13.2 points per game and 3.7 assists per game as Greer's running mate in the backcourt.

Billy Cunningham gave Philadelphia an All-Star presence off of the bench. Cunningham averaged 18.5 points and 7.3 rebounds per game in reserve.

The 76ers stormed to a 46-4 start, including a pair of 11-game winning streaks. Philadelphia finished the regular season with a 68-13 record. The 76ers smashed the existing league record for wins in a season by six games. They also established a new standard for single-season winning percentage. Philadelphia produced an average point differential of +9.4 points per game, the best margin in franchise history.

The 76ers passed their playoff tests. Philadelphia dispatched the Cincinnati Royals in the first round of the postseason, setting up another playoff matchup against Boston.

This year, the 76ers would not be denied. Philadelphia put a chokehold on the series with victories in the first three games. The 76ers closed out the Boston dynasty—for one year, anyway—with a resounding 140-116 victory in Game 5.

Philadelphia had just enough energy left over to beat the San Francisco Warriors 4-2 in the NBA Finals, capping the best season in franchise history.

Why a bunch of people will argue and why they're wrong

Argument: "The 1966-1967 Philadelphia 76ers should have a better ranking because they achieved as much in one season as the other great single-season teams and they did it against better competition."

Counter argument: Both the "achievement" and "competition" parts of the argument have holes.

The 1966-1967 Philadelphia 76ers did set a standard for wins in a season surpassed by just the 1971-1972 Los Angeles Lakers and by the Chicago Bulls in 1995-1996 and 1996-1997.

This will sound strange, but Philadelphia overachieved to win so many games. The 76ers finished their season with an average point differential of +9.4 points per game. Impressive. However, history shows that a team with an average point differential of +9.4 should win "only" 61 games during an 81-game season.

Put another way: This Philadelphia team had the least-dominant season of the four teams to win 68 or more games.

As for the "stronger competition" argument…It's not quite true. The numerical proof will come out when we get around to the great Boston Celtics teams of the 1960s.

Speaking of the Boston Celtics teams of the 1960s…

Argument: "The 76ers should have a worse ranking because their one title doesn't make them better than the Celtics of the Bill Russell era, who won 11 championships."

Counter argument: In truth, Boston's excellence pushed Philadelphia's championship team to a dominant level.

The POST ratings achieved by championship teams show a pattern. Teams generally achieve their highest ratings en route to their initial title or titles. Teams that win multiple titles generally see their ratings decline later in their reigns.

Call it the "Suffering Apprentice" theory.

In the musical piece "The Sorcerer's Apprentice"—think Mickey Mouse and the brooms—the apprentice doesn't know how to control his newfound sorcerer powers. As a result, he creates far more brooms than he needs and retrieves far too much water from the sorcerer's well.

Teams who obtain championship "powers" for the first time often perform like the sorcerer's apprentice. They win far more games by far more points than they might truly need to get the job done.

These teams dominate the top positions in the all-time NBA POST ratings. The 1970-1971 Milwaukee Bucks made darn sure they outplayed the defending champion New York Knicks during the regular season. The 1995-1996 Chicago Bulls possessed a Michael Jordan determined to prove wrong those who didn't think he could make a successful comeback. The 1971-1972 Los Angeles Lakers soared to great heights, spurred in part by eight NBA Finals losses in the preceding 12 years. The 1966-1967 Philadelphia 76ers couldn't leave anything to chance after a pair of heartbreaking playoff losses against the Boston Celtics.

Teams that win multiple championships eventually learn to use their "powers" wisely, just like the sorcerer in "The Sorcerer's Apprentice." The sorcerer never used his magic more than absolutely necessary. The Boston Celtic teams of the 1960s, the Chicago Bulls of the 1990s and the Los Angeles Lakers of the early part of the current decade all learned just how much of their "powers" they needed to exert to win championships.

The 1966-1967 Philadelphia 76ers played like a classic "Suffering Apprentice." They didn't know how much "magic" they needed to win an NBA championship. After all, Boston had won every title since 1959. So, the 76ers left nothing to chance. They summoned all of their collective powers and composed one of the most memorable scores in NBA history.

Postscript

This got ugly in a hurry.

Philadelphia finished the 1967-1968 season with a 62-20 record, the best mark in the NBA. The 76ers took a 3-1 lead over the hated Celtics in the Eastern Division finals. They needed just one more win to move on to the NBA Finals and a chance at a repeat championship.

Philadelphia never got that one win. Boston evened the series with easy victories in Game 5 and Game 6. The Celtics then stunned the 76ers with a 100-96 triumph in Game 7 in Philadelphia. Chamberlain, the NBA's assist champion during the 1967-1968 season, inexplicably refused to shoot throughout the final quarter of Game 7.

Chamberlain demanded a trade following the season, claiming he had not received a promised ownership stake in the team. Philadelphia obliged and sent Chamberlain to the Los Angeles Lakers.

The 76ers' championship team quickly unraveled from there. Philadelphia traded Walker away after the 1968-1969 season. Wali Jones left after the 1970-1971 campaign. Hal Greer began to show signs of age. Finally, courts ordered Billy Cunningham to leave the 76ers after the 1971-1972 season and honor a contract with the Carolina Cougars of the American Basketball Association.

Philadelphia finished the 1972-1973 season with a 9-73 record, just six years after it ruled the basketball world.

1966-1967 Philadelphia 76ers final statistics

Name	G	PPG	FG%	FT%	RPG	APG
Wilt Chamberlain	81	24.1	.683	.441	24.2	7.8
Hal Greer	80	22.1	.459	.788	5.3	3.8
Chet Walker	81	19.3	.488	.766	8.1	2.3
Billy Cunningham	81	18.5	.459	.686	7.3	2.5
Wali Jones	81	13.2	.431	.838	3.3	3.7
Luke Jackson	81	12.0	.438	.759	8.9	1.4
Larry Costello	49	7.8	.444	.902	2.1	2.9
Dave Gambee	63	6.5	.435	.856	3.1	0.7
Bill Melchionni	73	4.3	.391	.650	1.3	1.3
Matt Guokas	69	3.0	.389	.605	1.2	1.5
Bob Weiss	6	2.0	.500	.400	0.5	1.7
Team	81	125.2	.483	.680	70.4	26.4
Opponent	81	115.8	N/A	N/A	N/A	N/A

7. The 1969-1970 New York Knickerbockers
Record: 60-22
Overall ranking: 15th, 8.363 points above average
Other dominant New York Knickerbocker team of the era: 1972-1973 (89th overall, 6.060 points above average).

The key players

Willis Reed, 6-foot-10 center—The Knicks' center, captain, and leader. The 1969-1970 season would represent the peak of Reed's Hall of Fame career.

Walt Frazier, 6-foot-4 point guard—"Clyde" Frazier directed New York's balanced offense. Frazier had a breakthrough second professional season in 1968-

1969. He stood poised for big things in 1969-1970. Another future Hall of Fame inductee.

Bill Bradley, 6-foot-5 small forward—The future presidential candidate and New Jersey senator first made a name for himself as a basketball star. The 1969-1970 season was the third year of Bradley's Hall of Fame career.

Dave DeBusschere, 6-foot-6 power forward—DeBusschere led New York's stingy defense. He came to the Knicks via trade during the 1968-1969 season. He proved to be the final piece in New York's championship puzzle.

Why they're ranked here

New York began the 1969-1970 season seeking the franchise's first NBA title. A careful building process yielded a championship-caliber team by the late 1960s. The Knicks reached the Eastern Division finals in 1968-1969, but lost a six-game series against the eventual champion Boston Celtics.

The Celtics abdicated their throne following the 1969 championship. The retirement of Bill Russell, the center on all 11 Boston championship teams to that point, started a rebuilding process for the Celtics.

New York quickly filled the vacuum atop the NBA. The Knicks embarked on a then-record 18-game winning streak early in the 1969-1970 season. New York had a 23-2 record before Christmas.

The Knicks finished the regular season with a 60-22 mark, the best in the league and the best in franchise history. New York enjoyed an average point differential of +9.1 points per game, still a franchise record.

The Knicks won with remarkable teamwork and defense. Not one New York player finished among the league's top ten scorers, but three Knicks (Dave DeBusschere, Willis Reed, and Walt Frazier) made the NBA's five-player All-Defensive team.

Reed led the club with 21.7 points per game and 13.9 rebounds per game. He also received the league's Most Valuable Player award.

Frazier boosted his scoring average to 20.9 points per game. He also averaged 8.2 assists (second best in the league) and 6.0 rebounds.

DeBusschere added 14.6 points and 10.0 rebounds per game, along with his defensive presence.

Bill Bradley and shooting guard Dick Barnett provided mirror contributions. Bradley scored 14.5 points and dished out 4.0 assists per game. Barnett averaged 14.9 points and 3.6 assists.

New York eked past the Baltimore Bullets in seven games during the opening round of the playoffs. The Knicks had an easier time during the Eastern Division finals. New York dispatched the Milwaukee Bucks and rookie center Lew Alcindor (later Kareem Abdul-Jabbar) in five games.

The Knicks faced the star-studded Los Angeles Lakers in the NBA Finals. The teams split the first four games. Disaster then struck New York early in Game 5. Los Angeles bolted to a 25-15 lead and Reed left the game with a torn thigh muscle.

The Knicks somehow rallied to win the game 107-100, but the Lakers seemed to have all of the momentum. Reed did not play in Game 6. Los Angeles evened the series with a 135-113 victory.

Few thought Reed would play in the decisive Game 7. Fewer thought Reed could play effectively against Lakers center Wilt Chamberlain.

Reed sent the crowd in New York's Madison Square Garden into a frenzy when he stepped onto the floor to start Game 7. Reed proceeded to play perhaps the most dominant four-point game in basketball history. Reed made only two baskets—the first two of the game—but he played gallant defense against Chamberlain. The inspired Knicks closed their magical season with a 113-99 victory.

Why a bunch of people will argue and why they're wrong

Argument: "The 1969-1970 New York Knicks should have a better ranking because they had better players and competed against better competition than many of the teams ranked above them."

Counter argument: Indeed, one might think a team with four Hall of Famers on its roster would rank higher.

This might be a good time to point something out: Defense doesn't dominate. High-powered offensive teams typically achieve the most dominant POST ratings. Great offensive teams tend to win their games by greater margins. These rankings reflect those margins. The 1969-1970 Knicks' win-with-defense philosophy made their POST rating worse.

Some consolation for Knicks fans: One could call this team the most dominant defense-oriented team ever.

Argument: "The Knicks should have a worse ranking because they didn't have a true superstar."

Counter argument: Funny how the "star" argument works both ways. Win with a superstar or two and critics point out the shortcomings of the supporting cast. Win with balance and critics point out the lack of a dominant player.

All signs indicate any of the Knicks' great players could have posted dominant individual statistics had they so desired. Many of the teams on this top 10 list boast great players who sacrificed individual glory to create a dominant team. This New York team happened to have several potentially dominant players who sacrificed individual glory throughout their careers for the sake of team dominance.

Argument: "The Knicks should have a worse ranking than the Boston Celtics teams of the 1960s because New York didn't win it all until Bill Russell retired."

Counter argument: See the "Suffering Apprentice" theory in the section concerning the 1966-1967 Philadelphia 76ers.

Boston's greatness pushed the 1969-1970 Knicks to greater heights. New York didn't know what powers it would need to summon to win a championship during the 1969-1970 season, so the Knicks tried every trick in the book. The result: A thoroughly dominant season.

Furthermore, though Russell's retirement eliminated the *chief* obstacle between the Knicks and the NBA title, New York faced some of the best *overall* competition in league history.

The Knicks played few weaklings during their championship run. Thirteen of the league's 14 teams won at least 30 games during the 1969-1970 season. The team with the NBA's worst record, the San Diego Rockets, won more games (27) than any league-worst team since. Expansion did not dilute the quality of play. The NBA's two newest teams (the two-year-old Milwaukee Bucks and Phoenix Suns) both made the playoffs.

Newton's Third Law—"For every action there is an equal and opposite reaction"—generally holds true in the NBA. If the league's best team wins around 70 games, the league's worst team typically loses around 70 games. If the best team wins just 60 games, the worst team typically loses just 60 games. If the NBA's most dominant team posts an average point differential of +5.0, expect the league's least dominant team to finish with an average point differential close to -5.0.

Every team in the NBA finished with an average point differential between +4.6 and -4.5 during the 1969-1970 season. Except one. The Knicks (+9.1 points per game) produced the greatest difference between the absolute values of a season's best and worst average point differentials (+4.6) in league history.

Translation: New York achieved the basketball equivalent of a force powerful enough to break free from the earth's gravity, an appropriate accomplishment in a season that tipped off soon after man walked on the moon for the first time. The Knicks enjoyed a transcendent year in a league filled with competitive teams, something the Boston Celtic squads of the Bill Russell era never truly accomplished. The Celtics of the 1960s produced some transcendent teams and participated in some highly competitive NBA seasons, but never in the same year.

Postscript

The New York Knicks might well have defeated the "Most Dominant Ever" Milwaukee Bucks in the 1970-1971 NBA Finals. The Knicks defeated the Bucks four times in five tries during the 1970-1971 regular season.

New York never got its chance at a Finals showdown against Milwaukee. The Baltimore Bullets ended the Knicks' bid for a repeat championship with a seven-game triumph in the Eastern Conference finals.

New York returned to the NBA Finals in 1972, but ran into a Los Angeles Lakers team destined to claim a championship. The Lakers won the series in five games.

The Knicks returned the favor during the 1972-1973 NBA Finals. New York held Los Angeles under 100 points in the last four games of a 4-1 series victory.

The aging process quickly took its toll on the Knicks thereafter. Reed and DeBusschere would not play again after the 1973-1974 season. Frazier and Bradley left the Knicks two years later.

1969-1970 New York Knickerbockers final statistics

Name	G	PPG	FG%	FT%	RPG	APG
Willis Reed	81	21.7	.507	.756	13.9	2.0
Walt Frazier	77	20.9	.518	.748	6.0	8.2
Dick Barnett	82	14.9	.475	.714	2.7	3.6
Dave DeBusschere	79	14.6	.451	.688	10.0	2.5
Bill Bradley	67	14.5	.460	.824	3.6	4.0
Cazzie Russell	78	11.5	.498	.775	3.0	1.7
Dave Stallworth	82	7.8	.429	.716	3.9	1.7
Mike Riordan	81	7.7	.464	.691	2.4	2.5
Wilmer Hosket	36	3.3	.505	.788	1.8	0.5
Nate Bowman	81	2.9	.417	.519	3.2	0.6
Don May	37	2.6	.386	.947	1.4	0.5
Johnny Warren	44	2.5	.407	.686	0.9	0.7
Team	82	115.0	.477	.733	48.9	26.0
Opponents	82	105.9	N/A	N/A	N/A	N/A

8. The 1999-2000 Los Angeles Lakers

Record: 67-15

Overall ranking: 16th, 8.327 points above average

Other dominant Los Angeles Laker teams of the era: 2001-2002 (47th overall, 7.037 points above average); 1997-1998 (50th overall, 6.993 points above average).

The key players

Shaquille O'Neal, 7-foot-1 center—O'Neal emerged as the NBA's most dominant force during the late 1990s, but had not yet led a team to a championship.

He had won one scoring title and finished second in the league in scoring three times prior to the 1999-2000 season.

Kobe Bryant, 6-foot-7 shooting guard—Bryant jumped to the NBA straight out of high school in 1996. He developed into one of the league's most dynamic perimeter players as a 21-year-old by the 1999-2000 season.

Why they're ranked here

Shaquille O'Neal and Kobe Bryant both joined the Los Angeles Lakers in the summer of 1996. Los Angeles general manager Jerry West cleared enough salary cap space to sign O'Neal, the game's best young center, to a mammoth contract. West shrewdly traded for Bryant, fresh out of high school, soon after the NBA draft.

O'Neal and Bryant produced a 148-66 record during their first three seasons together, but failed to reach the NBA Finals.

Enter Phil Jackson. Jackson coached the Chicago Bulls to six NBA championships between 1991 and 1998. Jackson took a one-year sabbatical after the breakup of Chicago's championship team. He arrived in Los Angeles refreshed and ready to build his famed "triangle offense" around O'Neal.

O'Neal responded with his finest season. He averaged a career-high 29.7 points per game, along with 13.6 rebounds per contest. He won his first Most Valuable Player award.

Bryant missed the first 15 games of the season with an injury. He came back with a flourish. He averaged 22.5 points, 6.3 rebounds, and 4.9 assists, all career bests at the time.

Jackson surrounded his young stars with savvy veterans.

Ron Harper played on three of Jackson's championship teams in Chicago. He manned the point guard position for this Los Angeles team. A.C. Green returned to the Lakers to play power forward. Shooting guard Glen Rice struggled to fit into the triangle offense at times, but still provided a feared outside presence. Reserves like forwards Robert Horry and John Salley had past championship experience.

Most fans paid attention to Los Angeles' scoring prowess, but defense turned the Lakers into champions. Los Angeles allowed 92.3 points per game, down from a 96.6 average during the first three seasons of the O'Neal-Bryant era. O'Neal blocked 239 shots, the most since his rookie year.

The Lakers started fast and finished the season 67-15. Los Angeles posted the second-highest victory total in franchise history, behind just the 1971-1972 squad. The Lakers posted an average point differential of +8.5 points per game, the third-best margin in team history.

Los Angeles survived a rocky playoff road. The Lakers needed five games to get past the No. 8 seed Sacramento Kings in the best-of-five first round. Los Angeles almost blew a 3-1 series lead during the Western Conference finals against the Portland Trail Blazers. Portland led by 15 points in the fourth quarter of the seventh and decisive game, but the Lakers rallied for a memorable 89-84 victory.

Los Angeles wrapped up its first championship since 1988 with a 4-2 series win against the Indiana Pacers in the NBA Finals. Bryant starred in the pivotal game, a 120-118 overtime victory in Indianapolis that gave the Lakers a 3-1 series lead. Bryant scored 28 points and made several key baskets during the overtime after O'Neal fouled out.

Why a bunch of people will argue and why they're wrong

Argument: "The 1999-2000 Lakers should have a better ranking because Shaq and Kobe would go wild against players from a different era."

Counter argument: Maybe they would. In 1999-2000, they weren't as dominant as players and teams from other eras. Their +8.5 average point differential should have translated to "just" 64 wins. This Los Angeles team also was outscored in its playoff series against Portland and Indiana.

Argument: "The Lakers should have a worse ranking because they had just two superstars."

Counter argument: As noted when examining the star-light 1969-1970 New York Knicks, it's funny how this argument works both ways.

The 1999-2000 Lakers did boast just two star-quality players. Those two players had dominant seasons. The supporting cast played its role well enough to produce a dominant season.

Argument: "The Lakers should have a worse ranking because they didn't accomplish as much as some other dynasties."

Counter argument: Many historians will look back on this Los Angeles team and see unfulfilled potential. Yet the Lakers did click on all cylinders in 1999-2000. The result: A season more dominant than any produced by some the league's long-running dynasties. The 1999-2000 Los Angeles squad is one of just seven NBA champions to win 67 games or more. The Lakers faced the toughest schedule of those seven teams, based on opponents' average point differential. The accomplishments merit a spot in the all-time top 10.

Postscript

The Los Angeles Lakers' dynasty began to crumble after the team won its third consecutive NBA title with a sweep of the New Jersey Nets in the 2002 Finals.

O'Neal elected to wait until after his "summer vacation" to undergo needed surgery on his feet. Los Angeles struggled to a 3-9 start as its big center recuperated. The Lakers finished with a 50-32 record, good for just fifth place in the loaded Western Conference. The so-so finish meant Los Angeles would not enjoy home court advantage in any of its 2003 playoff series.

The Lakers' living-on-the-edge philosophy finally caught up with them during the Western Conference semifinals against the San Antonio Spurs.

Los Angeles nearly erased a 24-point deficit in the pivotal Game 5. The Lakers lost 96-94 only when Robert Horry's potential game-winning 3-pointer in the waning seconds rattled in and out of the unfriendly rim in San Antonio's home arena. The Spurs ended the series and the Lakers' title reign with a blowout win in Game 6.

Los Angeles tried to make amends for the 2002-2003 disappointment by making an enormous splash in the free agent market. The Lakers added two future Hall of Famers in power forward Karl Malone and point guard Gary Payton before the 2003-2004 season. Analysts spoke of a dream season.

The dream turned into a nightmare.

A Colorado teen accused Bryant of sexual assault after an encounter a few days after the Malone and Payton signings. Bryant would spend the 2003-2004 season making frequent flights to Colorado for courtroom appearances. The case never would go to trial, but Bryant took a beating in the court of public opinion.

The Lakers also encountered troubles on the basketball court. Malone struggled with a knee injury. Payton struggled to fit into Jackson's triangle offense. Bryant and O'Neal struggled to coexist.

Los Angeles somehow battled its way into the NBA Finals. There, the Lakers had nothing left for their matchup against the Detroit Pistons.

Malone re-injured his knee and could not play effectively. Bryant made a game-tying shot at the regulation buzzer of Game 2 that allowed Los Angeles to win in overtime, but otherwise endured a dismal Finals. Detroit won the series 4-1.

The long-simmering O'Neal-Bryant feud boiled over after the season.

Bryant, a free agent, never publicly declared he would not play for Jackson or with O'Neal. The Lakers didn't take any chances. Los Angeles executives made re-signing Bryant their No. 1 offseason priority. They did their best to create a Kobe-friendly environment.

First, the Lakers elected not to renew Jackson's contract. O'Neal expressed public disappointment over the decision and demanded a trade. Los Angeles acquiesced to O'Neal's request and shipped the Big Diesel east to the Miami Heat.

Bryant returned to the Lakers as the franchise's go-to player. He led Los Angeles to a 34-48 record. The Lakers failed to make the playoffs. Jackson got his job back for the 2005-2006 season.

1999-2000 Los Angeles Lakers final statistics

Name	G	PPG	FG%	FT%	RPG	APG
Shaquille O'Neal	79	29.7	.574	.524	13.6	3.8
Kobe Bryant	66	22.5	.468	.821	6.3	4.9
Glen Rice	80	15.9	.430	.874	4.1	2.2
Ron Harper	80	7.0	.399	.680	4.2	3.4
Rick Fox	82	6.5	.414	.808	2.4	1.7
Derek Fisher	78	6.3	.346	.724	1.8	2.8
Tyronn Lue	8	6.0	.487	.750	1.5	2.1
Robert Horry	76	5.7	.438	.788	4.8	1.6
A.C. Green	82	5.0	.447	.695	5.9	1.0
Brian Shaw	74	4.1	.382	.759	2.9	2.7
Sam Jacobson	3	3.3	.556	.000	0.3	0.7
Devean George	49	3.2	.389	.659	1.5	0.2
John Celestand	16	2.3	.333	.833	0.7	1.3
Travis Knight	63	1.7	.390	.607	2.0	0.4
John Salley	45	1.6	.362	.750	1.4	0.6
Team	82	100.8	.459	.696	47.0	23.4
Opponents	82	92.3	.416	.742	43.1	19.5

9. The 2006-2007 San Antonio Spurs

Record: 58-24

Overall ranking: 17th, 8.246 points above average

Other dominant San Antonio Spurs teams of the era: 2000-2001 (25th overall, 7.765 points above average); 2004-2005 (29th overall, 7.729 points above average); 1998-1999 (37th overall, 7.388 points above average); 2003-2004 (40th overall, 7.334 points above average); 2005-2006 (62nd overall, 6.643 points above average); 2001-2002 (85th overall, 6.167 points above average)

The key player

Tim Duncan, 7-foot-0 forward—The Big Fundamental earned two Most Valuable Player trophies and nine All-Star appearances during his first 10 NBA seasons. The Spurs have won four NBA championships and averaged 58 wins per full season during Duncan's career.

Why they're ranked here

The San Antonio Spurs spent the career of quiet superstar Tim Duncan building one of the most underrated dynasties in NBA history.

Appropriately, San Antonio got overshadowed by other teams for the majority of the franchise's most dominant year.

The Dallas Mavericks and the Phoenix Suns garnered most of the league's attention during the 2006-2007 season. Dallas posted a 67-15 record, the best mark in the NBA. Phoenix won 37 of 40 games at one stretch and led the league in scoring for the third season in a row.

The Spurs chugged along in the wake of the Mavericks and Suns. San Antonio reached the 50-game mark with a 33-17 record. Not bad, but not championship-caliber.

February brings two traditional events to San Antonio. The rodeo comes to town and the Spurs hit the road to go on a hot streak.

The 2006-2007 season proved no different. San Antonio started to lasso up victories as the road stretch came to an end. The rodeo trip spurred a run of 25 wins in 28 games. The Spurs started their surge with a 13-game winning streak.

San Antonio finished the regular season with a 58-24 record, the franchise's exact average win total during the Duncan era.

Other numbers revealed the 2006-2007 Spurs as anything but average. San Antonio produced an average point differential of +8.4 points per game, the best mark in the league and in franchise history, and the second-best mark of the 2000s. The Spurs led the league in defense, yielding just 90.1 points per game.

Duncan led San Antonio with 20.0 points, 10.6 rebounds, and 2.4 blocks per game, all close to his career norms.

Duncan got help from supporting players who probably will not join him in the Hall of Fame, but who thrived in precise roles. Point guard Tony Parker averaged 18.6 points and 5.5 assists per game, and joined Duncan on the All-Star team. Former All-Star shooting guard Michael Finley started alongside Parker in the backcourt. Small forward Bruce Bowen made the All-Defense team for the fourth consecutive season. Shooting guard Manu Ginobili moved to a reserve role and averaged a career-high 16.5 points per game.

The Spurs also had Robert Horry, the patron saint of role players.

"Big Shot Bob" earned his nickname by hitting crucial shots to lift three different franchises to NBA championships.

Horry also unwittingly delivered perhaps the biggest shot of the 2006-2007 playoffs. He hip-checked Phoenix point guard Steve Nash into the scorer's table during the final seconds of the Suns' 104-98 victory in Game 4 of the West semifinal between San Antonio and Phoenix, the two best teams remaining in the NBA playoffs. The Suns tied the de facto league championship series at two with their win. But the NBA suspended Phoenix star forward Amare Stoudemire and key reserve Boris Diaw for Game 5 because both players stepped onto the playing floor during the Horry-Nash incident. Horry got a two-game suspension for instigating the flare-up. Still, the net effect seemed to favor the Spurs.

San Antonio made the most of its good fortune. The Spurs beat the Suns 88-85 in Game 5 in Phoenix, coolly overcoming a double-digit deficit and a nation of basketball fans pulling for the shorthanded Suns. San Antonio then closed out the controversial series with a 114-106 home victory in Game 6.

The Spurs went on to defeat the Utah Jazz in the Western Conference finals and the Cleveland Cavaliers in the NBA Finals to claim their fourth championship in nine seasons.

Why a bunch of people will argue and why they're wrong

Argument: "The Spurs should have a better ranking because they won more total titles than six of the eight teams ranked ahead of them."

Counter argument: OK, that's a stretch. Not a lot of folks insist on listing any of the recent San Antonio squads among the eight greatest teams in NBA history, even though just three other *franchises* have won more titles.

Do the Spurs at least have a claim to jump one spot, past the 1999-2000 Los Angeles Lakers? The teams competed during the same era. San Antonio won four championships to Los Angeles' three.

Think of the Lakers-Spurs rivalry of the 2000s as Generation X's version of the Los Angeles Lakers-Boston Celtics rivalry of the 1980s.

The Los Angeles teams of the 2000s climbed the highest the fastest, just like the Boston teams of the 1980s. The San Antonio teams of the 2000s sustained a longer period of dominance, just like the Los Angeles teams of the 1980s.

At peak performance? Take the Celtics as the best of the 1980s. Take the Lakers as the best of the new century.

The 1999-2000 Los Angeles squad posted the best record (67-15) and best average point differential (+8.5 points per game) of the current decade. When both the Lakers and the Spurs possessed all of their key players, Los Angeles won more championships and boasted a better record in head-to-head playoff meetings.

Bottom line: The Spurs don't belong ahead of the 1999-2000 Los Angeles Lakers. Therefore, they don't fit anywhere else in the top eight, either.

That said, for those nodding your head and thinking, "No kidding," keep the following in mind: San Antonio entered the final two games of the 2006-2007 regular season with an average point differential of +9.1 points per game. The Spurs lost both of those games by double digits as their top players rested for the postseason. If San Antonio had maintained an average point differential of +9.1 points per game (it dropped to +8.4 after the two losses), the Spurs would have cracked the top five on this list.

Argument: "The Spurs were not the NBA's best team during the 2006-2007 regular season, so how can they rank among the best teams of all time?"

Counter argument: The Spurs had the best team. They just didn't bother to win the most games.

The Dallas Mavericks (67-15) and the Phoenix Suns (61-21) both totaled more victories than the Spurs. San Antonio had the most dominant season.

The Spurs' average point differential of +8.4 points per game far exceeded the average point differential for the Mavericks (+7.2 points per game) and the Suns (+7.3 points per game). Statistically, San Antonio should have won 64 games. Dallas should have won "just" 61 games. Phoenix should have won 59.

The Mavericks and Suns displayed classic signs of "Suffering Apprentices." Dallas and Phoenix clearly overachieved during the regular season, perhaps hoping their impressive records would leave the competition spellbound during the postseason.

The wizened Spurs reserved their powers for the playoffs. Five regular season losses by one possession or less? No cause for concern. A chance to reach 60 wins with victories in the last two regular season games? San Antonio instead elected to rest its top players.

The Spurs proved they had the best team during the postseason. San Antonio performed sorcery on the basketball court on its way to its fourth NBA title in nine years. The Spurs eliminated the Suns in that controversial West semifinal en route to the championship. The top-seeded Mavericks suffered a stupefying loss against the Golden State Warriors in the first round of the playoffs. The apprenticeship continues for Dallas and Phoenix.

Argument: "The Spurs do not belong ahead of a legendary dynasty like the Boston Celtics of the 1960s."

Counter argument: San Antonio has emerged as a legendary dynasty in its own right. The POST ratings show the Spurs of the Tim Duncan era produced the second-best 10-year stretch in NBA history, behind the Chicago Bulls of the 1990s and just ahead of the Boston Celtics of the 1980s and 1960s. Only five teams, including San Antonio, have won four or more championships with the same key players.

The Spurs rank better than the 1961-1962 Celtics (the most dominant of the Bill Russell-led Boston teams) because of strength of schedule.

San Antonio faced the toughest schedule of any team in this top 10, based on opponents' average point differential. The Spurs played most of their games against teams from a Western Conference that produced two 60-win clubs and an overall winning percentage of .526.

The 1961-1962 Celtics competed in an Eastern Division that produced a winning percentage of .559, but Boston played most of its games against teams from a weaker Western Division because of a scheduling quirk caused by the addition of the expansion Chicago Packers.

Put simply: On a representative night, the 2006-2007 San Antonio Spurs would play a team that would finish with a 43-39 record. On a representative night, the 1961-1962 Boston Celtics would face a team that would finish with a 36-44 record.

Advantage: Spurs.

Postscript

The Spurs should continue to contend for championships so long as they have Duncan in his prime.

2006-2007 San Antonio Spurs final statistics

Name	G	PPG	FG%	FT%	RPG	APG
Tim Duncan	80	20.0	.546	.637	10.6	3.4
Tony Parker	77	18.6	.520	.783	3.2	5.5
Manu Ginobili	75	16.5	.464	.860	4.4	3.5
Michael Finley	82	9.0	.412	.918	2.7	1.3
Brent Barry	75	8.5	.475	.880	2.1	1.8
James White	6	8.3	.439	.800	3.3	0.8
Bruce Bowen	82	6.2	.405	.589	2.7	1.4
Francisco Elson	70	5.0	.511	.775	4.8	0.8
Matt Bonner	56	4.9	.447	.711	2.8	0.4
Beno Udrih	73	4.7	.369	.883	1.1	1.7
Fabricio Oberto	79	4.4	.562	.647	4.7	0.9
Robert Horry	68	3.9	.359	.594	3.4	1.1
Jackie Butler	11	3.7	.457	.900	2.0	0.5
Melvin Ely	6	3.2	.300	.583	2.3	0.7
Jacque Vaughn	64	3.0	.425	.754	1.1	2.0
Eric Williams	16	2.6	.441	.571	0.9	0.4
Team	82	98.5	.474	.751	40.7	22.1
Opponents	82	90.1	.443	.740	39.1	17.3

10. The 1961-1962 Boston Celtics

Record: 60-20
Overall ranking: 20th, 8.054 points above average
Other dominant Boston Celtic teams of the era: 1959-1960 (34th overall, 7.449 points above average); 1964-1965 (39th overall, 7.361 points above average); 1966-1967

(45th overall, 7.155 points above average); 1963-1964 (57th overall, 6.867 points above average); 1962-1963 (79th overall, 6.260 points above average)

The key players

Bill Russell, 6-foot-10 center—Perhaps the most valuable player and most dominant defensive player ever. Boston won its first championship during Russell's rookie season, 1956-1957. Russell would retire following the 1968-1969 season after leading the Celtics to 11 titles in 13 seasons.

Bob Cousy, 6-foot-1 point guard—Cousy led Boston's feared fast break with a showman's style. He helped revive the Boston franchise when he joined the team in 1950. He would retire in 1963 as an eight-time NBA assist champion.

Tom Heinsohn, 6-foot-7 power forward—The "Tommy Gun" led the Boston teams of the early 1960s in scoring. Heinsohn entered the NBA the same year as Russell and actually won Rookie of the Year honors.

Sam Jones, 6-foot-4 shooting guard—Jones emerged as Boston's primary shooting guard during the 1961-1962 season, following the retirement of Bill Sharman.

K.C. Jones, 6-foot-1 point guard—Cousy's understudy at point guard. Jones played with Russell on two NCAA championship teams at the University of San Francisco in 1955 and 1956. He joined the Celtics with Russell for the 1956-1957 season.

Frank Ramsey, 6-foot-3 shooting guard—Ramsey pioneered the "Sixth Man" role. He would enter games off of the bench and provide a quick scoring boost.

Why they're ranked here

In a 1961-1962 season filled with staggering accomplishments, the Boston dynasty also reached its apex.

Philadelphia Warriors center Wilt Chamberlain scored 100 points in one game and finished the 1961-1962 season with a record 50.4 scoring average. Cincinnati Royals guard Oscar Robertson averaged a triple-double for the season, still the only player to do so.

Boston put together equally impressive team accomplishments. The Celtics began the season as the three-time defending NBA champions. Boston would eventually win eight consecutive titles and 11 in 13 years. The 1961-1962 season stands out over all of those championship seasons.

The Celtics went 60-20 in 1961-1962, the first team to win 60 games in a season. Boston enjoyed an average point differential of +9.2 points per game, the best average point differential of any Celtics team from the Russell era.

The Boston roster included a staggering six Hall of Famers: Heinsohn, Russell, Cousy, Ramsey, and the Joneses.

Russell garnered the third of his five Most Valuable Player awards. He averaged 18.9 points and 23.6 rebounds per game. Heinsohn led Boston in scoring with 22.1 points per game. Sam Jones, Ramsey, Cousy, and Tom Sanders all scored in double figures as well. Cousy finished third in the league in assists with 7.8 per game.

The Celtics won their division by a staggering 11 games, but encountered considerable difficulty in the playoffs.

Boston needed seven games to get past the Chamberlain and the Philadelphia Warriors in the Eastern Division finals. The Celtics edged the Warriors 109-107 in the decisive contest.

The Los Angeles Lakers nearly toppled Boston in the NBA Finals. Los Angeles took a 3-2 series lead and had a chance to clinch the title on its home floor in Game 6, but the Celtics came through with a 119-105 victory and forced a Game 7 back in Boston.

The game went down to the final moments. Lakers guard Frank Selvy got a chance to win it for Los Angeles with the score tied at 100 and time winding down in regulation. Selvy took an open shot from eight feet away, but his short jumper bounced off the front of the rim. Given a reprieve, the Celtics prevailed 110-107 in overtime for their fourth consecutive championship.

Why a bunch of people will argue and why they're wrong

Argument: "Why single out this Boston Celtic team over the other ten championship squads of the Bill Russell era?"

Counter argument: One could rank several other Boston teams of the Russell era as better than the 1961-1962 squad.

The 1960-1961 team had an additional Hall of Famer (Bill Sharman) and rolled through both of its playoff series in five games.

The 1964-1965 squad had a 62-18 record, the best mark of any Russell-led Boston team.

The 1961-1962 team gets the nod here. The 1961-1962 team had the best average point differential for any Russell-led Celtics team during a strong year for Boston's Eastern Division.

Argument: "The Boston teams of the Russell era won 11 championships in 13 years and deserve a better ranking for the accomplishment."

Counter argument: The following will make a lot of Boston devotees angry, but here goes: The Celtic teams of the Russell era achieved relatively unimpressive POST rankings because they did not face quality competition.

That does not mean the Russell-led Boston teams faced low-quality *teams*.

The Celtics won eight consecutive NBA titles at the height of the Russell era, spanning the 1958-1959 through 1965-1966 seasons. The NBA had either eight or nine teams in the league during those seasons. Therefore, only the best 100 or so basketball players in the world played in the NBA during the height of the Boston dynasty.

By comparison, 150 players have *starting* positions in today's 30-team NBA. Those who prefer old-school professional basketball correctly point out the higher quality of the *teams* in the NBA's Russell era.

Yet the numbers show none of those teams rose to provide true *competition* for the Celtics at the height of the Russell dynasty.

The Boston teams of the Russell era earned five spots in the POST top 75. The best non-Celtics POST ranking from the years spanning Boston's eight-peat? The 1963-1964 Cincinnati Royals, who check in at No. 170.

The Celtics posted an average point differential of at least +4.9 points per game every season between 1958-1959 and 1965-1966. Only two other teams during that span enjoyed seasons with an average point differential of +4.9 points per game or better. The Los Angeles Laker teams who annually challenged the Celtics in the NBA Finals during the height of the Russell era never achieved an average point differential of more than +3.1 points per game.

So, the NBA of Russell's time almost certainly consisted of quality *teams*, but only the Boston squads rose far above the "average" level for the era. The lack of true *competition* depressed the Russell-led Celtics' POST rankings.

More bluntly: How great could the Russell-led Celtics have been if the best team they had to beat was the 1963-1964 Cincinnati Royals?

Still, the Russell-led Boston teams get a spot in the top two, along with the 1990s Chicago Bulls, when one discusses the top *dynasties* in NBA history.

(The *greatest* dynasty? It depends on the time span measured. The Chicago teams of the Michael Jordan era put together the most dominant *10-year* stretch in NBA history, according to the POST ratings. The formula shows the Boston teams of the Russell era enjoyed the most dominant *15-year* stretch in league history.)

Argument: "The Celtics should have a worse ranking…"

Counter argument: …Only if a person has a bias favoring modern teams or presides over the George Mikan fan club.

One could claim bigger, stronger, more athletic modern players would run roughshod over players from the 1950s and 1960s. One could claim the Minneapolis Lakers of the early 1950s dominated their competition just as much as the Boston teams one decade later.

The POST ratings evaluate how a team performed relative to the norm of its era. The POST ratings place the Boston Celtics of the 1960s ahead of all but nine other league champions, past and present. Plus, it's hard to justify ranking the most dominant team from the NBA's most dominant dynasty much lower than tenth.

For the record, Boston edged the 1949-1950 Minneapolis Lakers and the 1982-1983 Philadelphia 76ers for the last spot on the list of the 10 most dominant teams in NBA history.

Postscript

You know the rest. The Celtics won six more championships before Russell's retirement after the 1968-1969 season.

1961-1962 Boston Celtics final statistics

Name	G	PPG	FG%	FT%	RPG	APG
Tom Heinsohn	79	22.1	.429	.819	9.5	2.1
Bill Russell	76	18.9	.457	.595	23.6	4.5
Sam Jones	78	18.4	.464	.818	5.9	3.0
Bob Cousy	75	15.7	.391	.754	3.5	7.8
Frank Ramsey	79	15.3	.428	.825	4.9	1.4
Thomas Sanders	80	11.2	.435	.749	9.5	0.9
K.C. Jones	80	9.2	.406	.634	3.7	4.3
Jim Loscutoff	79	5.3	.362	.536	4.2	0.6
Gary Phillips	67	4.0	.355	.581	1.6	1.0
Carl Braun	48	3.7	.377	.741	1.0	1.5
Gene Guarilia	45	3.6	.379	.641	2.8	0.2
Team	80	121.1	.423	.728	76.0	25.6
Opponents	80	111.9	N/A	N/A	N/A	N/A

II. The Heartbreakers

The five most dominant teams not to win an NBA title

1. The 1946-1947 Washington Capitols
Record: 49-11
Overall ranking: 7th, 8.885 points above average.
Other dominant Washington Capitol teams of the era: None.

Why they were dominant

The Washington Capitols dominated the first season in the league now known as the National Basketball Association.

The Capitols played in an organization then known as the Basketball Association of America. The BAA came into existence in 1946 when several owners of professional hockey teams sought a way to fill their spacious arenas on nights when their hockey teams played in other cities.

The owners of the BAA teams thought the top basketball players of the day would leap at the chance to play in large arenas in the country's biggest cities. Most of those players passed on that opportunity during the BAA's inaugural season. The top college prospects, players like dominant centers George Mikan and Bob Kurland, elected to join the established National Basketball League or to play Amateur Athletic Union basketball.

Washington got a jump on the rest of the BAA when it managed to sign an NBL star *and* a college standout.

Bob Feerick, a 6-foot-3 guard, jumped from Oshkosh of the NBL to the Capitols for the 1946-1947 season. Horace "Bones" McKinney, a 6-foot-6 forward, joined the Washington franchise at the conclusion of his outstanding college career at North Carolina.

The presence of Feerick and McKinney gave the Capitols a clear talent advantage over the rest of the new league.

Feerick finished third in the BAA in scoring at 16.8 points per game. He also finished the campaign as the only player in the league to make 40 percent of his shots in significant playing time.

McKinney contributed 12 points a game and earned a reputation as one of the most accurate perimeter shooters of the time.

Fred Scolari teamed with Feerick in the backcourt and contributed 12.6 points per game in a year when only 18 BAA players averaged more than 12 points per game.

Washington supported its three high-scoring players with the best defense in the league. The Capitols limited foes to 63.9 points per game, an NBA record that likely will stand forever.

A 29-year-old former high school coach quickly molded this talent together into a formidable unit. Arnold "Red" Auerbach directed his first professional team to a 49-11 record.

The Capitols reeled off a 17-game winning streak early in the season to jump ahead of the rest of the league. Washington finished the season with 10 more victories than any other team in the BAA.

The Capitols set several standards for excellence during that first season.

Washington won its first 27 home games and finished 29-1 at home, becoming the first of five teams to finish a season with just one home defeat.

The Capitols' overall winning percentage (.817) stood as a record until the 1966-1967 Philadelphia 76ers finished their 68-13 season with a winning percentage of .840.

Washington enjoyed an average point differential of +9.9 points per game. The Chicago Stags had the next-best average point differential at +3.7 points per game. No BAA or NBA team produced a better average point differential until the 1970-1971 Milwaukee Bucks came along.

The Capitols also set a league record for most consecutive road wins at the end of a season with six. The streak doesn't sound impressive, but it stood as a league record for 26 years.

Why they didn't win it all

Owners of professional hockey teams brought this professional basketball league into existence. The hockey owners also chose to use the National Hockey League's playoff format for the new basketball league.

The top three teams in each division made the BAA playoffs after the 1946-1947 season. Then things got weird. The two second-place teams played each other in one quarterfinal. The two third-place teams squared off in the other quarterfinal. The winners of those two series then met in the semifinal round.

The format left the two division winners to play against each other in the league semifinals. Thus, the Eastern Division champion Washington Capitols faced the Western Division champion Chicago Stags. Not in the league finals, but in the first playoff series for both teams.

Chicago boasted one of the BAA's top young players in Max Zaslofsky, a 6-foot-2 guard. Zaslofsky and backcourt mate Don Carlson both ranked among the league's top shooters. Chicago center Chuck Halbert stood 6-foot-9, one of the tallest players of the era.

The Stags won the best-of-seven series in surprisingly dominant fashion.

The series started in Washington, where the Capitols lost just once during the regular season. Chicago promptly won a pair of games in Washington, both by double-digit margins.

The Stags returned home and again beat the Capitols by double digits to take a 3-0 series lead.

No BAA/NBA team has come back from a 3-0 deficit to win a best-of-seven playoff series. Washington had the unfortunate honor of starting that legacy.

The Capitols extended the series to six games, but the Stags closed out the Washington's magnificent season with a 66-61 win in Chicago in Game 6.

The Philadelphia Warriors, who finished 14 games behind the Capitols in the Eastern Division, upset the Stags in the championship series to claim what historians now recognize as the first NBA title. Thus was established the time-honored NBA "tradition" of waiting until the postseason to turn up the intensity.

Postscript

Washington returned to the league finals after the 1948-1949 season, but the George Mikan-led Minneapolis Lakers defeated the Capitols in six games to claim the Laker franchise's first BAA/NBA title. Auerbach left Washington after the season because of a contract dispute. The franchise folded within two seasons.

Auerbach would wind up with the struggling Boston Celtics franchise at the beginning of the 1950-1951 season. Auerbach might have presided over the most dominant team not to win a league title, but he developed a reputation as a pretty fair postseason coach during his tenure in Boston.

1946-1947 Washington Capitols final statistics

Name	G	PPG	FG%	FT%	RPG	APG
Bob Feerick	55	16.8	.401	.762	N/A	1.3
Freddie Scolari	58	12.6	.294	.811	N/A	1.0
Horace McKinney	58	12.0	.279	.690	N/A	1.2
Johnny Norlander	60	10.4	.319	.652	N/A	0.8
John Mahnken	60	9.3	.255	.681	N/A	1
Irv Torgoff	58	8.4	.273	.730	N/A	0.5
Bob Gantt	23	3.1	.326	.464	N/A	0.2
Al Negratti	11	2.8	.188	.625	N/A	0.5

Marty Passaglia	43	2.8	.231	.563	N/A	0.2
Francis O'Grady	55	2.7	.238	.717	N/A	0.4
Ben Goldfaden	2	1.0	.000	.500	N/A	0.0
Ken Keller	25	0.9	.333	.500	N/A	0.0
Al Lujack	5	0.8	.125	.400	N/A	0.0
Gene Gillette	14	0.6	.091	.667	N/A	0.1
Team	60	73.8	.297	.706	N/A	6.3
Opponents	60	63.9	N/A	N/A	N/A	N/A

2. The 1993-1994 Seattle Supersonics
Record: 63-19
Overall ranking: 9th, 8.615 points above average.
Other dominant Seattle Supersonic teams of the era: 1994-1995 (24th overall, 7.809 points above average); 1995-1996 (38th overall, 7.385 points above average); 1996-1997 (49th overall, 7.001 points above average).

Why they were dominant

The Seattle Supersonics seemed ready to assume to mantle of the NBA's most dominant team following Michael Jordan's surprising first retirement after the Chicago Bulls' 1992-1993 "three-peat" championship season.

Seattle executed a masterful rebuild-on-the-fly project during the late 1980s and early 1990s. The franchise consistently made the playoffs and still acquired several talented young players.

The Sonics selected 6-foot-10 forward Shawn Kemp and 6-foot-4 point guard Gary Payton with first round draft picks in 1989 and 1990, respectively.

The Kemp selection represented a gamble. Kemp did not play college basketball and entered the NBA as a 19-year-old. The Payton selection represented the obvious. Payton earned several national college player of the year awards during his senior season at Oregon State.

Together, Kemp and Payton became the Sonics' inside-outside foundation. Seattle surrounded Kemp and Payton with players obtained in shrewd trades. The Sonics dealt players like Xavier McDaniel, Dale Ellis, and Olden Polynice just as they started to show signs of age. Seattle brought in players like sharpshooter Ricky Pierce and versatile big man Sam Perkins during the primes of their careers.

All of the pieces started to fit together when George Karl took over as coach midway through the 1991-1992 season. Karl employed a fast-paced offense and a trapping defense that made full use of his team's youth and depth. Karl directed the Sonics to a 27-15 finish to the 1991-1992 season. Seattle went 55-27 and won two rounds in the playoffs in 1992-1993.

The Sonics added two more valuable pieces prior to the 1993-1994 campaign.

Seattle traded defensive stopper Derrick McKey to the Indiana Pacers in exchange for high-scoring forward Detlef Schrempf, a two-time Sixth Man of the Year honoree.

The Sonics also brought in Kendall Gill to fill the team's need for a shooting guard.

Seattle overwhelmed its competition with its depth and talent during the 1993-1994 season. The Sonics assumed the best record in the NBA on February 27 and never looked back.

The Sonics won with balance and defense.

Six Seattle players averaged more than 12 points a game, led by Kemp at 18.1 per outing.

Payton and Nate McMillan formed a tenacious backcourt defensive duo. Both averaged more than two steals per game. Seattle forced over 400 more turnovers than it committed. The Sonics also forced over 200 more turnovers than any other team in the league.

Seattle finished the regular season with a then-franchise best 63-19 record, five games better than any other team in the NBA. They posted an average point differential of +9.0, two full points better than any other team in the league.

Why they didn't win it all

Seattle earned the No. 1 seed for the 1994 Western Conference playoffs. The Sonics drew a matchup against the Denver Nuggets, the No. 8 seed in the eight-team bracket.

The Nuggets had experienced a 20-62 train wreck of a season just three years earlier, but now boasted one advantage against Seattle. The Sonics did not possess a true center to match up against 7-foot-2 Denver big man Dikembe Mutombo.

Seattle's lack of size didn't matter in the first two games of the best-of-five series. The Sonics opened their playoff run with a 106-82 home win. Seattle took a 2-0 series lead with a 97-87 victory in Game 2.

The Nuggets had history going against them at this point. No No. 1 seed had lost a playoff series against a No. 8 seed. Only two other teams had won a best-of-five playoff series after losing the first two games on the road.

Denver refused to fold. The Nuggets cruised to a 110-93 win in Game 3. Denver forced a decisive Game 5 with a 94-85 overtime win in Game 4.

The final game took place in Seattle, where Seattle had a 37-4 record during the regular season. The Sonics led for most of the contest, but couldn't shake the pesky Nuggets. A late Denver surge sent the game into overtime.

The Nuggets then applied the final touches to one of the biggest upsets in NBA postseason history. Kemp scored with 2:29 left in overtime to put Seattle ahead 94-93, but the Sonics would not score again. Mutombo made a pair of timely blocks to preserve a Denver lead in the final moments. Mutombo also corralled the game's final rebound. He collapsed to the floor, shrieked, and held the ball aloft to celebrate his team's win.

Postscript

The stunning loss seemed to hang over the Seattle franchise for the rest of the Kemp-Payton era.

The Sonics slipped to a 57-25 record during the 1994-1995 season. Seattle suffered another surprising first round playoff exit, this time against an unheralded Los Angeles Lakers team.

The Sonics finally broke through to the NBA Finals after the 1995-1996 season. Seattle compiled a franchise-best 64-18 record. The Sonics slipped by the Utah Jazz in seven games in the Western Conference finals after building a 3-1 series lead.

Seattle proved a mere speed bump for the Chicago Bulls during the NBA Finals. Chicago brought its 72-10 team to the championship round. The Bulls won a pair of spirited games at home and then took the drama out of the series with a 108-86 Game 3 victory in Seattle. Chicago wrapped up the series in six games.

The Sonics kept the Kemp-Payton nucleus together for one more season. Seattle went 57-25 during the 1996-1997 campaign, but lost against the Houston Rockets in seven games in the Western Conference semifinals.

The Kemp-Payton era ended when Seattle traded away Kemp and acquired another high-scoring forward, Vin Baker, in a multi-team deal. The Sonics would register a 61-21 record during the 1997-1998 season, but lost in the second round of the playoffs. Seattle missed the playoffs altogether the following season, ending the franchise's hopes of winning a title with the nucleus that came of age during the 1993-1994 season.

1993-1994 Seattle Supersonics final statistics

Name	G	PPG	FG%	FT%	RPG	APG
Shawn Kemp	79	18.1	.538	.741	10.8	2.6
Gary Payton	82	16.5	.504	.595	3.3	6.0
Detlef Schrempf	81	15.0	.493	.769	5.6	3.4
Ricky Pierce	51	14.5	.471	.896	1.6	1.8
Kendall Gill	79	14.1	.443	.782	3.4	3.5
Sam Perkins	81	12.3	.438	.801	4.5	1.4
Vincent Askew	80	9.1	.481	.829	2.3	2.4

Nate McMillan	73	6.0	.447	.564	3.9	5.3
Michael Cage	82	4.6	.545	.486	5.4	0.5
Chris King	15	3.7	.396	.577	1.0	0.7
Alphonso Ford	6	2.7	.538	.500	0.0	0.2
Ervin Johnson	45	2.6	.415	.630	2.6	0.2
Steve Scheffler	35	2.1	.609	.950	0.7	0.2
Rich King	27	1.5	.441	.500	0.7	0.3
Team	82	105.9	.484	.745	41.2	25.8
Opponents	82	96.9	.453	.741	39.9	22.0

3. The 1985-1986 Milwaukee Bucks
Record: 57-25
Overall ranking: 11th, 8.473 points above average.
Other dominant Milwaukee Buck teams of the era: 1980-1981 (54th overall, 6.944 points above average); 1984-1985 (66th overall, 6.530 points above average).

Why they were dominant

Don Nelson coached a string of outstanding Milwaukee Bucks teams during the 1980s. The 1985-1986 squad stands out above them all.

Milwaukee positioned itself for success during the 1985-1986 season with a transaction back in 1984. The Bucks traded forwards Marques Johnson, Junior Bridgeman, and Harvey Catchings to the Los Angeles Clippers in exchange for Terry Cummings, Craig Hodges, and Ricky Pierce.

Johnson and Bridgeman had helped Milwaukee win five consecutive division titles, but their productivity declined soon after the trade because of injury and age.

Cummings and Pierce only got better. Cummings, a 6-foot-9 forward, assumed Johnson's role as the team's top frontcourt player. He would lead the Bucks in scoring in four of the next five seasons. Pierce, a high-scoring 6-foot-4 guard, became Milwaukee's top reserve. He would win the NBA's Sixth Man of the Year award twice as a Buck.

Milwaukee already had one of the NBA's best backcourts with quiet superstar shooting guard Sidney Moncrief and point guard Paul Pressey.

Moncrief, Pressey, and the new infusion of talent produced a 59-23 mark during the 1984-1985 season and a 57-25 campaign in 1985-1986.

The 1985-1986 season ranks as the franchise's most impressive of the era. The Bucks won 57 games in a season when the Boston Celtics won 67 games, the Los Angeles Lakers won 62, and every team in the NBA won at least 23.

Milwaukee went 33-8 at home and an impressive 24-17 on the road. Only Boston and Los Angeles bettered the Bucks' road record.

Milwaukee boasted one of the most balanced lineups in the NBA. Moncrief led the way with 20.2 points per game. Cummings added 19.8 per contest and led the team in rebounds. Pressey, Pierce, and Hodges also averaged in double figures. A pair of seven-footers (Randy Breuer and Alton Lister) alternated at center.

The Bucks ranked in the NBA's top five in both points per game and points allowed per game. Milwaukee enjoyed an average point differential of +9.0 points per game, second in the league only to Boston and the best average point differential for the franchise since the early 1970s.

Why they didn't win it all

Milwaukee picked the wrong decade to build a dominant squad in the Eastern Conference.

The Bucks' 1985-1986 Central Division title marked the franchise's seventh consecutive division crown. The Bucks averaged almost 55 wins per year during those seven seasons, but Milwaukee never reached the NBA Finals during that span. The dominant Boston Celtics and Philadelphia 76ers teams of the era took turns knocking the Bucks out of the playoffs.

Milwaukee had to play both Philadelphia and Boston during the 1985-1986 postseason. The Bucks swept New Jersey in the first round to set up a matchup against the 76ers, who eliminated Milwaukee from the playoffs in 1981, 1982, and 1985.

The Bucks lost Game 1 at home and played from behind for most of the series. Milwaukee finally advanced when Philadelphia great Julius Erving missed a shot at the buzzer that could have won Game 7 for the 76ers.

The Bucks went from facing a buzzer-beater to facing a buzz saw. Boston swept Milwaukee in the Eastern Conference finals en route to its 16th NBA title. The Bucks lost Game 3 at home by a 111-107 margin. The Celtics won every other game in the series by at least 11 points to eliminate Milwaukee from the playoffs for the third time in four seasons.

Postscript

One of the most dominant teams in NBA history saw its period of excellence end with a whimper.

Moncrief, the franchise's standard bearer throughout the 1980s, played just 39 games during the 1986-1987 season because of injuries. His scoring average dropped to 11.8 points per game. He never returned to his pre-injury level of play.

Nelson coaxed 50 wins out of the 1986-1987 Bucks, but the franchise's string of division titles ended. Nelson also departed after the season. He soon would surface with the Golden State Warriors.

Milwaukee's fortunes slowly sagged as its top players aged. The Bucks made the playoffs during their first four seasons under new coach Del Harris, but won just one postseason series.

The final collapse came during the 1991-1992 season. Milwaukee tried to build around a too-small Dale Ellis and a too-old Moses Malone, and managed just a 31-51 record.

1985-1986 Milwaukee Bucks final statistics

Name	G	PPG	FG%	FT%	RPG	APG
Sidney Moncrief	73	20.2	.489	.859	4.6	4.9
Terry Cummings	82	19.8	.474	.656	8.5	2.4
Paul Pressey	80	14.3	.488	.806	5.0	7.8
Ricky Pierce	81	13.9	.538	.858	2.9	2.2
Craig Hodges	66	10.8	.500	.872	1.8	3.5
Alton Lister	81	9.8	.551	.602	7.3	1.2
Randy Breuer	82	8.4	.477	.712	5.6	1.4
Charlie Davis	57	7.7	.474	.813	3.0	1.0
Kenny Fields	78	6.4	.513	.689	2.6	1.0
Jeff Lamp	44	6.3	.449	.859	2.8	1.5
Mike Glenn	38	6.2	.495	.959	1.5	1.0
Jerry Reynolds	55	3.7	.444	.558	1.5	1.6
Paul Mokeski	45	3.2	.424	.735	3.1	0.7
Bryan Warrick	5	2.0	.400	1.000	0.6	1.2
Derrick Rowland	2	1.5	.333	.500	0.5	0.5
Earl Jones	12	1.1	.417	.750	0.8	0.3
Team	82	114.5	.493	.764	44.0	26.3
Opponents	82	105.5	.467	.740	42.6	23.8

4. The 1990-1991 Portland Trail Blazers

Record: 63-19

Overall ranking: 12th, 8.421 points above average.

Other dominant Portland Trail Blazer teams of the era: 1991-1992 (55th overall, 6.942 points above average); 1989-1990 (74th overall, 6.365 points above average).

Why they were dominant

"The Team That Didn't Draft Michael Jordan" still nearly became "The Team of the 1990s."

The Portland Trail Blazers lost in the NBA Finals after the 1989-1990 and 1991-1992 seasons. Portland also led the NBA in victories during the 1990-1991 season, but lost in the Western Conference finals.

Observers made a habit of tracing the team's near-misses to a 1984 draft day decision. The Trail Blazers used the No. 2 overall pick to select University of Kentucky center Sam Bowie. The Chicago Bulls went next and "settled" for University of North Carolina guard Michael Jordan.

Truth be told, Portland made few draft mistakes during the mid-1980s. The Trail Blazers chose shooting guard Clyde Drexler from the University of Houston with the No. 14 selection in the 1983 draft. Two years later, Portland selected little-known point guard Terry Porter from lesser-known Division III school Wisconsin-Stevens Point. Thus, the Trail Blazers were set in the backcourt for the next decade.

Drexler would set the Portland franchise record for career points during his 12-plus years with the Trail Blazers. Porter would set the franchise record for career assists and participate in two All-Star games.

Drexler and Porter emerged as stars by the 1988-1989 season. The franchise also had added complementary players like center Kevin Duckworth and forward Jerome Kersey.

The mix of talent didn't produce many wins in 1988-1989. Portland fired coach Mike Schuler after a 25-22 start. The Trail Blazers fared even worse under new coach Rick Adelman. They finished 39-43.

Portland reversed its fortunes with a summer trade. The Trail Blazers sent Bowie to the New Jersey Nets for rugged power forward Buck Williams. Portland further bolstered its frontcourt with the addition of rookie forward Clifford Robinson. The additions instantly transformed Portland into a power.

The Trail Blazers posted a franchise-best 59-23 record during the 1989-1990 season. Portland then took advantage of a postseason path made clear when the Phoenix Suns upset the top-seeded Los Angeles Lakers in the Western Conference semifinals. The Trail Blazers in turn defeated the Suns to reach the NBA Finals for the first time since 1977.

Portland lost the championship series 4-1 against the Detroit Pistons, but began the 1990-1991 campaign with lofty expectations. The Trail Blazers brought their nucleus back. Portland also added veteran guard Danny Ainge, a mainstay on the Boston Celtics' mid-1980s title teams, as the final piece to the franchise's championship puzzle.

The Trail Blazers lived up to the preseason hype at the beginning of the 1990-1991 campaign. Portland won its first 11 games and 19 of its first 20. The Trail Blazers would enjoy a franchise-record 16-game winning streak later in the season.

The rest of the league never caught up. Portland finished 63-19, breaking the year-old franchise record for wins in a season. The Trail Blazers won the Pacific Division and finished the regular season with the NBA's best record for the first time since 1978. Portland led the league in road wins with 27. The Trail Blazers tied the Utah Jazz for most home wins with 36. The Trail Blazers finished third in the league in scoring and enjoyed a franchise-record average point differential of +8.7 points per game.

Seven players averaged double figures in scoring on this balanced team. Drexler led the way at 21.5 points per game. Porter added 17.0. Duckworth contributed 15.8. Williams averaged 11.7 points and led the league in field goal percentage.

Drexler, Duckworth, and Porter all played in the All-Star Game. Adelman coached the Western Conference All-Star team. The franchise drew its 10 millionth fan on November 27. The franchise recorded its 600th consecutive sellout on January 6. The fans continued to pack the stands the rest of the year, enjoying their team's march to an expected championship.

Why they didn't win it all

The first signs of trouble popped up during the first round of the 1991 playoffs. The Seattle Supersonics, with the inside-outside combination of Shawn Kemp and Gary Payton in its embryonic stages, pushed top-seeded Portland to five tough games. The Trail Blazers survived with a 119-107 victory in the decisive fifth game.

Portland eventually advanced to a matchup against the Los Angeles Lakers in the Western Conference finals.

Los Angeles immediately took control of the series with a 111-106 victory in Portland in Game 1. The home teams easily won the next four games of the series, resulting in a 3-2 Lakers lead heading into Game 6 in Los Angeles' Great Western Forum.

This one stayed close throughout. The Lakers nursed a 91-90 lead into the final seconds. Porter had a shot to give the Trail Blazers the lead, but missed off the rim. The ball caromed off of several players and finally wound up in the vicinity of Magic Johnson, the Lakers' Hall of Fame floor leader. Johnson brilliantly flung the loose ball over his head toward the empty end of the floor, thus preventing a Portland foul. The remaining seconds of the game, the series, and the Trail Blazers' season ticked away.

Postscript

Portland did come back strong during the 1991-1992 season. The Trail Blazers led the Western Conference with a 57-25 record. Portland plowed through the Western Conference playoffs and returned to the NBA Finals.

The Trail Blazers faced the Chicago Bulls in the championship series, the same team they would have played had they reached the NBA Finals in 1991. Now, however, the circumstances had changed. Portland would have enjoyed a home court advantage and an edge in postseason experience had the teams met in the 1991 playoffs. Chicago now reigned as NBA champion and enjoyed home court advantage for the 1992 Finals.

The Bulls immediately made a statement with a 122-89 rout in Game 1. Michael Jordan, the player Portland let get away, set an NBA Finals record with 35 points and a memorable shrug in the first half.

Portland stole Game 2 in overtime, but Chicago refused to cede control of the series. The Bulls cruised to a 94-84 victory in Game 3 in Portland. The Trail Blazers again tied the series with a 93-88 win in Game 4. Jordan answered with a 46-point performance during Chicago's 119-106 Game 5 triumph in Portland. The series appeared over as the Bulls returned to Chicago needing just one win in two home games to defend their title.

Portland had other ideas. The Trail Blazers dominated the first three quarters of Game 6 and led 79-64 entering the final period.

The last hit to Portland's championship dreams came from an unlikely source. A brigade of Bulls reserves went on a 14-2 run to start the fourth quarter, slicing the Trail Blazers' lead to 81-78.

Jordan and sidekick Scottie Pippen took over from there. Jordan and Pippen scored the Bulls' last 19 points during a series-clinching 97-93 triumph.

The 1992 Finals marked the end of Portland's run as an elite team. Drexler missed 33 games because of a leg injury during the 1992-1993 season. The Trail Blazers finished third in the Pacific Division. They lost against San Antonio in the first round of the playoffs. Television analysts pronounced the end of "The Dynasty That Never Was."

Events would prove the analysts correct. The aging Trail Blazers lost against the eventual champion Houston Rockets in the first round of the 1994 playoffs.

The Clyde Drexler era in Portland finally ended when the Trail Blazers traded their franchise player to Houston just before the trade deadline during the 1994-1995 season. Drexler would go on to help the Rockets win their second consecutive NBA title. Portland would go on to a new building process.

1990-1991 Portland Trail Blazers final statistics

Name	G	PPG	FG%	FT%	RPG	APG
Clyde Drexler	82	21.5	.482	.794	6.7	6.0
Terry Porter	81	17.0	.515	.823	3.5	8.0
Kevin Duckworth	81	15.8	.481	.772	6.6	1.1

Jerome Kersey	73	14.8	.478	.709	6.6	3.1
Clifford Robinson	82	11.7	.463	.653	4.3	1.8
Buck Williams	80	11.7	.602	.705	9.4	1.2
Danny Ainge	80	11.1	.472	.826	2.6	3.6
Walter Davis	32	6.1	.446	.913	1.8	1.3
Mark Bryant	53	5.1	.488	.733	3.6	0.5
Drazen Petrovic	18	4.4	.451	.682	1.0	1.1
Danny Young	75	3.8	.380	.911	1.0	1.9
Alaa Abdelnaby	43	3.1	.474	.568	2.1	0.3
Wayne Cooper	67	2.2	.393	.786	2.8	0.3
Team	82	114.7	.485	.753	45.9	27.5
Opponents	82	106.0	.456	.777	41.9	25.0

5. The 1996-1997 Utah Jazz
Record: 64-18
Overall ranking: 19th, 8.056 points above average.
Other dominant Utah Jazz teams of the era: 1994-1995 (31st overall, 7.651 points above average); 1995-1996 (81st overall, 6.236 points above average); 1997-1998 (97th overall, 5.845 points above average).

Why they were dominant

The Utah Jazz's window of opportunity to win a championship during the Karl Malone-John Stockton era seemed to close during the summer of 1993. The Jazz lost in the first round of the playoffs against the Seattle Supersonics, taking a giant step back from the franchise's appearance in the 1992 Western Conference finals. Malone turned 30 during the summer. Stockton had turned 30 the previous year. NBA observers prepared to tune out the Jazz.

Malone and Stockton already had secured their places in NBA history. Malone already had finished second in the league in scoring four times. Stockton had just won the sixth of his nine consecutive assist titles. Both played on the United States' Olympic "Dream Team" and won gold medals at the 1992 Summer Games in Barcelona.

A trade and a playoff upset helped Malone and Stockton add to their legacies in the mid-1990s.

The trade brought Jeff Hornacek to Utah in exchange for Jeff Malone. Malone had served as the third option in Utah's offense. Hornacek, a deadly shooter, would prove a better fit in the Jazz's pick-and-roll-based scheme. Jeff Malone would be out of the NBA by 1996.

The playoff upset—the Denver Nuggets' shocking victory over top-seeded Seattle—enabled Utah to reach the Western Conference finals in 1994. The Jazz probably would have lost a playoff series against the Sonics, but they defeated the upstart Nuggets in the second round. The fortuitous playoff run silenced those who saw Utah as a team in decline.

The Jazz suddenly emerged as a serious championship contender during the 1996 postseason. Utah smashed Midwest Division champion San Antonio 95-75 in Game 1 of the Western Conference semifinals. The Jazz went on to win the series 4-2. Utah then rallied from a 3-1 deficit against top-seeded Seattle in the Western Conference finals and extended the series to seven games before falling.

All of the planets aligned properly to allow the Jazz to dominate the Western Conference during the 1996-1997 season. Defending conference champion Seattle suffered from a post-NBA Finals loss hangover. The Houston Rockets had the three-headed monster of Hakeem Olajuwon, Clyde Drexler, and Charles Barkley, but the Rockets also showed signs of age. The Los Angeles Lakers had newly signed center Shaquille O'Neal and newly drafted rookie Kobe Bryant, but the Lakers also showed signs of youth. The San Antonio Spurs' season ended before it began when center David Robinson missed 76 games because of an injury.

In Utah, Stockton and Malone continued to do the same things they had done since the mid-1980s. Now, they did their thing better than anyone else.

The Jazz got in swing with a franchise-record 15-game winning streak early in the season. Utah reeled off another 15-game winning streak during the season's final month.

The Jazz finished with a franchise-best 64-18 record. They led the Western Conference in victories for the first time. Utah compiled an impressive 38-3 home record, second in the NBA behind only the Chicago Bulls' 39-2 home ledger. The Jazz were the only team in the league to make more than half of their field goal attempts. No team has matched the feat since.

Utah finished second in the NBA in points per game, just a fraction of a point behind the Bulls. The team posted an average point differential of +8.8 points per game, another franchise record.

Malone averaged 27.4 points and 9.9 rebounds per game. He again finished second to Michael Jordan in the NBA scoring race, but he did win his first MVP award.

Stockton's nine-year reign as the NBA's assist leader ended, but he did finish second in the league with 10.5 assists per game.

Malone and Stockton also finished sixth and seventh, respectively, in the league field goal percentage standings.

Hornacek contributed 14.5 points per game and made almost 90 percent of his free throws. Shooting guard Bryon Russell and center Greg Ostertag rounded out the lineup. Rugged veteran forward Antoine Carr led Utah's reserves.

The Jazz mowed through the Western Conference playoffs. Utah swept the Los Angeles Clippers in Round 1. The Jazz then earned a surprisingly easy 4-1 triumph against the Los Angeles Lakers in the second round.

Utah faced Houston for the right to advance to the NBA Finals. The Rockets defeated the Jazz in the playoffs en route to their championships in 1994 and 1995.

Things changed this time. Utah dominated the games on its home court as Houston had no answer for Malone. The Jazz went to Houston for Game 6 with a 3-2 lead in the series. The Rockets led throughout most of the contest. Utah tied it with a late flurry. The Jazz wound up with the last possession and Stockton made the most of it. He buried a long 3-pointer at the buzzer to give Utah a 103-100 victory and the franchise's first NBA Finals berth.

Why they didn't win it all

Five reasons: Michael Jordan, Michael Jordan, Michael Jordan, Michael Jordan, and Michael Jordan.

Game 1 of the 1997 NBA Finals. Malone went to the free throw line with 9.2 seconds to go and the score tied at 82 in the opening game of the series between Utah and Chicago. Malone missed both charity tosses. Chicago rebounded and Jordan hit a 20-footer at the buzzer to win the game.

Game 5 of the 1997 NBA Finals. Jordan played despite flu-like symptoms that left him, "queasy and low on energy." Utah had won two consecutive games to tie the series at two. The Jazz had a chance to pull ahead in the series with another home win. Jordan wouldn't let it happen. He scored 38 points in 44 minutes, including the tiebreaking basket in the final minute of the Bulls' crucial 90-88 win.

Game 6 of the 1997 NBA Finals. Jordan scored 39 points and grabbed 11 rebounds as Chicago wrapped up the series and its fifth championship with a 90-86 win. Jordan split a double team and passed to Steve Kerr for the go-ahead basket in the final minute.

Game 2 of the 1998 NBA Finals. Chicago and Utah met in an NBA Finals rematch. This time, the Jazz enjoyed home court advantage. They had fresher legs after a sweep of the Los Angeles Lakers in the Western Conference finals. They led the series 1-0 after an overtime win in Game 1.

Jordan changed things in a flash. He converted a critical three-point play in the final minute of Game 2, breaking a tie score and lifting Chicago to a 93-88 win.

Game 6 of the 1998 NBA Finals. Chicago led the series 3-2, but Utah had the home court and an 86-83 lead with 41.9 seconds left. A back injury had rendered Bulls All-Star Scottie Pippen ineffective.

Cue Mr. Jordan.

He quickly scored on a drive to slice the Jazz lead to 86-85.

Then he stripped the ball from Malone with 18.5 seconds left.

Then he sank a 20-footer from the left wing with 6.6 seconds left. The basket gave Jordan 45 points for the game, an 87-86 victory, and Chicago's sixth championship in eight years.

The Bulls broke up their roster following the season, but the Jazz's window of championship opportunity also had closed.

Postscript

Utah led the Western Conference standings for most of the lockout-delayed 1998-1999 season, but the San Antonio Spurs made a furious closing kick and nosed out the Jazz for the No. 1 seed for the playoffs.

Utah had to face an exciting young Sacramento Kings team in the first round of the postseason. The Kings pushed the Jazz to five games, with Utah needing overtime to win the finale. The Jazz had little left for the Western Conference semifinals. They lost against the Portland Trail Blazers in six games.

The script repeated itself during the 1999-2000 season. Utah outlasted Seattle in a five-game first round playoff series, but couldn't keep up with Portland in the second round.

The Dallas Mavericks applied the final death knell to Utah's championship aspirations. Dallas rallied from a 2-0 deficit and beat the Jazz 3-2 in the opening round of the 2001 playoffs. Calvin Booth's basket in the final seconds gave the Mavericks an 84-83 Game 5 victory on the Jazz's home floor.

The Malone-Stockton Jazz reached the playoffs two more times. They lost in the first round on both occasions.

Stockton retired after the 2003 season as the NBA's all-time leader in career assists and steals.

Malone played one additional season with the Los Angeles Lakers, hoping to win the elusive championship ring. The Lakers reached the NBA Finals, but lost against the Detroit Pistons in five games as Malone missed most of the series with a knee injury. Malone retired the following winter as the second-leading scorer in NBA history.

1996-1997 Utah Jazz final statistics

Name	G	PPG	FG%	FT%	RPG	APG
Karl Malone	82	27.4	.550	.755	9.9	4.5
Jeff Hornacek	82	14.5	.482	.899	2.9	4.4
John Stockton	82	14.4	.548	.846	2.8	10.5
Bryon Russell	81	10.8	.479	.701	4.1	1.5
Antoine Carr	82	7.4	.483	.780	2.4	0.9
Greg Ostertag	77	7.3	.515	.678	7.3	0.4
Shandon Anderson	65	5.9	.462	.687	2.8	0.8
Howard Eisley	82	4.5	.451	.787	1.0	2.4
Chris Morris	73	4.3	.408	.722	2.2	0.6
Ruben Nembhard	8	4.0	.414	.800	1.0	1.5
Adam Keefe	62	3.8	.513	.689	3.5	0.5
Stephen Howard	42	3.6	.573	.597	1.8	0.2
Greg Foster	79	3.5	.453	.831	2.4	0.4
Jamie Watson	13	2.5	.440	.833	1.4	0.8
Brooks Thompson	2	0.0	.000	.000	0.0	0.5
Team	82	103.1	.504	.769	40.2	26.8
Opponents	82	94.3	.438	.750	37.3	19.4

III. The Right Place at the Right Time

The five least dominant teams to win an NBA title

1. The 1957-1958 St. Louis Hawks
Record: 41-31
Overall ranking: 519th, 0.734 points above average.

Why they weren't so dominant

    The St. Louis Hawks emerged as the Boston Celtics' chief rival for NBA dominance during the late 1950s.
    The Hawks filled the role almost by default.
    St. Louis played in the NBA's downtrodden Western Division during the late 1950s.
    The Hawks' competition:
* The Minneapolis Lakers, in a down cycle after the retirement of center George Mikan and before the arrival of high-flying forward Elgin Baylor
* The Fort Wayne/Detroit Pistons, rapidly aging after NBA Finals appearances in 1955 and 1956 and in transition after the franchise moved to Detroit.
* The Rochester/Cincinnati Royals, who staggered through the late 1950s haunted by the tragic loss of forward Maurice Stokes (paralysis brought on by encephalitis), all the while biding time waiting to select guard Oscar Robertson in the 1960 draft.
    St. Louis had the pieces in place to take over the division by the start of the 1956-1957 season. Star forward Bob Pettit won his first scoring title the previous year. Jack Coleman and Charlie Share also averaged double figures in the frontcourt. The Hawks acquired skilled guards Slater Martin (formerly a member of the Lakers' early-1950s championship teams) and Jack McMahon (from the Royals) in trades.
    St. Louis also shipped its first round pick in the 1956 draft to Boston in exchange for two future Hall of Famers: forward and St. Louis hometown hero Ed Macauley, and rookie center Cliff Hagen.
    (The Celtics used the draft pick to select a University of San Francisco center with questionable offensive skills. His name: Bill Russell).
    St. Louis' loaded roster started slowly at the beginning of the 1956-1957 season. The shaky start resulted in the dismissal of coach Red Holzman after 33 games. Reserve player Alex Hannum took over as coach for the final 31 games.

He led the Hawks to a 15-16 finish, good enough for a final record of 34-38 and a tie for first place in the weak Western Division.

St. Louis suddenly clicked in the playoffs. The Hawks won their first six games of the 1957 postseason. Two victories to earn the Western Division tiebreaker. A 3-0 sweep of the Lakers in the Western Division finals. A 125-123 double-overtime triumph at Boston in Game 1 of the NBA Finals.

The 1957 Finals would go down as one of the most memorable in NBA history. The Celtics would win their first championship with a 125-123 double overtime victory in Game 7 in Boston Garden. The Hawks had a chance to force a third overtime, but Pettit missed a last-second layup after catching Hannum's length-of-the-floor pass off of the backboard. St. Louis spent the next year looking forward to another crack at the Celtics in a championship series.

St. Louis repeated as Western Division champion in 1957-1958, but didn't dominate the way one would expect from a title contender. The Hawks finished 41-31, tied with Syracuse for the second-best mark in the league.

St. Louis' 41-31 record equates to a 47-35 mark for an 82-game season. The Hawks' record seems even less impressive considering:

* No other team in the Western Division finished with a winning record.
* Every team in the Eastern Division finished with a better record than the second-place teams in the Western Division (Detroit and Cincinnati).
* St. Louis got to play its weaker Western Division brethren 12 times apiece (the Eastern Conference teams got nine games apiece against the Western Division teams), but produced just the 41 wins.

The Hawks finished the regular season with an average point differential of just +1.3 points per game. Three other teams did better during the 1957-1958 season. St. Louis did manage a 23-8 record at home and a 9-4 mark on neutral courts, but just a 9-19 ledger in road games.

Why they still won it all

The Hawks remained the class of the Western Division, despite the flawed season.

Pettit averaged 24.6 points (third-best in the league) and 17.4 rebounds (second-best). Hagen contributed 19.9 points per game and finished second in the league in field goal percentage during his second season.

St. Louis topped Detroit 4-1 in the Western Division finals, controlling the series from start to finish. The Hawks earned a rematch against the Celtics in the NBA Finals.

The 1958 Finals started along the same pattern as the previous year. St. Louis stole a two-point win in Game 1 in the Boston Garden. The Celtics responded with a vengeance, rolling to a blowout win in Game 2.

The series turned the Hawks' way in Game 3. Bill Russell injured his ankle during the Hawks' 111-108 victory. Russell would continue to play, but without his usual quickness and mobility.

Other key Boston players sustained key injuries. Star point guard Bob Cousy played through a foot injury, though he did play well enough in a surprise start at center to lead the Celtics to a 109-98 Game 4 win.

Boston's leading scorer, Bill Sharman, tweaked a knee early in Game 5. The Celtics tried to slow the pace, but the Hawks adjusted and won 102-100 to take a 3-2 lead in the series.

St. Louis returned home for Game 6 with a chance to wrap up the championship. Russell again tried to play, but managed just 20 minutes on his heavily wrapped ankle.

The Celtics still hung close. The Hawks needed a 50-point night from Pettit to stay in front. Pettit scored 19 of his points in the fourth quarter, including a pair of free throws with 16 seconds left that sealed St. Louis' series-clinching 110-109 victory.

The Hawks owned the franchise's first and only title, even though they were outscored by 29 points during the NBA Finals.

The 1957-58 St. Louis squad now holds a semi-exalted place in NBA history as one of two other teams to win a championship during the Russell-led Celtics dynasty. In truth, the Hawks possessed a team that squeaked by in a lousy division and won one championship series with the assistance of several key Boston injuries.

St. Louis reached two more NBA Finals during the Pettit era. Boston won both series decisively. The 1960 NBA Finals went seven games, but the Celtics won the clincher 122-103. Boston put away the 1961 NBA Finals in five games.

1957-1958 St. Louis Hawks final statistics

Name	G	PPG	FG%	FT%	RPG	APG
Bob Pettit	70	24.6	.410	.749	17.4	2.2
Cliff Hagan	70	19.9	.443	.768	10.1	2.5
Ed Macauley	72	14.2	.428	.724	6.6	2.0
Slater Martin	60	12.0	.336	.746	3.8	3.6
Charlie Share	72	8.6	.396	.648	10.4	1.8
Jack McMahon	72	7.9	.300	.606	2.7	4.6
Win Wilfong	71	7.8	.361	.685	4.1	2.3
Jack Coleman	72	7.6	.413	.641	6.7	1.6

Medford Park	71	5.4	.366	.728	2.6	1.1
Frank Selvy	38	3.6	.263	.610	2.3	0.9
Worthy Patterson	4	1.8	.375	.500	0.5	0.5
Dwight Morrison	13	1.6	.346	.750	2.0	0.0
Team	72	107.5	.388	.715	75.6	21.4
Opponents	72	106.2	N/A	N/A	N/A	N/A

2. The 1977-1978 Washington Bullets

Record: 44-38

Overall ranking: 510th, 0.818 points above average.

Why they weren't so dominant

The second half of the 1970s produced the NBA's Age of Parity.

Five different teams won NBA titles between 1975 and 1979. Four of those teams won the only championships their respective franchises have captured in their current locales. Four of those teams defeated an opponent with a superior record in the NBA Finals. None of those teams posted the league's best regular-season record during their championship seasons.

The 1977-1978 NBA champion Washington Bullets typified the league's Age of Parity.

The Bullets ushered in the era by losing the 1975 NBA Finals in a sweep against the Golden State Warriors. Washington finished the 1974-1975 regular season with a sparkling 60-22 record. Golden State finished 47-35.

The Bullets built their strong teams of the 1970s around skilled 6-foot-9 forward Elvin Hayes and burly 6-foot-9 center Wes Unseld. Hayes won a scoring title as a rookie with the San Diego Rockets. He won multiple rebounding titles as a Bullet. Unseld won the league MVP award during his rookie year (1968-1969). He also won a rebounding title during the 1974-1975 season.

Washington tweaked the frontcourt's supporting cast after the loss in the 1975 Finals. Dick Motta replaced K.C. Jones as coach after the 1976 postseason. The Bullets brought in players like guard Kevin Grevey and forward Mitch Kupchak (draft) and guard Tom Henderson (trade). Forward Phil Chenier, the No. 2 scorer on the 1975 team, shifted to a supporting role.

Washington made a key free agent acquisition before the 1977-1978 season. The Bullets signed high-scoring forward Bob Dandridge, a key player on the Milwaukee Bucks' dominant teams during the early 1970s.

Injuries prevented the Bullets from hitting their marks for most of the 1977-1978 season. Chenier would play just 36 games. Four other regulars would miss at least seven games. Washington signed just-released guard Charles Johnson in January so the team would have eight players available to play.

The Bullets struggled home with a 44-38 record. Washington finished eight games behind San Antonio in the Central Division and 11 games behind Eastern Conference front-runner Philadelphia. Seven teams in all exceeded the Bullets' victory total.

Washington did its struggling during a down year for the Eastern Conference. Only five teams in the East finished with a winning record. Seven teams finished above .500 in the West. No team in the West won fewer than 31 games. Three teams fared worse in the East.

Six Bullets averaged double figures in scoring, led by Hayes at 19.7 points per game and Dandridge with 19.3, but none finished among the league leaders

Washington finished the season with an average point differential of merely +0.9 points per game. Seven teams matched or bettered that mark.

Bullets fans didn't see anything special on the horizon for this group. Attendance at Washington's Capital Centre dropped about 500 fans per game.

Why they still won it all

The Bullets did have some things going for them as the 1978 postseason started. Washington had depth and balance. Six players averaged double figures in scoring. Three others—Unseld, Johnson, and Larry Wright—also provided vital contributions.

The Bullets also had playoff experience. Washington's core had produced 10 consecutive playoff appearances. No other team in the 1978 postseason could make that claim.

The door to the 1978 championship swung wide open late in the season.

The Portland Trail Blazers had seemed on course to win their second consecutive title. Portland boasted a 50-10 record when a foot injury forced star center Bill Walton to the sidelines. The Trail Blazers still finished the regular season with a league-best 58-24 record, but lost against the Seattle Supersonics in the Western Conference semifinals.

Washington started its own postseason trek with a sweep of Atlanta in the first round. The Bullets then knocked off division champion San Antonio 4-2 to reach the Eastern Conference finals. Washington's 121-117 victory in Game 2 on the Spurs' home floor proved the pivotal game of the series.

Next up: The Philadelphia 76ers, the defending Eastern Conference champions. The series followed a pattern similar to Washington's win against San Antonio. The Bullets stole Game 1 in Philadelphia and won three narrow victories in the Capital Centre to claim the series. Washington wrapped up the East title with a 101-99 victory in Game 6. Unseld scored the winning basket on a tip-in in the final seconds.

The Bullets advanced to the NBA Finals to meet another surprise team. The Seattle Supersonics started 5-17 before naming Lenny Wilkens to replace Bob Hopkins as coach. Wilkens led Seattle to 42 wins in its last 60 games and a franchise-best 47-35 record. The Sonics upset division champions Portland and Denver to win the Western Conference.

A scheduling conflict at Seattle's home arena, the Seattle Center Coliseum, proved fortuitous for Washington. The NBA Finals schedule used at the time called for a 2-2-1-1 home-and-home format. The scheduling dilemma forced a change to a 1-2-2-1-1 format. The Sonics also decided to play Game 4 of the series in the spacious Seattle Kingdome instead of the Coliseum, where they had a 21-game winning streak going into the Finals.

The game in the Kingdome took place May 30 before a then-NBA Finals record crowd of 39,457. The Sonics fans expected to see their team take a 3-1 lead in the series.

Instead, Washington rallied from a 15-point deficit and won the game 120-116 in overtime to square the series at 2-2.

Seattle moved within one game of the championship with a 98-94 Game 5 victory back in the Coliseum. Washington answered with a 117-82 Game 6 thrashing in the Capital Centre. The rout set a record for largest margin of victory in an NBA Finals game at the time. "It ain't over until the fat lady sings," Motta said.

The teams flew back across the country for Game 7 in Seattle. Johnson and Dandridge scored 19 points apiece to stake Washington to a lead entering the stretch run. Unseld took over from there. He sank a pair of game-clinching free throws in the final minute of the Bullets' 105-99 triumph. He would earn the NBA Finals MVP award.

Seattle and Washington validated their 1978 NBA Finals appearances to some degree by returning to the championship series the following season. The Sonics avenged the 1978 loss by winning the 1979 Finals in five games.

The Bullets posted the best record in the Eastern Conference during the 1978-1979 season and needed minimal luck to return to the NBA Finals. Their 1978 championship required good fortune in the form of Bill Walton's injury, Seattle's scheduling dilemmas, and the good fortune to play in the NBA's Age of Parity.

1977-1978 Washington Bullets final statistics

Name	G	PPG	FG%	FT%	RPG	APG
Elvin Hayes	81	19.7	.451	.634	13.3	1.8
Bob Dandridge	75	19.3	.471	.788	5.9	3.8

Mitch Kupchak	67	15.9	.512	.697	6.9	1.1
Kevin Grevey	81	15.5	.448	.789	3.6	1.9
Phil Chenier	36	14.1	.443	.790	2.8	2.0
Tom Henderson	75	11.4	.432	.746	2.6	5.4
Larry Wright	70	9.2	.496	.710	1.5	3.7
Charlie Johnson	39	8.3	.408	.824	2.4	2.1
Wes Unseld	80	7.6	.523	.538	11.9	4.1
Greg Ballard	76	4.9	.425	.772	3.5	0.8
Phil Walker	40	4.5	.354	.667	1.3	1.4
Joe Pace	49	3.9	.479	.613	2.7	0.5
Team	82	110.3	.461	.711	50.8	23.8
Opponents	82	109.4	.467	.758	46.9	26.1

3. The 1954-1955 Syracuse Nationals
Record: 43-29
Overall ranking: 463rd, 1.204 points above average.

Why they weren't so dominant

Perfect timing—pun intended—helped the Syracuse Nationals win the 1954-1955 NBA title.

Syracuse emerged as an elite team during a brief gap between eras in NBA history. George Mikan retired following the 1953-1954 season after leading the Minneapolis Lakers to five championships in six seasons. Bill Russell, who would lead the Boston Celtics to 11 titles in 13 seasons, would not come on the scene until the 1956-1957 campaign.

The 1954-1955 Syracuse squad helped bridge the gap between Mikan and Russell.

The 1954-1955 season also saw the introduction of the 24-second shot clock. The new rule revolutionized the game. Teams averaged 10 more shots per contest. Scoring skyrocketed from 79.5 points per game to 93.1 points per game.

The inventor of the shot clock? None other than Syracuse owner Daniel Biasone.

A shot clock theoretically benefits the superior team by increasing the number of possessions in a game. Biasone's Nationals had developed into a superior team in the years leading up to the 1954-1955 season.

Syracuse posted a winning season in four of its first five NBA seasons. The Nationals advanced to the NBA Finals during their first NBA season, but lost against Minneapolis and Mikan in six games.

Syracuse returned to the NBA Finals after the 1953-1954 season. The Nationals again lost to the Lakers, but pushed Minneapolis to its closest championship series of the Mikan era. The series went seven games before the Lakers prevailed 87-80 in the finale.

Syracuse succeeded because of Dolph Schayes, a versatile 6-foot-8 forward. Schayes joined the Nationals during the 1948-1949 season, the last year of the National Basketball League. Schayes continued to shine once the NBL and Basketball Association of America merged to form the NBA. Schayes would become the first player in NBA history to surpass 15,000 points for his career. He would retire after a then-record 16 seasons. The 1954-1955 season began with Schayes ready to enter the prime of his career.

Paul Seymour served as Syracuse's captain, assist leader, and second-leading scorer. Seymour, another veteran from the NBL days, made most of the All-NBA teams during the mid-1950s.

The Nationals had good size on the front line for the era with players like Red Rocha, Red Kerr, and Earl Lloyd. George King played opposite Seymour in the backcourt.

Syracuse fulfilled expectations by winning the Eastern Division title during the 1954-1955 season. Yet the Nationals did not dominate the way they perhaps should have with Mikan retired and a shot clock in use.

Syracuse finished with a 43-29 record, just short of a 50-win pace over the modern 82-game NBA schedule. The Nationals went just 10-16 in road games. (In their defense, no other team in the league won more than 10 road games, either).

The Nationals' Eastern Division did boast a better overall record than the Western Division, but no other team in the East had a record comparable to Syracuse's. The Nationals finished the season as an above-average team in a division full of average teams.

Syracuse finished the year with an average point differential of just +1.4 points per game, second in the league, but a full point behind the Fort Wayne Pistons. The Nationals did lead the league in defense, but finished sixth out of eight teams in points per game.

The Nationals overachieved to an extent to win 43 games. One generally would expect a 40-32 season from a team with an average point differential of +1.4 points per game. By contrast, the 1958-1959 Nationals finished the season with an average point differential of +4.0 points per game, but compiled a 35-37 record.

Why they still won it all

Syracuse enjoyed tremendous success against the Fort Wayne Pistons during the 1954-1955 season. The Nationals went 7-2 against the Western Division champion Pistons, their best record against any team.

Syracuse needed every one of those seven wins against Fort Wayne. Had the Nationals gone "just" 6-3 against the Pistons, Fort Wayne would have finished with the best record in the NBA. The teams instead tied with 43-29 records. The teams met in the NBA Finals. Syracuse received home court advantage by virtue of that 7-2 regular season mark against the Pistons.

And what an advantage. The Nationals never had lost a home game against Fort Wayne in franchise history.

Syracuse continued its home mastery over the Pistons with narrow wins in the first two games of the series.

Fort Wayne rebounded on its "home" court in Indianapolis. (A bowling tournament took over the Pistons' true home facility in Fort Wayne). Frank Brian scored 16 points to pace Fort Wayne to a 96-89 victory in Game 3. The Pistons put a then-remarkable seven players in double figures during a 109-102 triumph in Game 4. Fort Wayne made it three consecutive "home" wins with a 74-71 victory in Game 5. Syracuse guard Dick Farley missed a potential game-winning shot in the final seconds.

The Nationals returned to Syracuse needing home victories in Game 6 and Game 7 to win the championship. The Nationals forced a decisive seventh game with a 109-104 win in Game 6. Schayes scored 28 points to keep Syracuse's season alive.

The Nationals' title dreams nearly turned into a nightmare when the Pistons stormed to a 17-point lead during the first half of Game 7. In the pre-shot clock era, Fort Wayne might have milked away the clock in the second half and left Syracuse as NBA champions.

Instead, the Pistons had to keep shooting. The Nationals kept chipping away. Schayes hit two free throws with 1:23 to go to put Syracuse ahead for the first time at 91-90. George Yardley, Fort Wayne's leading scorer, answered with one free throw on the ensuing possession to tie it at 91.

George King then put himself in the right place at the right time for the team at the right place at the right time. King made a free throw with 12 seconds left to put the Nationals ahead 92-91. King then made a steal with five seconds remaining to secure Syracuse's first and only NBA championship.

1954-1955 Syracuse Nationals final statistics

Name	G	PPG	FG%	FT%	RPG	APG
Dolph Schayes	72	18.5	.383	.833	12.3	3.0
Paul Seymour	72	14.6	.362	.811	4.3	6.7
Red Rocha	72	11.3	.368	.782	6.8	2.5
Johnny Kerr	72	10.5	.419	.682	6.6	1.1
Earl Lloyd	72	10.2	.365	.750	7.7	2.1
Connie Simmons	36	9.6	.357	.632	6.1	1.7
George King	67	8.9	.377	.611	3.4	4.9
Bill Kenville	70	7.1	.357	.766	3.5	2.1
Dick Farley	69	5.9	.385	.677	2.4	1.6
Billy Gabor	3	5.7	.318	.600	1.7	3.7
Jim Tucker	20	5.3	.336	.711	4.9	0.6
Wally Osterkorn	19	2.9	.206	.500	3.7	0.9
Team	72	91.1	.372	.750	54.6	24.7
Opponents	72	89.7	N/A	N/A	N/A	N/A

4. The 1975-1976 Boston Celtics

Record: 54-28

Overall ranking: 363rd, 2.225 points above average.

Why they weren't so dominant

An aging Boston Celtics team overachieved and somehow won one last championship before age, injuries, and attrition took their inevitable toll.

The typical pro basketball fan assigns that description to the 1968-1969 Celtics, who won the NBA title during Bill Russell's final season despite a fourth-place finish in the Eastern Conference.

In truth, the description better fits the 1975-1976 Celtics, who produced a championship season despite relatively tame credentials.

Boston quickly reconstructed a championship team within a few years of Russell's retirement. Celtics president Red Auerbach selected point guard Jo Jo White with his first round draft pick in the summer of 1969. One summer later, Auerbach filled the team's vacancy in the middle with the choice of undersized center Dave Cowens.

White would score 14,000 points during his career. Cowens would become one of the first big men to play effectively inside and on the perimeter. He would win the league's Most Valuable Player award after the 1972-1973 season.

Versatile forward John Havlicek, who played the role of "super-sub" on Boston's championship teams during the 1960s, emerged as the leading scorer for the Celtics' teams of the 1970s.

Auerbach rounded out the roster with shrewd acquisitions of savvy big men like future NBA coaches Paul Silas and Don Nelson.

The Celtics returned to the top of the Eastern Conference regular season standings by the 1971-1972 season. Boston set a franchise record with a 68-14 ledger during the 1972-1973 campaign. The Celtics finally broke through and regained the NBA title with an exciting seven-game NBA Finals victory against the Milwaukee Bucks after the 1973-1974 season.

The new Boston dynasty already showed signs of age as the 1975-1976 season began. Havlicek would turn 36 during the season. Injuries soon would shorten Cowens' career. Nelson would retire after the campaign.

Auerbach gave his team a preseason boost, trading Paul Westphal to acquire high-scoring guard Charlie Scott.

Boston went 54-28 and posted the best record in the Eastern Conference during the 1975-1976 season. It did so with smoke and mirrors. The Celtics finished the season with an average point differential of +2.3 points per game. Three teams did better, including the Cleveland Cavaliers and Washington Bullets in the Eastern Conference. One generally would expect a 47-35 season from a team with an average point differential of +2.3 points per game.

Boston finished the season seventh in the league in points scored and points allowed in an 18-team league. None of Celtics made the All-NBA first team. (Havlicek and Cowens did make the second team; Silas, Cowens, and Havlicek were first team All-Defense).

Why they still won it all

Boston had a slightly above-average team in a season filled with average teams.

The NBA reached some degree of equilibrium by the 1975-1976 season after rapid expansion during the late 1960s and early 1970s briefly filled the league with haves and have-nots.

Every team in the NBA, with one exception, finished the 1975-1976 season with an average point differential between +2.5 and -2.9 points per game. Every team in the NBA, with one exception, won between 24 and 54 games.

The one exception: The Golden State Warriors, the defending NBA champions. The Warriors seemed on course to roll to their second consecutive title. Golden State finished the 1975-1976 regular season with a league-best 59-23 record. The Warriors achieved an average point differential of +6.7 points per game, 4.2 points per game better than any other team in the league.

A funny thing happened to Golden State on its way to the title. The Warriors suffered a stunning seven-game loss against the Phoenix Suns in the Western Conference finals. Golden State finished 17 games ahead of Phoenix in the Pacific Division during the regular season, but the Suns rallied from a 3-2 deficit to win the West.

The upset of the Warriors cleared the path for Boston to win its 13th NBA title.

The Celtics eliminated the Buffalo Braves and league Most Valuable Player Bob McAdoo in the first round of the playoffs. Boston then beat Cleveland in six games in the Eastern Conference finals, benefiting from a mid-series injury to Cavaliers center Jim Chones.

The Celtics dominated the first two games of the NBA Finals against Phoenix, scoring a pair of double-digit home victories. The Suns responded with a pair of tough wins on their home court. The series returned to the Boston Garden for the pivotal fifth game.

The Celtics roared ahead 32-12 after nine minutes and would extend their lead to 22 points later in the half.

The Suns remained composed and whittled the deficit to 15 points by halftime. Phoenix's defense tightened some more and limited Boston to 34 points during the last two quarters. The Suns finally forced overtime when Paul Westphal—traded from Boston to Phoenix in the offseason—scored five points in the final minute of regulation.

The contest remained deadlocked after one overtime. Things got even more dramatic during the second extra session.

Suns forward Curtis Perry gave Phoenix a stunning 110-109 edge on a basket with five seconds remaining. Havlicek answered for Boston. Havlicek, playing despite a foot injury, banked in a difficult shot from the left side to give the Celtics a 111-110 advantage. Boston fans swarmed to court to celebrate the apparent victory.

Not yet. The officials placed one second back on the clock. Phoenix took a time out it didn't have, resulting in a technical foul, a White free throw, and a 112-110 Celtics lead. The Suns did get the ball at midcourt under the technical foul rules of the time. Phoenix took advantage of the rules loophole and forced a third overtime on Gar Heard's miraculous 25-footer at the buzzer.

Boston finally pulled away in the third extra session. Unheralded reserve Glenn McDonald, who would play just nine more NBA games after the 1976 Finals, scored six points in the third OT to lift the Celtics to a 128-126 victory.

The teams returned to Phoenix two nights later, where Boston closed out the series with an anticlimactic 87-80 win.

The 1975-1976 Celtics emerged as champions after a memorable postseason, but did so with a rather ordinary team.

1975-1976 Boston Celtics final statistics

Name	G	PPG	FG%	FT%	RPG	APG
Dave Cowens	78	19.0	.468	.756	16.0	4.2
Jo Jo White	82	18.9	.449	.838	3.8	5.4
Charlie Scott	82	17.6	.449	.797	4.4	4.2
John Havlicek	76	17.0	.450	.844	4.1	3.7
Paul Silas	81	10.7	.426	.709	12.7	2.5
Don Nelson	75	6.4	.462	.789	2.4	1.0
Glenn McDonald	75	5.6	.419	.714	1.8	0.9
Steve Kuberski	60	5.4	.467	.895	3.9	0.7
Kevin Stacom	77	5.3	.439	.747	2.1	1.7
Jim Ard	81	3.5	.364	.710	3.6	0.6
Jerome Anderson	22	2.8	.556	.688	0.6	0.3
Tom Boswell	35	2.7	.441	.583	2.0	0.5
Ed Searcy	4	1.5	.333	1.000	0.0	0.3
Team	82	106.2	.446	.780	52.9	24.1
Opponents	82	103.9	.449	.742	45.1	22.4

5. The 1994-1995 Houston Rockets
Record: 47-35
Overall ranking: 357th, 2.251 points above average.

Why they weren't so dominant

More than a few basketball fans wrote off the Houston Rockets' 1993-1994 NBA championship as a fluke.

Detractors wondered if Houston could have defeated the three-time defending champion Chicago Bulls had Michael Jordan not retired before the start of the 1993-1994 season.

They wondered if the Rockets could have defeated the Seattle Supersonics in a playoff meeting had the top-seeded Sonics not faltered in the first round of the playoffs

They dismissed Houston's seven-game victory over the New York Knicks in the NBA Finals as inartistic, as basketball at its ugliest.

The Rockets seemed intent on proving the critics right during the 1994-1995 regular season.

Houston still had the nucleus of its 1993-1994 team. Hakeem Olajuwon continued to play like the best center in the NBA. Power forward Otis Thorpe still rebounded like a machine. Guards Vernon Maxwell and Kenny Smith continued to provide outside shooting touch when teams paid too much attention to Olajuwon. Third-year forward Robert Horry and second-year guard Sam Cassell continued to improve after contributing during the championship run. Mario Elie led the Rockets' tough corps of reserves.

Houston just couldn't generate much momentum during the first half of the season. The Rockets reached the All-Star break with a decent 29-17 record, but ranked sixth in the Western Conference standings.

Houston made a heart-thumping move on February 14, just two days after the All-Star Game. The Rockets sent Thorpe and a first round draft pick to the Portland Trail Blazers in exchange for Portland franchise icon Clyde Drexler, along with forward Tracy Murray.

The trade made sentimental sense. Drexler and Olajuwon played together at the University of Houston and helped the Cougars reach the 1983 NCAA championship game. The Rockets celebrated the transaction by thumping the Los Angeles Clippers 124-104 a few hours after the trade.

Sentiment aside, the trade made little basketball sense. Drexler had established himself as one of the top shooting guards in basketball. Yet the Rockets already had a capable—if erratic—shooting guard in Vernon Maxwell. The loss of Thorpe also left Houston without its second-best rebounder and without a true power forward.

Those problems manifested themselves throughout the remainder of the regular season. The Rockets went 17-18 in 35 games with Drexler. The stumbling finish left Houston with a 47-35 final regular season record. The Rockets finished with 11 fewer wins than their 1993-1994 championship team. Houston finished 15 games behind San Antonio for the Midwest Division title. The Rockets received the No. 6 seed for the Western Conference playoffs.

Houston's individual players produced scoring numbers comparable to their 1993-1994 numbers. Drexler's scoring average declined marginally during his games with the Rockets. The reason for the slide came on defense. Houston allowed just 96.8 points per game (fifth in the NBA) during the 1993-1994 season, good for an average point differential of +4.3 points per game. The Rockets gave up 101.4 points per game (14th in the NBA) during the 1994-1995 campaign, resulting in an average point differential of just +2.1 points per game. Eleven teams posted better average point differentials.

The effects of Houston's slide showed when the NBA handed out its regular season awards. San Antonio center David Robinson dethroned Olajuwon as the league Most Valuable Player and as the league's first-team All-NBA center. Olajuwon also lost his spot on the league's All-Defensive team.

Olajuwon soon would have the last laugh.

Why they still won it all

Houston did produce some favorable numbers during the 1994-1995 regular season, for those who bothered to notice.

The Rockets finished sixth in the league in overall field goal percentage (.480), a figure that is more impressive when one takes into account the team's league-leading 646 3-pointers. Houston finished tied for second in the league in defensive field goal percentage (.453).

The Rockets also proved they could win on the road during the regular season. Houston compiled a 22-19 road record, one of just seven teams to finish over .500 on the road during the 1994-1995 season.

None of those numbers seemed relevant once the postseason began. Houston faced the No. 3 seed Utah Jazz in the first round of the playoffs. The Jazz finished 60-22, the second-best record in the league.

The teams split the first two games in Salt Lake City. Utah appeared poised to eliminate the defending champions after a 95-82 victory in Game 3.

Suddenly, the Olajuwon-Drexler combination clicked the way the Rockets had hoped when they paired the two on Valentine's Day. Drexler scored 41 points on just 18 shots and Olajuwon added 40 as Houston stayed alive with a 123-106 decision in Game 4.

Utah seemed undeterred when the teams returned to Salt Lake City for the decisive fifth game. The Jazz led by 12 points with one minute left in the third quarter. Utah still held an 82-75 advantage midway through the fourth quarter.

The Jazz then went seven consecutive possessions and 4:19 without a point. The Rockets began a parade to the free throw line. Houston made 16 of 20 free throws in the final 3:50 and rallied for a stunning 95-91 victory. Olajuwon finished with 33 points, including the club's only field goal in the final 3:50. Drexler added 31 points.

Next up for the Rockets: The Phoenix Suns, regarded by many as the most talented team in the West. Phoenix won the first two games at home. The Suns then stole Game 4 in Houston by a 114-110 score to take a 3-1 lead in the series.

Phoenix held a 92-90 late in the fourth quarter of Game 5, but Olajuwon sank a baseline basket to force overtime. The Rockets pulled away in the extra session and stayed alive—again—with a 103-97 triumph. Houston forced a decisive seventh game with a 116-103 home in win Game 6.

Earlier in the series, Suns star Charles Barkley said of the Rockets, "They won't die. We're going to have to kill them." Phoenix nearly landed a killing blow early in Game 7, roaring to a 26-13 lead after one quarter. The Suns still led 51-41 at the break.

The Rockets had yet another comeback in them. Houston surged ahead 81-79 by the start of the fourth quarter. The game remained nip-and-tuck throughout the final period. Mario Elie finally stuck the dagger with a 3-pointer from the left corner with 7.1 seconds left, putting the Rockets ahead 113-110. Houston held on to win, 115-114. The Rockets became the fifth team in NBA history to rally from a 3-1 deficit and win a playoff series.

Remarkably, things only would get easier for Houston during the rest of the postseason.

The Rockets set the tone for the Western Conference finals against the top-seeded San Antonio Spurs with victories in the first two games in San Antonio. The Spurs briefly recovered with a pair of wins in Houston, tying the series at two. The Rockets responded with a blowout 111-90 victory in Game 5 in San Antonio. They closed out the series with a taut 100-95 triumph in Game 6 in Houston. Olajuwon humbled the Spurs' David Robinson during the series, outscoring the NBA's regular season MVP by a 212-146 margin over the six games.

The Rockets met the Orlando Magic in the NBA Finals. The Magic boasted young center Shaquille O'Neal, who had averaged 29.3 points per game during the regular season to win his first scoring title. Orlando proved its playoff mettle by eliminating the Chicago Bulls (and newly un-retired Michael Jordan) in the Eastern Conference semifinals and by outlasting the Indiana Pacers in a seven-game Eastern Conference final.

The Magic had not seen playoff mettle like Houston's.

Game 1 of the NBA Finals showcased the Rockets' resiliency. Orlando jumped ahead 57-37 with four minutes left in the first half. Houston recovered and led by as many as nine in the third quarter.

The Magic appeared poised to close out the game with a 110-107 lead and the ball with 15 seconds to go. Orlando's Nick Anderson had four chances to sink a game-clinching free throw, but missed all four attempts. Houston's Kenny Smith drilled a 3-pointer with 1.6 seconds remaining to send it to overtime. There, Olajuwon provided the margin of victory in a 120-118 win with a tip-in of a Drexler miss with 0.3 seconds left.

The series all but ended with the Rockets' stunning Game 1 triumph. Houston cruised to a 117-106 victory in Game 2 to take a 2-0 lead with three games coming up at The Summit. Horry's clutch 3-pointer late in Game 3 made the difference in a 106-103 win. Olajuwon concluded his memorable postseason with 35 points in Game 4, including a 3-pointer that provided the exclamation point to the clinching 113-101 victory.

The Rockets of the mid-1990s didn't produce the numbers of a dominant team, but they produced unbelievable numbers in games that mattered.

Houston went 8-0 in possible elimination games during its two-year championship run. The Rockets also concluded the 1995 postseason with seven consecutive road victories.

Sometimes, greatness need not require dominance.

1994-1995 Houston Rockets final statistics

Name	G	PPG	FG%	FT%	RPG	APG
Hakeem Olajuwon	72	27.8	.517	.756	10.8	3.5
Clyde Drexler	35	21.4	.506	.809	7.0	4.4
Otis Thorpe	36	13.3	.563	.528	8.9	1.6
Vernon Maxwell	64	13.3	.394	.688	2.6	4.3
Kenny Smith	81	10.4	.483	.851	1.9	4.0
Robert Horry	64	10.2	.447	.761	5.1	3.4
Sam Cassell	82	9.5	.426	.843	2.6	4.9
Mario Elie	81	8.8	.500	.842	2.4	2.3
Carl Herrera	61	6.8	.523	.624	4.6	0.7
Chucky Brown	40	6.2	.601	.607	4.7	0.8
Pete Chilcutt	68	5.3	.445	.738	4.6	1.0
Tracy Murray	25	3.5	.400	.625	0.9	0.2
Scott Brooks	28	3.4	.538	.857	0.5	0.8
Tim Breaux	42	3.0	.372	.653	0.8	0.4
Zan Tabak	37	2.0	.453	.614	1.5	0.1
Charles Jones	3	1.0	.333	.500	2.3	0.0
Adrian Caldwell	7	0.7	.250	.500	1.4	0.0
Team	82	103.5	.480	.749	40.5	25.1
Opponents	82	101.4	.453	.751	43.3	23.7

IV. The Bottom of the Barrel

The 10 least dominant teams in NBA history

1. The 1992-1993 Dallas Mavericks
Record: 11-71
Overall ranking: 1,153rd, 14.575 points below average.
Other not-so-dominant Dallas Maverick teams of the era: 1993-1994 (1,115th overall, 8.200 points below average); 1991-1992 (1,099th overall, 7.420 points below average).

Why they're ranked here

The Dallas Mavericks seemed like a franchise on the rise when they extended the eventual NBA champion Los Angeles Lakers to seven games in the 1987-1988 Western Conference finals.

Just four years later, the Mavericks embarked on the least dominant season in NBA history.

Dallas' 1987-1988 team gradually crumbled. The Mavericks traded players like star forward Mark Aguirre and promising frontliner Detlef Schrempf for aging players. Dallas traded its top draft picks for more aging players. Proven forward Sam Perkins left the team via free agency. Talented forward Roy Tarpley carried the Mavericks to the 1987-1988 Western Conference finals, but missed large chunks of the next few seasons because of injuries and substance abuse suspensions.

Dallas retreated from a 53-29 record during the 1987-1988 season to a 28-54 mark by 1990-1991. The NBA suspended Tarpley for life on October 16, 1991, cementing the Mavericks' decision to start a rebuilding process.

Dallas hoped to start the process with Ohio State guard Jim Jackson, the club's top pick in the 1992 NBA draft. But Jackson and the Mavericks could not agree on a contract. Jackson would not join the team until late in the 1992-1993 season.

Jackson's holdout left Dallas coach Richie Adubato with a roster of veteran point guard Derek Harper and not much else. The Mavericks started the season with one win in their first 16 games. They had a 2-22 record on New Year's Day. They took a 4-45 record into the All-Star break.

Dallas fired Adubato after 29 games. The Mavericks turned the coaching reins over to Garfield Heard, who proceeded to fare even worse: a 2-30 mark in his first 32 games. Heard presided over a then-club worst 19-game losing streak between February 5 and March 19.

Dallas' season turned around—relatively speaking—after the team's record fell to 4-50. The Mavericks held a press conference to announce the surprise signing of Jackson.

Dallas lost seven consecutive games after the announcement, and then ran off a "hot streak" of seven wins in 21 games. Jackson enjoyed a stretch of seven consecutive games with 20 points or more once he got acclimated to the NBA.

The Mavericks won three of their last six games, including the final two games of the season, to finish 11-71. Dallas' last-ditch surge left the record for fewest wins in a single season in the hands of the 1972-1973 Philadelphia 76ers, who finished 9-73.

The Mavericks' final carnage included some staggering numbers.

Dallas lost 58 games by double-digit margins.

The Mavericks finished the season with an average point differential of -15.2 points per game, far and away the worst in NBA history.

Dallas fielded the league's worst defense (114.5 points allowed per game) and second-worst offense (99.3 points scored per game).

The Mavericks had the worst shooting team in the NBA and allowed the highest field goal percentage.

Adding injury to insult: The 1992-1993 Mavericks set a franchise record with 246 player games lost to illness of injury.

It all added up to the least dominant season in NBA history.

Why a bunch of people will argue and why they're wrong

Argument: "The 1992-1993 Dallas Mavericks should not rank as the least dominant team of all time because they didn't have the worst record in NBA history."

Counter argument: Many NBA fans first think of the 1972-1973 Philadelphia 76ers when listing the least dominant teams in NBA history. The 1972-1973 Philadelphia team finished with a 9-73 record, the only team in modern league history to finish with fewer than 10 wins over a full season.

The 1992-1993 Dallas disaster did produce 11 wins. The Mavericks endured the least dominant season ever by all other measures.

Dallas finished the season with an average point differential of -15.2 points per game. No other team in NBA history has posted an average point differential worse than -13.0. By all rights, the Mavericks should have won about 10 games. (The 1972-1973 Philadelphia 76ers statistically should have won 15 games). Dallas overachieved to win 11.

The Mavericks also played the plurality of their games against teams in the Midwest Division, the league's weakest division in 1992-1993.

A gap of almost three points exists between the 1992-1993 Dallas Mavericks' POST ranking and the next-worst team on the list. Other teams won fewer games, but the Mavericks still rank far and away as the least dominant team ever.

Argument: "The Mavericks should not rank as the least dominant team of all time because athletes from the 1990s would dominate athletes from the 1950s."

Counter argument: As a late-night comedian might say, "Not these athletes from the 1990s."

In seriousness: Sure, if one put the 1992-1993 Mavericks in a time machine and transported them back to 1950, the team indeed might win an NBA title against shorter, slower opposition. Or at least make the playoffs.

But the POST ratings measure teams relative to the norm of their eras. By 1992-1993 standards, Dallas produced the least dominant NBA season of all time.

Postscript

Dallas tried to rebuild from the rubble of the early 1990s around its "Three Js": point guard Jason Kidd, shooting guard Jimmy Jackson, and small forward Jamal Mashburn.

Jackson and Mashburn both developed into 20-point per game scorers. Kidd won a share of the Rookie of the Year award for the 1994-1995 season and became one of the top point guards in basketball.

The Mavericks made a 23-win improvement to 36-46 during the 1994-1995 season. Dallas appeared poised for more progress in 1995-1996. The Mavericks enticed their fans by winning their first four games.

Soon, however, a fourth J popped up in Dallas: Jealousy.

Jackson and Mashburn allegedly became more and more selfish on the court. Jackson and Kidd allegedly got into a tiff over their relationships with singer Toni Braxton. The team unraveled. The Mavericks slipped to a 26-56 record in 1995-1996. The franchise traded away all three Js during the 1996-1997 season.

The trade of Kidd to the Phoenix Suns started the franchise's turnaround. Dallas received skilled shooting guard Michael Finley in the deal. Mavericks coach and general manager Don Nelson added two more key pieces before the 1998-1999 season. Nelson acquired flashy point guard Steve Nash from Phoenix. He drafted raw but talented 7-foot forward Dirk Nowitzki.

All of the new pieces jelled during the 2000-2001 season. The Mavericks improved from a 40-42 record to a 53-29 mark. Dallas rallied from an 0-2 deficit to stun the Utah Jazz in the first round of the playoffs. The Mavericks marked the tenth anniversary of the 1992-1993 disaster by posting a 60-22 mark during the 2002-2003 season, the best record in the NBA.

1992-1993 Dallas Mavericks final statistics

Name	G	PPG	FG%	FT%	RPG	APG
Derek Harper	62	18.2	.419	.756	2.0	5.4
Jim Jackson	28	16.3	.395	.739	4.4	4.7
Sean Rooks	72	13.5	.493	.602	7.4	1.3
Terry Davis	75	12.7	.455	.594	9.3	0.9
Doug Smith	61	10.4	.434	.757	5.4	1.7
Randy White	64	9.7	.435	.750	5.8	0.8
Tim Legler	30	9.6	.437	.803	1.9	1.5
Mike Iuzzolino	70	8.7	.462	.765	2.0	4.7
Walter Bond	74	8.0	.402	.772	2.6	1.6
Tracy Moore	39	7.2	.414	.869	1.3	1.2
Dexter Cambridge	53	7.0	.484	.687	3.2	1.1
Brian Howard	68	6.5	.442	.766	3.1	1.0
Morlon Wiley	33	5.8	.405	.667	1.7	3.0
Lamont Strothers	9	5.6	.328	.800	1.6	1.4
Donald Hodge	79	5.0	.403	.683	3.7	0.9
Walter Palmer	20	3.0	.474	.667	2.2	0.3
Radisav Curcic	20	2.9	.390	.722	2.5	0.6
Stephen Bardo	23	2.2	.306	.706	1.6	1.3
Team	82	99.3	.435	.705	42.7	20.5
Opponents	82	114.5	.501	.766	46.4	25.0

2. The 1970-1971 Cleveland Cavaliers

Record: 15-67
Overall ranking: 1,152nd, 11.790 points below average.
Other not-so-dominant Cleveland Cavalier team of the era: 1971-1972 (1,112th overall, 7.906 points below average).

Why they're ranked here

The season that produced the most dominant team in NBA history (the 1970-1971 Milwaukee Bucks) also produced one of professional basketball's least dominant squads.

The Cleveland Cavaliers entered the NBA as part of a three-team expansion for the 1970-1971 season.

Cleveland assembled a first-year roster with few names of note.

Walt Wesley, a 6-foot-11 center, never had averaged double figures in points during his career. He would lead the expansion Cavaliers in scoring.

Bobby Smith managed just 7.3 points per game as a rookie for the San Diego Rockets in 1969-1970. He would emerge as Cleveland's top outside shooter.

John Johnson, a rookie forward from Iowa, would average 16.6 points and participate in the All-Star Game. But he certainly could not carry the team.

The Cavaliers did acquire serviceable guard Butch Beard, who would play for Golden State's 1974-1975 championship team. Beard didn't play for anyone during the 1970-1971 season. He spent the season completing his military obligation.

Cleveland selected some other veterans in the expansion draft. One of those players immediately retired. The Cavaliers traded away two others away.

The Cavaliers' makeshift roster proceeded to lose its first 15 games. The first win came by a 105-103 margin against the Portland Trail Blazers, another expansion team. Cleveland lost 12 more games before beating Buffalo—the third 1970-1971 expansion team—for its first home win.

The Cavaliers didn't beat an established NBA team until they beat the Philadelphia 76ers in the 42nd game of the season. Cleveland had a 2-34 record at one point. The Cavaliers managed just one three-game winning streak all season. Second-year player John Warren scored a basket in the wrong goal during a game against Portland.

Cleveland did "improve" during the second half of the season and finished with a 15-67 record.

The Cavaliers' other statistics suggest things could have ended in far worse fashion. Nine of those 15 wins came against expansion brethren Buffalo and Portland. Cleveland finished with an average point differential of -11.2 points per game. No other team in the league had an average point differential worse than -6.6 points per game. The Cavaliers finished last in the NBA with just 102.1 points per game. Every other team in the league averaged at least 105.5 points.

Why a bunch of people will argue and why they're wrong

Argument: "The 1970-1971 Cleveland Cavaliers should rank as the least dominant team in NBA history because they had the imperfect combination of inferior talent that achieved bad results against a weak schedule."

Counter argument: This Cleveland team indeed might rank as the least dominant of all time had the 1970-1971 season ended after, say, 36 games. The Cavaliers had a 2-34 record at that point, with blowout losses in most of the games.

The season did continue. Cleveland managed better results the rest of the way. The Cavaliers improved from their historically bad pace through 36 games to a run-of-the-mill bad pace the rest of the way. Cleveland would have finished with a 5-77 record had it continued its 36-game pace over the full campaign. Such a season would have ended all arguments over the NBA's least dominant team.

On the other hand, the Cavaliers would have "enjoyed" a 23-59 debut season had they won games at the same rate they did during their last 46 games. Cleveland's improved play over the last 46 games saved it from the all-time cellar.

Argument: "The Cavaliers should have a better ranking because several other teams lost more games and had inferior average point differentials."

Counter argument: This Cleveland team rarely comes up in discussions about the NBA's least dominant squads. Six teams won fewer games over 82-game seasons. Seven squads posted inferior average point differentials. Expansion teams generally get a philosophical exemption from worst-ever debates, anyway.

So, why is the Cavaliers' POST rating so bad?

The POST rating for this Cleveland team has a characteristic unlike the POST ratings for every other team in this chapter. The Cavaliers' POST rating value (-11.790) is worse than their average point differential (-11.2). The nine other teams in this chapter and virtually all of the not-so-dominant teams in NBA history have POST rating values better than their average margin of defeat.

What happened to Cleveland's rating? The NBA did its expansion teams a favor during the 1970-1971 season. The three new teams (Buffalo, Portland, and the Cavaliers) all played each other 12 times apiece. Cleveland did not play more than six games against any other team. The Cavaliers did not play more than four games against any team that would make the playoffs.

Cleveland also played in the NBA's weakest division. The Baltimore Bullets won the Cavaliers' Central Division with a 42-40 record. The two other teams in the division besides Cleveland combined for a 69-95 record.

The schedule probably saved Cleveland from a 70-loss season. The Cavaliers went a reasonable 9-15 against Buffalo and Portland. Cleveland went 6-52 against everyone else. The latter pace would have yielded an 8-74 record over a full campaign.

The schedule gave the Cavaliers a few extra wins, but also made their POST rating worse than all but one team in NBA history.

Postscript

The Cleveland organization didn't panic after the Year 1 disaster. The Cavaliers built slowly under coach Bill Fitch. Cleveland selected high-scoring guard Austin Carr in the 1971 draft. The Cavaliers promptly improved by eight wins to a 23-59 mark in 1971-1972.

Cleveland kept adding pieces. The Cavaliers traded for the right to draft forward Jim Brewer in 1973. Cleveland drafted another skilled forward, Campy Russell, in 1974. The Cavaliers traded for center Jim Chones and guard Dick Snyder prior to the 1974-1975 season. Cleveland peeked out of the Central Division cellar for the first time with a 40-42 record in 1974-1975.

All of the players listed above averaged double figures in scoring during the 1975-1976 season to help Cleveland win its first—and to date, only—division title. The Cavaliers advanced to the Eastern Conference finals, but an injury to Chones ensured a six-game loss against the Boston Celtics.

The injury to Chones started the franchise back on a downward spiral. Cleveland's victory total gradually declined through the rest of 1970s. The team finally bottomed out with another 15-67 season in 1981-1982. The franchise has endured a roller coaster existence since.

Still, the franchise's starting point ranks as its lowest point.

1970-1971 Cleveland Cavaliers final statistics

Name	G	PPG	FG%	FT%	RPG	APG
Walt Wesley	82	17.7	.455	.687	8.7	1.0
John Johnson	67	16.6	.422	.805	6.8	4.8
Bingo Smith	77	15.2	.448	.761	5.6	3.4
McCoy McLemore	58	11.7	.388	.773	8.0	3.0
Johnny Warren	82	11.5	.423	.829	4.2	4.2
Dave Sorenson	79	11.3	.445	.803	6.2	2.1
Luke Rackley	74	7.6	.466	.637	5.3	0.9
Bobby Washington	47	7.4	.397	.743	2.2	4.0
Len Chappell	6	6.8	.395	.786	3.0	0.2
Bobby Lewis	79	5.9	.370	.717	2.6	3.1
Joe Cooke	73	4.3	.393	.814	1.6	1.3
Johnny Egan	26	4.0	.408	.893	1.2	2.2
Cliff Anderson	23	3.4	.322	.683	1.6	0.7
Larry Mikan	53	3.0	.333	.618	2.6	0.8
Gary Suiter	30	1.4	.352	.444	1.4	0.1
Gary Freeman	11	1.4	.583	.500	0.7	0.4
Team	82	102.1	.424	.746	48.6	25.2
Opponents	82	113.3	.465	.773	50.9	28.1

3. The 1997-1998 Denver Nuggets
Record: 11-71
Overall ranking: 1,151st, 11.579 points below average.
Other not-so-dominant Denver Nugget teams of the era: 1998-1999 (1,066th overall, 6.285 points below average); 1996-1997 (1,065th overall, 6.282 points below average).

Why they're ranked here

The Denver Nuggets experienced the most remarkable decade of any team in the NBA during the 1990s in a macabre kind of way.

Denver started the decade off with a hyper-fast-paced 1990-1991 squad that ran its way to one of the worst seasons in NBA history.

The Nuggets improved enough by 1994 to win a playoff series and advance within one game of the Western Conference finals.

The Denver roster promptly imploded once again, resulting in another historically bad team by the 1997-1998 campaign.

The Nuggets started on the road to ruin after the 1995-1996 season. Center Dikembe Mutombo, the centerpiece of Denver's rebuilding efforts, became a free agent and signed with the Atlanta Hawks. The team also allowed sharpshooting but controversial guard Mahmoud-Abdul Rauf to leave for the Sacramento Kings.

The loss of the two players put a huge hole in the team's core of young talent. The franchise went through 23 players during the 1996-1997 season, trying to rediscover the proper mix. The Nuggets regressed to a 21-61 record. Talented forward Antonio McDyess, the player the team hoped to re-build around, made an emotionally difficult decision to sign as a free agent with the Phoenix Suns.

The franchise entered the 1997-1998 season with a roster full of young players, but this group of young players did not posses talent equal to the young group of players who came to Denver in the early 1990s.

Everything then proceeded to go wrong for the Nuggets.

The team acquired forward Eric Williams via a summer trade with the Boston Celtics. Williams averaged 19.8 points through Denver's first four games, but injured his knee during the fourth game. He would miss the rest of the season.

Versatile forward LaPhonso Ellis led Denver in scoring with 21.9 points per game during the 1996-1997 season, but injured his knee late in the year. He returned for the 1997-1998 campaign, but would not regain his pre-injury form.

Newcomer Johnny Newman led the healthy players with 14.7 points per game. The rest of the inexperienced players on the Nuggets' roster all had some positive moments, but not nearly enough.

Denver's horrid 1990-1991 team lost because it played minimal defense. The 1997-1998 Nuggets lost because they couldn't score. Denver finished last in the league with 88.3 points per game and a shooting percentage of .417. The Nuggets' defense didn't perform much better. Denver allowed opponents to score 100.8 points per game and to shoot at a .473 clip. Both marks ranked in the league's bottom five.

Denver produced an average point differential of -11.8 points per game, the third-worst average differential in league history.

Williams' presence would have helped Denver score more, but might not have made a difference in final record. Denver started 0-4 with Williams. The Nuggets lost their first eight games without him, resulting in an 0-12 start.

The lowlight of the season: A single season record-tying 23-game losing streak. The Nuggets went 55 days between wins during a stretch spanning December and January. The Nuggets' longest winning streak lasted two games.

Despite the long losing streaks, Denver stayed just ahead of the record-setting 9-73 pace established by the 1972-1973 Philadelphia 76ers. The Nuggets avoided the inglorious spot in the record book when they earned their 10th victory in their 77th game. Denver would win one more game and crawl home with an 11-71 record.

Why a bunch of people will argue and why they're wrong

Argument: "The 1997-1998 Denver Nuggets should have a worse ranking…just because."

Counter argument: Let's face it: There isn't exactly a movement going on to declare the 1997-1998 Denver Nuggets the least dominant team of all time. Denver lost a lot of games and did so in unspectacular fashion.

Several media outlets tracked the progress of the Dallas Maverick teams of the early 1990s when those squads threatened to finish with a record worse than the 9-73 mark posted by the 1972-1973 Philadelphia 76ers. Few of those outlets conducted a "Countdown to history" involving the 1997-1998 Nuggets.

Dallas fans, Cleveland fans, and Nugget critics could point to the 23-game losing streak as a basis for suggesting this Denver team deserves the distinction as the least dominant team of all time.

The Nuggets did have a historically bad season, but the two teams with worse POST ratings produced much less impressive overall credentials.

Argument: "The Nuggets should have a better ranking because the 1972-1973 Philadelphia 76ers lost more often by more points."

Counter argument: Denver ranks worse here because the Nuggets had a slightly weaker schedule. The elite teams in the 1972-1973 Philadelphia 76ers'

Eastern Conference had better numbers than the elite teams in the Denver's Western Conference in 1997-1998.

Philadelphia's POST rating got some help from playing a 68-win Boston Celtics team seven times during the 1972-1973 season. Utah led the Western Conference with 62 wins in 1997-1998. The Nuggets got to play the Jazz only four times.

At the other end of the spectrum, the below-average teams on the 76ers' schedule also had better numbers than the below-average teams on the Nuggets' schedule. Four teams in the Western Conference had less than 20 wins in 1997-1998. No team other than Philadelphia won fewer than 20 games in the Eastern Conference in 1972-1973.

Those strength of schedule numbers make Philadelphia's POST rating better than Denver's.

Argument: "The 1997-1998 Nuggets weren't even the worst team in Denver history."

Counter argument: Ask an average NBA fan to name the worst team in Denver history and most will refer to the 1990-1991 Nuggets team that scored often and got scored upon even more.

The 1990-1991 Denver team got plenty of attention because of its wild, fast-paced style. The 1990-1991 Nuggets played in some incredibly high scoring games and lost by some eye-popping margins.

The 1997-1998 Nuggets labored in anonymity, but had an inferior season by almost any measure. Denver won more considerably more games in 1991 (20). The 1990-1991 squad produced an average point differential of "only" -10.9 points per game.

Fans will remember the 1990-1991 Denver team as a historical oddity. The Nuggets team that came along seven years later was simply historically bad.

Postscript

McDyess returned for the 1998-1999 season, lifting Denver from atrocious to merely bad. The franchise muddled along for a few years, taking care to rely on young players, but winning few games.

The turning point came during the 2002-2003 season. The Nuggets assembled what shaped up as another historically awful roster, headed by an unknown coach by the unpronounceable name of Jeff Bzdilik. Denver filled its roster with players entering the final years of their contracts. The Nuggets planned to use the resulting salary cap space to kick-start the rebuilding process.

Bzdilik exceeded some expectations by winning 17 games with the makeshift roster during the 2002-2003 season. Better yet, Denver got the No. 3 overall pick in the 2003 draft. The Nuggets used the pick to select Carmelo Anthony, a talented 19-year-old forward who led Syracuse to the 2003 NCAA championship.

Anthony proved one of those rare impact rookies. He averaged 21.0 points per game during his first year. He got better as he got older. He led a young, exciting Denver team to playoff appearances during each of his first four seasons.

1997-1998 Denver Nuggets final statistics

Name	G	PPG	FG%	FT%	RPG	APG
Eric Williams	4	19.8	.393	.689	5.3	3.0
Johnny Newman	74	14.7	.431	.820	1.9	1.9
LaPhonso Ellis	76	14.3	.407	.805	7.2	2.8
Cory Alexander	23	14.0	.435	.846	4.3	6.0
Bobby Jackson	68	11.6	.392	.814	4.4	4.7
Danny Fortson	80	10.2	.452	.776	5.6	1.0
Anthony Goldwire	82	9.2	.423	.806	1.8	3.4
Tony Battie	65	8.4	.446	.702	5.4	0.9
Eric Washington	66	7.7	.404	.783	1.9	1.2
Bryant Stith	31	7.6	.333	.872	2.1	1.6
Dean Garrett	82	7.3	.428	.648	7.9	1.1
Harold Ellis	27	6.1	.559	.635	1.9	0.7
Priest Lauderdale	39	3.7	.417	.551	2.6	0.5
George Zidek	6	3.0	.267	.833	2.2	0.2
Kiwane Garris	28	2.4	.338	.760	0.7	1.0
Joe Wolf	57	1.5	.331	.500	2.2	0.5
Team	82	89.0	.417	.772	39.0	18.9
Opponents	82	100.8	.473	.754	42.6	24.2

4. The 1972-1973 Philadelphia 76ers
Record: 9-73

Overall ranking: 1,150th, 11.418 points below average.

Other not-so-dominant Philadelphia 76er teams of the era: 1973-1974 (1,049th overall, 5.875 points below average).

Why they're ranked here

The Philadelphia 76ers needed just six years to go from the pinnacle of professional basketball to the absolute rock bottom.

Philadelphia set a then-NBA record with 68 wins during its 1966-1967 championship season. The 76ers reached the opposite extreme with a 9-73 record during the 1972-1973 season, a record for fewest wins during a modern 82-game season that still stands.

The breakup of Philadelphia's championship team occurred swiftly and completely. Wilt Chamberlain, the center and centerpiece of the 1966-1967 championship team, demanded and received a trade to the Los Angeles Lakers during the summer of 1968. Chamberlain's successors could not to begin to replace his contributions. Darrall Imhoff, acquired in the trade for Chamberlain, lacked the talent. Holdover Luke Jackson excelled at forward, but struggled when asked to play center.

Piece by piece, the championship team broke apart. Wali Jones and Chet Walker departed via trades. Hall of Fame guard Hal Greer stayed, but age took its toll on his play.

The final blow came after the club went 30-52 during the 1971-1972 season and missed the playoffs for the first time since the franchise moved to Philadelphia in 1963. Courts ordered Billy Cunningham and his 23.3 points per game to leave the 76ers and honor a contract with the Carolina Cougars of the American Basketball Association.

The Philadelphia franchise expected a rebuilding year in 1972-1973. No one expected the disaster that unfolded.

New coach Roy Rubin alienated several veterans with one of his first moves. He named rookie Fred Boyd the starting point guard over Greer.

That move and several others failed to pan out.

The 76ers had something of a balanced offense. Nineteen players suited up for Philadelphia during the 1972-1973 season. Ten of them would average double-figures in scoring. Yet the numbers almost always added up to defeat. Fred Carter led the team in scoring at 20.0 points per game, but the 6-foot-3 guard hardly could carry the team.

The 76ers started 0-15. The losses came by close margins at first and then got worse and worse.

Philadelphia "celebrated" the New Year by embarking on a 20-game losing streak starting January 9. The skid established a since-broken league record for consecutive losses.

Philadelphia fired Rubin and handed the coaching reins over to reserve guard Kevin Loughery when the team had a 4-47 record at the All-Star break. The 76ers responded by losing their first 11 games under Loughery.

The team would close the season, appropriately, with 13 consecutive losses. The 9-73 finish set still-standing records for lowest winning percentage in any NBA season and for fewest wins over an 82-game schedule.

(The 1947-1948 Providence Steamrollers, who won just six games in a 48-game schedule, still hold the record for fewest wins during a BAA or NBA season. The 76ers finished with a .110 winning percentage; the Steamrollers a robust .125.)

For perspective, consider the 1950-1951 Washington Capitols won 10 games in 35 tries before folding.

Philadelphia lost games because it couldn't play defense. The 76ers gave up an average of 116.2 points per game, worst in the league by 2.8 points. Philadelphia's players couldn't shoot straight, either. The 76ers made just 42 percent of their shots, the worst mark in the NBA.

Philadelphia finished with an average point differential of -12.1 points per game, the second-worst margin in league history. The 76ers won no more than one game against any team in the NBA. Philadelphia finished a record 59 games behind the Atlantic Division champion Boston Celtics.

Why a bunch of people will argue and why they're wrong

Argument: "The 1973-1973 Philadelphia 76ers should rank as the least dominant team of all time because they have the magic number by which all not-so-dominant teams are measured: the 9-73 record."

Counter argument: The 9-73 record makes the 76ers the answer to many trivia questions, but doesn't make them the least dominant team in NBA history.

Wins and winning percentage make up just a portion of the POST rating. Consider the abovementioned 1947-1948 Providence Steamrollers, who won just six games and own the second-worst single-season winning percentage in NBA history. The Steamrollers couldn't even crack the top ten on the list of the league's least dominant teams.

Philadelphia's relatively good—for a 9-73 team—average point differential gives it a POST rating superior to that of the 1992-1993 Dallas Mavericks. The 76ers' reasonably difficult schedule makes their POST rating better than that of the 1970-1971 Cleveland Cavaliers and 1997-1998 Denver Nuggets.

Philadelphia played 32 games against teams that won at least 50 games in 1972-1973. The 1997-1998 Nuggets played just 30 games against such teams. The 1970-1971 Cavaliers played just 12.

Philadelphia played in the NBA's best division in 1972-1973. The Boston Celtics went 68-14. The New York Knicks went 57-25 and won the NBA title. The 76ers played those teams 13 times.

The inept Cleveland and Denver teams played in the worst divisions in the NBA during their historically bad seasons. Those squads played a total of just eight games against the top teams in their divisions.

One final edge for Philadelphia "over" Cleveland: The Cavaliers got to play 24 games against fellow expansion teams in Buffalo and Portland. The 76ers got no such special dispensation.

One final edge for Philadelphia "over" Denver: Philadelphia had the lone sub-20 win team in the NBA during the 1972-1973 season. Five teams won fewer than 20 games during the 1997-1998 season.

Argument: "If the 76ers played such a good schedule, shouldn't they have a better ranking than some other teams on this list?"

Counter argument: No.

The 76ers' historically bad average point differential deservedly makes their POST rating worse than every team in NBA history save three.

Philadelphia did play a tough schedule and gets rewarded with a ranking superior to a pair of teams (the 1970-1971 Cleveland Cavaliers and 1997-1998 Denver Nuggets) that played weaker schedules and finished with comparable average point differentials.

The rest of the teams on this list finished with average point differentials far superior to the 76ers', achieved against reasonably tough schedules.

The 76ers belong right here.

Postscript

Philadelphia rebuilt almost as quickly as it collapsed. Gene Shue came aboard as coach for the 1973-1974 season. He somehow coaxed a 25-57 record out of a cast similar to the 1972-1973 roster.

The rebuilding process then accelerated rapidly. The courts ordered Cunningham to return to Philadelphia for the 1974-1975 season. Cunningham averaged 19.5 points per game. The 76ers improved to 34-48.

High-scoring power forward George McGinnis and quick-shooting guard World B. Free came aboard for the 1975-1976 season. Philadelphia won 46 games and reached the playoffs.

The franchise returned to championship contention during the 1976-1977 season. The 76ers purchased electrifying forward Julius Erving from the New York Nets prior to the campaign. "Doctor J" averaged 21.6 points per game during his first season in Philadelphia and thrilled fans with his high-flying, above-the-rim game. Erving led the 76ers to a 50-32 record and a berth in the NBA Finals.

Philadelphia lost the 1977 championship series against the Portland Trail Blazers. The 76ers would lose in the finals again in 1980 and 1982 before finally breaking through to win the NBA title with Erving in 1983.

1972-1973 Philadelphia 76ers final statistics

Name	G	PPG	FG%	FT%	RPG	APG
Fred Carter	81	20.0	.421	.704	6.0	4.3
John Block	48	17.9	.441	.781	9.2	2.0
Tom VanArsdale	30	17.7	.393	.833	6.2	2.1
Bill Bridges	10	14.0	.376	.708	12.2	2.3
Kevin Loughery	32	13.9	.396	.823	3.5	4.6
Leroy Ellis	69	13.7	.441	.801	10.8	2.0
Don May	26	11.9	.441	.855	5.5	1.7
Emanuel Leaks	82	11.0	.404	.720	8.3	1.2
John Trapp	39	10.7	.412	.741	4.8	1.2
Fred Boyd	82	10.5	.392	.680	2.6	3.7
Jeff Halliburton	31	9.5	.436	.758	2.6	2.2
Dave Sorenson	48	5.9	.456	.747	3.6	0.6
Hal Greer	38	5.6	.392	.821	2.8	2.9
Dale Schlueter	78	5.4	.524	.699	4.5	1.3
Mike Price	57	5.1	.415	.809	2.1	1.2
Dennis Awtrey	3	2.3	.429	.250	4.7	0.7
Mel Counts	7	1.4	.313	.000	2.3	0.4
Luther Green	5	0.6	.000	.333	0.6	0.0
Bob Rule	3	0.0	.000	.000	0.7	0.3
Team	82	104.1	.420	.750	50.9	20.6
Opponents	82	116.2	.473	.749	57.1	27.3

5. The 1982-1983 Houston Rockets
Record: 14-68
Overall ranking: 1,149th, 10.986 points below average.
Other not-so-dominant Houston Rocket teams of the era: None

Why they're ranked here

This horror show on hardwood would prove worth the inconvenience.

The 1982-1983 Houston Rockets produced the least dominant season in franchise history, but also set the foundation for three future NBA Finals appearances and a pair of championships.

Coincidentally, the 1982-1983 struggles stemmed from an NBA Finals appearance. Hall of Fame center Moses Malone led Houston on a surprise run during the 1980-1981 postseason. The Rockets finished the regular season with a 40-42 record, but Malone led Houston all the way to the NBA Finals. The

Rockets fell 4-2 against the Boston Celtics, but Malone established himself as the premier frontcourt player in basketball.

Malone won the league's Most Valuable Player award during the 1981-1982 season and helped Houston to a 46-36 finish.

The Philadelphia 76ers took note of Malone's excellence and decided he would provide the final answer to their championship aspirations. Philadelphia offered Malone a six-year contract worth $13.2 million, a staggering sum at the time.

New Rockets owner Charlie Thomas decided Malone was not worth $13.2 million and allowed his franchise center to join the 76ers. Thomas immediately discovered Malone apparently *was* worth 32 wins. Houston collapsed to a 14-68 record during its first season without Malone, at the time an NBA record for the most dramatic single-season decline in wins.

Several other things had to go wrong to produce the 1982-1983 debacle. The Rockets technically had two Hall of Fame players on their roster: bruising forward Elvin Hayes and sharpshooting guard Calvin Murphy. But both players would call it a career after the 1982-1983 campaign. Both would produce solid numbers during their final seasons, but far below their career standards.

No player on the 1982-1983 Rockets would average more than Allen Leavall's 14.8 points per outing. Houston would finish last in the league with a .448 shooting percentage. The Rockets also languished in the bottom half of the league in most defensive statistics, resulting in an average point differential of -11.6 points per game.

Houston had a relatively uneventful season, as disasters go. The Rockets never lost more than 10 games in a row. They never truly threatened to match 1972-1973 Philadelphia 76ers' 9-73 record, the benchmark for futility.

The Rockets took their losses in 1982-1983 and then embarked on a swift, lasting turnaround.

Why a bunch of people will argue and why they're wrong

Argument: "The 1982-1983 Houston Rockets should have a worse ranking."

Counter argument: Like the 1997-1998 Denver Nuggets, there isn't exactly a grass-roots movement demanding a dishonored place in NBA history for the 1982-1983 Houston Rockets.

Quite frankly, unless one loves all things related to the Dallas Mavericks, Cleveland Cavaliers, Denver Nuggets, or Philadelphia 76ers, or despises all things connected to the Houston Rockets, one cannot make much of a case to demote this Rockets team. Houston won more games than all but one of the teams rated below them. The Rockets finished with a better average point differential than all of the teams ranked below them. Houston also played a competitive schedule.

Fourteen of the 23 NBA teams, including seven of the 12 in the Rockets' Western Conference, would finish with winning records during the 1982-1983 campaign.

Argument: "The Rockets should have a better ranking because they merely had a tough-luck season in a time of transition."

Counter argument: Many an NBA general manager has prefaced a rebuilding season by saying great success in the future will make the struggles of the here-and-now forgotten.

No team shows the truth in that axiom more than the 1982-1983 Houston Rockets.

Houston played in the NBA Finals in 1981. The franchise would reach the league's championship in 1986.

The Rockets completely deconstructed in the interim, but few remember the bad times now. Ask an NBA fan about the Houston Rockets of the 1980s and the fan likely will respond with an anecdote from the 1981 or 1986 playoff runs.

The 1982-1983 Rockets often get excused from the list of truly terrible NBA teams because of the franchise's success before and after the poor season. Yet this Houston team does deserve its spot on the roll call of the wretched. The 1982-1983 Houston squad had the second-worst record of the 1980s and the fourth-worst average point differential of all time. The Rockets played a solid schedule, but not strong enough to make their POST rating better than it is.

Postscript

The Rockets got their biggest win of the 1982-1983 season after the games ended. Houston won a coin flip with the Indiana Pacers to determine the No. 1 overall pick in the 1983 draft. The Rockets used the top pick to select 7-foot-4 center Ralph Sampson, an All-American player at the University of Virginia.

Sampson helped Houston improve to a 29-53 record during the 1983-1984 season. He didn't help the Rockets get good enough to escape the Western Conference cellar. Houston again participated in a coin flip to determine the draft's No. 1 overall pick. The Rockets again won the top choice. Houston again used the pick to select a center. The Rockets chose 7-foot Akeem (later Hakeem) Olajuwon from the University of Houston.

Sampson and Olajuwon became known as "The Twin Towers." They led Houston to a surprise appearance in the NBA Finals after the 1985-1986 season.

Sampson declined quickly after the 1985-1986 season. Olajuwon got better and better. Olajuwon emerged as the NBA's top player during Michael Jordan's brief retirement in the mid-1990s. Olajuwon led Houston to consecutive NBA titles in 1994 and 1995.

No one in Houston complained much then about the 14-68 record in 1982-1983.

1982-1983 Houston Rockets final statistics

Name	G	PPG	FG%	FT%	RPG	APG
Allen Leavell	79	14.8	.415	.832	2.5	6.7
James Bailey	69	14.1	.497	.700	6.8	0.9
Elvin Hayes	81	12.9	.476	.683	7.6	2.0
Calvin Murphy	64	12.8	.447	.920	1.2	2.5
Terry Teagle	73	10.4	.428	.696	2.7	2.1
Joe Bryant	81	10.0	.448	.703	3.4	2.3
Wally Walker	82	9.7	.449	.621	4.5	2.4
Caldwell Jones	82	9.5	.453	.786	8.1	1.7
Major Jones	60	5.7	.457	.549	4.4	0.7
Tom Henderson	51	5.1	.407	.789	1.4	2.7
Chuck Nevitt	6	3.8	.733	.250	2.8	0.0
Jeff Taylor	44	3.6	.400	.652	1.8	2.5
Billy Paultz	57	3.6	.445	.456	2.9	1.0
Calvin Garrett	4	2.5	.364	1.000	1.8	0.8
Team	82	99.3	.448	.725	42.3	23.5
Opponents	82	110.9	.503	.750	47.7	27.5

6. The 1988-1989 Miami Heat
Record: 15-67
Overall ranking: 1,148th, 10.913 points below average.
Other not-so-dominant Miami Heat team of the era: 1989-1990 (1,137th overall, 9.439 points below average).

Why they're ranked here

The Miami Heat came into existence as part of a four-team expansion, including franchises in Charlotte, Minneapolis, and Orlando, announced April 22, 1987.

The Heat began play during the 1988-1989 season. Miami fans should have sensed trouble ahead for that first season when the Heat used the first overall pick in the expansion draft to select Arvid Kramer. The Dallas Mavericks had cut Kramer during a tryout camp eight years earlier. He had not played in an NBA game since the 1979-1980 season. He would not play in another.

Another ominous sign came on opening night. Miami lost its first game by 20 points to the traditionally weak Los Angeles Clippers. The Heat proceeded to lose their first 17 games, setting a league record for most consecutive losses to start a season.

Miami finally got its first win—against the Clippers, naturally—in an 89-88 squeaker in Los Angeles. Things didn't get much better the rest of the way. The Heat would suffer through a 10-game losing streak, plus a pair of seven-game skids. Miami did manage a three-game winning streak during a homestand in late March, but finished the season with a 15-67 mark.

The Heat nickname did not fit when describing the team's shooting. Miami averaged 97.8 points per game, 5.7 points less than any other team in the league. The Heat also finished with the league's worst shooting percentage (.453). Miami did play decent defense, but still posted an average point differential of -11.2 points per game.

The Heat had a method to their badness. The Miami brain trust made a commitment to build the franchise with young players, regardless of how much the team struggled during its early seasons.

The expansion draft selection of Kramer reflected that philosophy. Kramer never played a game in a Heat uniform. The Dallas Mavericks gave Miami a future first round pick in exchange for the Heat promising to take Kramer instead of one of the team's other available players.

Another example of the Heat commitment to youth: Three rookies finished among Miami's top four scorers during the 1988-1989 season. Guard Kevin Edwards led the team with 13.8 points per game. Rookie forward Grant Long produced 11.9 points per contest. First-year center Rony Seikaly added 10.9 points per outing.

Journeyman players like guards Rory Sparrow and Jon Sundvold, and forward Billy Thompson filled the rotation during that first year. Miami would replace those players with young talent over the next few seasons.

For one season, the mix of youth and players-to-be-replaced-by-youth produced a team for the ages in the not-so-dominant sense.

Why a bunch of people will argue and why they're wrong

Argument: "The 1988-1989 Miami Heat deserve a worse ranking because their 0-17 start made them the reference point for bad teams for several years."

Counter argument: The average fan remembers the 1988-1989 Miami Heat as a historically bad team because it established an easy-to-recognize mark: the 17-game losing streak to start the franchise's existence. Miami spent the late 1980s and early 1990s as the punch line to many an NBA joke, the role generally held by the Los Angeles Clippers.

Take away the 0-17 start and the rest of Miami's "accomplishments" during the 1988-1989 season proved relatively average for a not-so-dominant team. Miami won 15 games and never threatened the 1972-1973 Philadelphia 76ers 9-73 mark. The Heat finished the season with an average point differential of -11.2 points per game, significantly better than the teams with less favorable rankings.

Miami also played a difficult schedule, in reality if not statistically. The four teams in the NBA's late-1980s expansion rotated between the Eastern Conference and Western Conference during their first seasons in the league. The NBA hoped to give the fans in its new markets a chance to see all of the league's stars.

Miami played in the Western Conference during the 1988-1989 season. Heat fans got to see Magic Johnson and the Los Angeles Lakers multiple times because of the alignment. The Miami players had to spend the season jetting back and forth between south Florida and the West Coast. The arrangement probably pleased the Heat fans. It didn't help the Miami players.

Argument: "The Heat should have a better ranking because several other teams produced worse overall seasons."

Counter argument: Other teams did produce worse overall seasons. Miami earned "bonus points" for its historically poor start.

If one divides the 1988-1989 Heat schedule into two parts, one sees two distinct seasons: bad and incredibly bad. Miami lost its games by an average of 15.1 points per game during its season-opening losing streak. The Heat would have finished the season with a POST rating of approximately -14.8—worse than the 1992-1993 Dallas Mavericks' rating—had the campaign continued at a similar pace.

Miami finished the season with "improvement": a 15-50 record and an average point differential of -10.2 points per game over its last 65 contests. The "strong" finish creates a final profile that might look better than the final profile of some other teams we'll meet later in this chapter.

Yet no team started worse than the 1988-1989 Miami Heat. The staggering start made Miami's POST rating worse than that of all but five teams in NBA history.

Postscript

Miami stuck with its build-with-youth plan until the mid-1990s. The Heat added sharpshooter Glen Rice for the 1989-1990 season. Another accurate shooter, Steve Smith, came aboard for the 1991-1992 campaign. Point guards Vernell "Bimbo" Coles and Brian Shaw gave Miami a starting five of young, talented players.

The build-with-youth plan got the Heat into the playoffs by the 1991-1992 season. Miami made the playoffs again following the 1993-1994 season. There, the team pushed the top-seeded Atlanta Hawks to five games in a best-of-five first round series.

The build-with-youth plan didn't fail, but didn't look like a success when compared to the good fortune of two other late-1980s expansion teams. The Heat's relative early success meant the franchise never enjoyed a top overall draft pick. The Charlotte Hornets and Orlando Magic did obtain No. 1 overall picks. They used those selections to surpass Miami.

Charlotte won the No. 1 pick in the 1990 draft and the No. 2 selection in 1992. The Hornets obtained forward Larry Johnson and center Alonzo Mourning with those picks. Charlotte got good enough to win a playoff series by the 1992-1993 season

Orlando landed the No. 1 pick in the 1992 and 1993 drafts. The Magic turned those picks into center Shaquille O'Neal and guard Anfernee Hardaway. Orlando reached the NBA Finals by the 1994-1995 season.

Miami changed its approach when Pat Riley took over the team before the 1995-1996 season. The original Heat core had slipped to a 32-50 record during the 1994-1995 season, so Riley scrapped the build-with-youth plan. Riley traded for Mourning and veteran guard Tim Hardaway. He reconstructed the roster with additional tough, veteran players. Mourning kept the team among the Eastern Conference elite until 2000, when kidney problems curtailed his effectiveness.

1988-1989 Miami Heat final statistics

Name	G	PPG	FG%	FT%	RPG	APG
Kevin Edwards	79	13.8	.425	.746	3.3	4.4
Rory Sparrow	80	12.5	.452	.879	2.7	5.4
Grant Long	82	11.9	.486	.749	6.7	1.8
Rony Seikaly	78	10.9	.448	.511	7.0	0.7
Billy Thompson	79	10.8	.487	.696	7.2	2.2
Jon Sundvold	68	10.4	.455	.825	1.3	2.0
Pat Cummings	53	8.8	.500	.742	5.3	0.9
Sylvester Gray	55	8.0	.420	.673	5.2	2.1
Dwayne Washington	54	7.6	.424	.788	2.3	4.2
Clinton Wheeler	8	7.0	.571	.800	1.5	2.6
Anthony Taylor	21	6.9	.397	.750	1.6	2.0
Kelvin Upshaw	9	6.3	.413	.667	1.4	2.2
John Shasky	65	5.5	.488	.689	3.6	0.3
Todd Mitchell	22	5.4	.466	.600	2.1	0.9
Scott Hastings	75	5.1	.436	.850	3.1	0.8
Craig Neal	32	2.8	.386	.619	0.6	2.7

Dave Popson	7	1.6	.333	.500	1.6	0.3
Team	82	97.8	.453	.702	42.9	23.9
Opponents	82	109.0	.488	.773	43.3	25.1

7. The 1986-1987 Los Angeles Clippers
Record: 12-70
Overall ranking: 1,147th, 10.806 points below average.
Other not-so-dominant Los Angeles Clipper teams of the era: 1987-1988 (1,141st, 9.978 points below average); 1988-1989 (1,134th overall, 9.282 points below average); 1985-1986 (1,078th overall, 6.657 points below average).

Why they're ranked here

The Buffalo Braves-San Diego/Los Angeles Clippers franchise traces its legacy of ineptitude to this team.

The Braves/Clippers franchise had a tradition of mediocrity prior to the 1986-1987 season. Since then, the team has achieved even less.

The Clippers moved from San Diego to Los Angeles for the 1984-1985 season. The club tried to build around center Bill Walton during its time in San Diego. Walton spent most of those years on the injured list. The team never won more than 36 games with Walton in the fold.

The Clippers dealt Walton to the Boston Celtics prior to the 1985-1986 season. Los Angeles acquired Cedric Maxwell in the transaction. The trade followed a pattern that saw the Clippers obtain several aging players who had performed key roles on successful teams. Los Angeles also traded for players like guards Norm Nixon and Marques Johnson. Those players possessed notable names, but had passed their primes.

The trades meant giving up young players and draft picks. The Clippers dealt away players like Tom Chambers and Terry Cummings. They gave up a draft pick the Los Angeles Lakers used to select Byron Scott.

The Clippers used one of the few picks they did keep to select Benoit Benjamin, literally and figuratively one of the biggest disappointments in NBA history. Benjamin, a 7-foot center, boasted plenty of potential. He never came close to using it.

The roster makeup didn't matter much during the 1986-1987 season, because the notable players spent much of the season on the injured list.

Nixon injured a tendon above his knee during a summer softball game. He missed the entire year.

Johnson ruptured a disc in his back when he ran into Benjamin on the court during the season's tenth game. He missed the rest of the season.

Maxwell showed signs of age. He played in just 35 games.

The injuries forced forward Mike Woodson to assume the role of go-to scorer. Woodson would average 18.0 points per game, but did not get nearly enough help.

The other positive was the play of Michael Cage, the team's power forward. Cage would average a double-double with 15.7 points and 11.5 rebounds per game.

Aside from those two bright spots, the team spent the season in the dark. The Clippers lost 16 consecutive games at one stretch. Los Angeles lost its last 14 games and finished with a 12-70 record, 25 games out of next-to-last place

The Clippers finished last in the league in both field goal percentage and field goal percentage allowed, resulting in an average point differential of -11.4 points per game.

The first truly horrid Los Angeles Clippers team remains the least dominant in franchise history.

Why a bunch of people will argue and why they're wrong

Argument: "The least dominant franchise in NBA history deserves a harsher ranking on the list of the league's least dominant teams."

Counter argument: The Clippers franchise would hold the No. 1 spot for all-time achievement on a list of the least dominant franchises in NBA history. Los Angeles compiled the league's least dominant five-year and 15-year stretches, according to the POST ratings.

Yet none of the individual Clippers teams sank to the level of single-season futility achieved by the teams ranked lower on this list. Los Angeles did not challenge the 9-73 benchmark established by the 1972-1973 Philadelphia 76ers. The Clippers' average point differential of -11.2 points per game is much better than the average point differential for four of the six teams rated worse.

Los Angeles ranks more favorably than the 1970-1971 Cleveland Cavaliers and the 1988-1989 Miami Heat because of schedule strength. The Cavaliers and Heat played games against fellow expansion teams, thereby making their POST ratings worse. The Clippers played all of their games against established teams.

Argument: "Why pick this Clippers team as the least dominant of all the not-so-dominant Clipper teams?"

Counter argument: From this vantage point, all of the Los Angeles Clipper teams seem equally bad.

Looking back, however, the 1986-1987 squad does stand out. The wart on a witch's nose.

The 1986-1987 Clippers had a winning percentage of .146. All subsequent Clipper teams posted a winning percentage of at least .180.

The 1986-1987 Clippers produced an average point differential of -11.2 points per game. Only one team Clippers team fared worse.

The 1986-1987 Clippers played weaker opponents than the Clipper shipwrecks of recent vintage. The Western Conference of the 1980s was decidedly weaker than the Eastern Conference. The situation reversed starting with the 1998-1999 season. The Clippers have posted some bad seasons since the start of the 1998-1999 campaign, but get credit in the POST formula for facing stronger competition.

Bottom line: The 1986-1987 Clippers not only steered the franchise off course, but also produced the most off-course year in the franchise's voyage.

Postscript

The Clippers did follow the 1986-1987 disaster with a somewhat successful rebuilding process.

Los Angeles selected gifted forward Danny Manning with the first pick of the 1988 draft. The Clippers obtained bruising forward Charles Smith in the same draft.

Los Angeles tried to add Danny Ferry in the 1989 draft. Ferry refused to sign with the team, cementing the public image of a bumbling, inept franchise.

The Clippers managed to obtain Ron Harper from the Cleveland Cavaliers in exchange for the rights to Ferry—in retrospect, perhaps the best trade in franchise history. Ferry never developed into a player worthy of the No. 2 pick in the draft. Harper contributed several strong seasons during his stay in Los Angeles. The trade also yielded a draft pick the Clippers used to select Loy Vaught, a solid contributor for several seasons.

The Clippers combined a healthy Manning, a solid supporting cast, and proven coach Larry Brown late in the 1991-1992 season. Brown led Los Angeles to a 23-12 finish and a spot in the playoffs. The Clippers swapped Smith for point guard Mark Jackson for the 1992-1993 season and again made the playoffs.

Los Angeles then scuttled its finally sailing ship. Brown resigned after the 1993 playoffs. Manning demanded a trade and got one late in the 1993-1994 season. Players like Harper and Jackson departed as soon as possible. Harper and Jackson had no desire to remain in the losing atmosphere. The Clippers had no desire to pay those players what they deemed their market worth.

The Clippers returned to their pattern of acquiring big-name but past-their-prime players, most notably forward Dominique Wilkins. Soon, the franchise reverted to its pattern of losing most of its games.

1986-1987 Los Angeles Clippers final statistics

Name	G	PPG	FG%	FT%	RPG	APG
Mike Woodson	74	17.1	.437	.828	2.2	2.6
Marques Johnson	10	16.6	.439	.714	3.3	2.8
Michael Cage	80	15.7	.521	.730	11.5	1.6
Cedric Maxwell	35	13.6	.519	.776	7.2	3.5
Larry Drew	60	12.4	.432	.837	1.7	5.4
Benoit Benjamin	72	11.5	.449	.715	8.1	1.9
Darnell Valentine	65	11.2	.410	.815	2.3	6.9
Quintin Dailey	49	10.6	.407	.768	1.7	1.6
Rory White	68	9.2	.480	.653	2.9	1.2
Kenny Fields	44	8.7	.445	.809	3.3	1.4
Kurt Nimphius	38	7.8	.472	.648	3.5	0.5
Earl Cureton	35	7.7	.487	.544	6.4	1.5
Lancaster Gordon	70	7.5	.406	.737	1.8	2.0
Geoff Huston	19	6.8	.455	.529	0.9	5.3
Tim Kempton	66	4.4	.471	.693	2.9	0.8
Steffond Johnson	29	2.6	.422	.526	1.5	0.2
Dwayne Polee	1	2.0	0.250	.000	0.0	0.0
Team	82	104.5	.452	.742	41.1	24.0
Opponents	82	115.9	.518	.746	46.7	29.5

8. The 1949-1950 Denver Nuggets
Record: 11-51
Overall ranking: 1,146th, 10.771 points below average.
Other not-so-dominant Denver Nugget teams of the era: None.

Why they're ranked here

First, a historical clarification: This team has no connection with the Denver Nuggets of today.

The current Denver Nuggets began life in 1966 as the Denver Rockets of the American Basketball Association. The Rockets changed their nickname to Nuggets prior to the 1975-1976 season.

The original Denver Nuggets came into existence in 1948 as part of the National Basketball League. The NBL folded after the 1948-1949 season, but the Nuggets and five other NBL teams joined the Basketball Association of America. The merger formed the National Basketball Association—the NBA.

The Denver franchise lasted just one season in the NBA. The Nuggets went 11-51 and dropped out of the league.

Denver started its season with a 15-game losing streak. Things never got much better. The Nuggets never won more than two games in a row.

Denver posted an average point differential of -11.4 points per game. No other team would produce an average point differential worse than -10.0 points per game until the Cleveland Cavaliers came along for the 1970-1971 season. The Nuggets averaged a respectable-for-the-time 77.7 points per game, but allowed a league-worst 89.1 points per game.

Denver did not employ a single player of note. Only two players who completed the season in Colorado (leading scorer Kenny Sailors and third-leading scorer Dillard Crocker) would play another game in the NBA. Sailors would play just one more season; Crocker two. Neither would come close to matching the statistics they posted in Denver.

The Nuggets had a respectable 9-15 record at home, but went just 1-26 in true road games. Denver schedule accentuated the team's difficulties. The new NBA had no other teams located farther west than St. Louis and Minneapolis. Denver played in the Western Division, consisting of two teams from Indiana and three from Wisconsin. No other team in the league faced such demanding travels.

The Nuggets lost their last 11 games and mercifully went out of existence.

Why a bunch of people will argue and why they're wrong

Argument: "The 1949-1950 Denver Nuggets should have a worse ranking because they likely had less talent than any team in NBA history."

Counter argument: Point taken. NBA observers generally concede that professional basketball teams in the 1950s played at a level inferior to that of subsequent decades. The Nuggets clearly had the least-talented team of the era and therefore the least-talented team of all time.

The POST ratings gauge dominance, or lack thereof, within a given team's season. Denver needed just 62 tries to win 11 games during the 1949-1950 season. Other teams have fared far worse. The Nuggets had an average point differential of -11.4 points. Again, other teams have fared far worse.

Would the 1949-1950 Denver Nuggets lose a best-of-seven series against every other team in NBA history? Probably. Do they fare more favorably than seven other teams in NBA history when compared to the "average" teams of their respective eras? Definitely.

Argument: "Does this historical footnote of a team really deserve to take up a spot on this list?"

Counter argument: These Denver Nuggets played in the NBA, so they get in.

The Nuggets' schedule cements their position as one of the least dominant teams in NBA history. Denver made frequent trips to odd locales like Anderson,

Indiana, and Sheboygan, Wisconsin. The travels probably didn't keep the Nugget players very fresh, but should have helped them win more games.

Denver played in the Western Division, far and away the NBA's worst during the 1949-1950 season. Teams in the Western Division, excluding Denver, won just 46.2 percent of their games. Teams in the Central Division won 61.1 percent of their games. Teams in the Eastern Division won at a 48.5 percent clip.

Four of the six teams in the Western Division, including the Nuggets, would fold at the conclusion of the season.

Denver got to play 35 of its 62 games against the weaker Western Division and still managed one of the worst seasons imaginable.

Had the 1972-1973 Philadelphia 76ers not gone 9-73, the 1949-1950 Denver Nuggets probably would hold the 76ers' place as the historical standard for teams gone bad.

Postscript

The beginning was the end.

1949-1950 Denver Nuggets final statistics

Name	G	PPG	FG%	FT%	RPG	APG
Kenny Sailors	57	17.3	.349	.721	N/A	4.0
Dillard Crocker	53	13.6	.292	.735	N/A	1.6
Bob Brown	62	11.7	.361	.683	N/A	1.6
Duane Klueh	33	10.0	.364	.725	N/A	1.9
Floyd Volker	37	9.6	.308	.577	N/A	2.8
Jack Toomay	62	9.6	.397	.705	N/A	1.5
Jimmy Darden	26	8.1	.321	.688	N/A	2.6
Jack Cotton	54	5.1	.292	.509	N/A	1.2
Al Guokas	41	4.8	.317	.532	N/A	2.1
Bob Royer	42	4.7	.338	.707	N/A	2.0
Ed Bartels	13	4.5	.256	.548	N/A	1.5
Bill Herman	13	4.3	.385	.545	N/A	1.2
Jake Carter	13	3.4	.289	.692	N/A	1.2
Earl Dodd	9	1.7	.222	.600	N/A	0.7
Jim Browne	31	1.5	.354	.481	N/A	0.3
Team	62	77.7	.334	.678	N/A	16.8
Opponents	62	89.1	N/A	N/A	N/A	N/A

9. The 1999-2000 Los Angeles Clippers
Record: 15-67
Overall ranking: 1,145th, 10.767 points below average.
Other not-so-dominant Los Angeles Clipper teams of the era: 1998-1999 (1,123rd overall, 8.569 points below average); 1997-1998 (1,096th overall, 7.380 points below average).

Why they're ranked here

Everything went right for the Los Angeles Clippers during the 1996-1997 season, resulting in a playoff berth.

Everything went wrong for the franchise during the next three years, culminating in a historically bad season in 1999-2000.

Hard-working forward Loy Vaught gave the Clippers something of an identity in the mid-1990s. Vaught averaged a double-double during the 1996-1997 season, helping a balanced Los Angeles team qualify for the playoffs.

The deterioration of the team began when a back injury derailed Vaught's career.

The Clippers had awarded Vaught a generous contract and hoped to build the team around him. Instead, Vaught would play just 10 more games in his career.

Shooting guard Malik Sealy also departed after the 1996-1997 season. He signed as a free agent with the Detroit Pistons.

Thus, Los Angeles lost the top two scorers from a playoff team at one blow. The Clippers showed the effects of such devastating personnel losses during the 1997-1998 season, winning just 17 games.

The Clippers did receive the No. 1 draft pick for the 1998 draft, but used the opportunity to signal the start of another rebuilding process. The franchise selected Michael Olowokandi, a raw 7-foot center. Olowokandi possessed talent, but lacked the experience and, as it turned out, the desire to make an impact.

Los Angeles' league record-tying 17-game losing streak at the start of the lockout-delayed 1998-1999 season reaffirmed the decision to start over with young players.

In retrospect, the Clippers' roster for the 1999-2000 season looks respectable. Forwards Maurice Taylor and Lamar Odom averaged in double figures. So did guards Derek Anderson and Tyrone Nesby. Olowokandi and guards Troy Hudson and Jeff McInnis also would enjoy solid pro careers. All played for the 1999-2000 Clippers.

The combination simply didn't click during the 1999-2000 season. None of the young, talented players could carry a team on offense yet. The young Clippers didn't play much defense, either. Los Angeles finished next-to-last in the league in both offense (92.0 points per game) and defense (103.5 points per game). The

Clippers finished with an average point differential of -11.5 points per game, the worst margin in the franchise's sorry history.

Los Angeles finished with a 15-67 record. Three of those wins came against the Golden State Warriors, who would finish with a 19-63 record. The Clippers did not defeat any other team on their schedule more than once.

Los Angeles fired coach Chris Ford after the team sagged to an 11-34 record. Things got worse under replacement Jim Todd. Los Angeles went 4-33 down the stretch, including a 17-game losing streak.

The Clippers played their home games in the new Staples Center during the 1999-2000 season. The building's primary tenant, the Los Angeles Lakers, went 67-15 and won the NBA title. The presence of the Clippers meant Staples Center home teams managed just a .500 record during the regular season.

Why a bunch of people will argue and why they're wrong

Argument: "The 1999-2000 Los Angeles Clippers should rank as the least dominant Clipper team of all time."

Counter argument: Almost. Not quite.

The 1999-2000 Clippers set a dubious franchise record with an average point differential of -11.5 points per game. One could use that statistic to say the 1999-2000 Clippers should rank lower than any team other in franchise history.

Strength of schedule saves the 1999-2000 Clippers. The Western Conference emerged as the NBA's strongest conference during the 1998-1999 season. The division between East and West grew more obvious during the 1999-2000 campaign. Western Conference teams won 34 more total games than East teams during the 1999-2000 season. The Clippers played 52 of their 82 games against Western Conference teams.

By comparison, the 1986-1987 Clippers played the majority of their games against the then-weaker Western Conference. Teams in the West won 28 fewer total games than teams in the East during the 1986-1987 season. The Clippers played even more of their games against teams in the West that season (60 of 82).

The 1999-2000 Clippers' tougher schedule negates their franchise-worst average point differential

Argument: "The Clippers should have a better ranking because of the talent clearly present on the roster."

Counter argument: The Clippers admittedly represent an anomaly on this list. The other nine not-so-dominant teams discussed here took the floor with rosters full of has-beens and never-weres.

This Clippers team had a bunch of too-youngs. Los Angeles would have won considerably more games during the 1999-2000 season had the players on the roster performed at the level they would reach just a few years later. No other team on this list can make that claim.

The Clippers simply didn't have enough experience to succeed in 1999-2000. They posted accordingly poor results and "earned" the POST rating they have.

Postscript

The Clippers brought in more young, talented players between 2000 and 2002. Forwards Elton Brand and Quentin Richardson, and flashy guards Jeff McInnis and Corey Maggette came aboard soon after the 1999-2000 disaster.

"Even we can't screw this up," Los Angeles general manager Elgin Baylor reportedly exulted after a successful 2001 draft.

The Clippers haven't exactly screwed this up, but they haven't truly succeeded, either.

Los Angeles improved to 31 wins in 2000-2001 and 39 in 2001-2002.

The progress created playoff hopes for the 2002-2003 season. Not surprisingly, the team couldn't meet the expectations in the powerful Western Conference. The team played competitively, but couldn't crack the postseason.

The team surprised many observers by signing Brand to a maximum-salary deal, but the franchise still showed signs of instability. The team went through several coaches. It allowed Richardson, Maggette, and McInnis to leave as free agents.

Brand's presence kept the team competitive. He finally got some help for the 2005-2006 campaign and led the Clippers to a winning season.

1999-2000 Los Angeles Clippers final statistics

Name	G	PPG	FG%	FT%	RPG	APG
Maurice Taylor	62	17.1	.464	.711	6.5	1.6
Derek Anderson	64	16.9	.438	.877	4.0	3.4
Lamar Odom	76	16.6	.438	.719	7.8	4.2
Tyrone Nesby	73	13.3	.398	.791	3.8	1.7
Michael Olowokandi	80	9.8	.437	.651	8.2	0.5
Troy Hudson	62	8.8	.377	.811	2.4	3.9
Eric Piatkowski	75	8.7	.415	.850	3.0	1.1
Jeff McInnis	25	7.2	.430	.765	2.9	3.6
Eric Murdock	40	5.6	.385	.638	1.9	2.7
Brian Skinner	33	5.4	.507	.662	6.1	0.3
Keith Closs	57	4.2	.487	.590	3.1	0.4
Charles Jones	56	3.4	.328	.739	1.1	1.7
Pete Chilcutt	24	3.0	.492	1.000	3.3	0.7

Etdrick Bohannon	11	2.4	.538	.600	2.7	0.5
Anthony Avent	49	1.7	.302	.719	1.5	0.2
Marty Conlon	3	0.7	.500	.000	0.7	0.0
Mario Bennett	1	0.0	.000	.000	2.0	0.0
Team	82	92.0	.426	.746	40.6	18.0
Opponents	82	103.5	.477	.741	45.6	24.1

10. The 1990-1991 Denver Nuggets

Record: 20-62
Overall ranking: 1,144th, 10.318 points below average.
Other not-so-dominant Denver Nugget team of the era: 1991-1992 (1,102nd overall, 7.527 points below average).

Why they're ranked here

The Denver Nuggets produced consistent results throughout the 1980s. Coach Doug Moe encouraged a fast-paced style of play. The club reached the playoffs nine times under his guidance.

Moe produced consistent winners, but no champions. Denver reached the Western Conference finals just once during his tenure. The team began to show signs of age by the 1989-1990 season. The Nuggets went 43-39 and lost in the first round of the playoffs for the second consecutive season. Alex English, the franchise's all-time leading scorer, announced his retirement. Moe also traded away high-scoring point guard Lafayette "Fat" Lever.

Denver's management responded to the team's decline with a couple of head-scratching moves.

First, the Nuggets fired Moe. Then, new general manager Bernie Bickerstaff gave the aging Nuggets a coach who emphasized up-tempo basketball even more than Moe.

Paul Westhead had coached tiny Loyola Marymount University to the NCAA tournament quarterfinals during the 1989-1990 season. Westhead used a system of constant fast breaks and 3-point shots at LMU. He promised to use the same system with the Nuggets.

Westhead's teams excelled at pushing the tempo, but not much else. Westhead might have succeeded with sharpshooters English and Lever in his lineup. Without them, Westhead had an aging roster ill-suited for a fast-paced style of play.

Denver started the season 0-7. The team lost games by space-age scores like 162-158 and 173-143. The Nuggets bottomed out at 6-28. They finished with a then-franchise-worst 20-62 mark.

Players like too-short guard Michael Adams (26.5 points per game) and too-old forwards Orlando Woolridge (25.1 points per game) and Walter Davis (18.7 points per game) produced their career-best scoring years in Westhead's system. They also proved incapable of stopping anyone on defense.

The Nuggets allowed over 100 points in every game during the 1990-1991 season. They set an NBA record for average points per game allowed in a season.

Denver did lead the league in scoring by a wide margin with 119.9 points per game. The team also finished last in the league by a wider margin by allowing 130.8 points per game. Shooting statistics show how the Nuggets' supposed offensive prowess was fool's gold. Denver finished last in the league in shooting percentage with a mark of .440.

The Nuggets deserved every bit of their reputation as a poor defensive team. Denver allowed opponents to shoot at a .512 clip. No other team in the league allowed opponents to make half of their shots.

No team since has allowed opponents to score so frequently or so freely.

Why a bunch of people will argue and why they're wrong

Argument: "The 1990-1991 Denver Nuggets should have a worse ranking because they were spectacularly worse than several of the teams on this list."

Counter argument: The Nuggets played spectacularly poorly during the 1990-1991 season. The other teams in the NBA's all-time bottom ten suffered through worse seasons overall.

Denver won 20 games, more than every other not-so-dominant team discussed earlier. The Nuggets produced an average point differential of "only" -10.9 points per game, again better than every other team in the not-so-dominant ten.

Denver got plenty of attention in a "stop and look at the car crash" fashion because of the way it lost its games during the 1990-1991. The publicity helps many fans remember the team as one of the least dominant in NBA history, but several other less-notorious teams played worse.

Argument: "In that case, the Nuggets should have a better ranking."

Counter argument: For the record, Denver beat out the 1947-1948 Providence Steamrollers and the Vancouver Grizzlies of the mid-1990s to earn the last spot on the list of the NBA's 10 least dominant teams. No other team has a POST rating within shouting distance of a spot on this list.

The Providence Steamrollers went 6-42 during the 1947-1948 season and produced an average point differential of -11.0 points per game. On the surface, Providence had a less-dominant season than the 1990-1991 Nuggets.

A look at the Steamrollers' schedule shows otherwise. Six of the eight teams in the Basketball Association of America finished with 26 to 29 victories during the league's 48-game season.

Thus, either Providence played a remarkably tough schedule, with 40 of 48 games against teams with winning records, or the Steamrollers simply had the one below-average team in a league full of otherwise equal clubs. Either way, Providence's POST rating is better than Denver's. The Nuggets fielded a clearly inferior team in a relatively average NBA season.

The expansion Vancouver Grizzlies went 14-68 during the 1996-1997 season and finished with an average point differential of -10.2 points per outing. The 1996-1997 Grizzlies and 1990-1991 Nuggets played similar schedules. Denver's average point differential of -10.9 points per game gives the Nuggets a POST rating worse than Vancouver's.

Postscript

Denver made a stunning rise to the second round of the playoffs by the 1993-1994 season. The franchise then endured an equally stunning fall and produced a less-dominant team by the end of the 1990s.

The Nuggets had selected high-scoring guard Chris Jackson from Louisiana State during the 1990 draft. The train wreck 1990-1991 season gave the franchise the No. 4 choice in the 1991 draft. Denver used the pick to obtain center Dikembe Mutombo from Georgetown.

Westhead completely changed his philosophy with Mutombo aboard. The Nuggets suddenly became a slow-it-down, defense-oriented squad, with Mutombo anchoring the middle. Denver allowed 130.8 points during the 1990-1991 season. The figure dropped to 107.6 points per game during the 1991-1992 campaign, but the Nuggets only scored 99.7 points per game. The franchise fired Westhead after the 24-58 season.

Dan Issel came aboard as coach with a mandate to play the team's young talent. Versatile forward LaPhonso Ellis joined the team for the 1992-1993 season and started every game. Players like Reggie Williams, Robert Pack, and Bryant Stith developed into dependable performers.

Denver improved to 36-46 during the 1992-1993 season. The Nuggets squeaked into the playoffs as a giddy No. 8 seed in 1993-1994.

Denver then produced one of the most stunning upsets in NBA playoff history. The Nuggets rallied from a 2-0 series deficit to defeat the top-seeded Seattle Supersonics 3-2 in the first round of the postseason. Denver won the decisive game in overtime on Seattle's home floor. The Supersonics had compiled an NBA-best 63-19 record during the regular season.

Denver almost rallied from a 3-0 deficit against the Utah Jazz in the Western Conference semifinals. The Nuggets came back with three consecutive wins to force a seventh game, but lost it 91-81.

The surprising playoff run increased expectations for the young Denver team. And eventually ruined it.

The Nuggets made the playoffs again after the 1994-1995 season, this time as a disappointing No. 8 seed, and lost three consecutive games against the top-seeded San Antonio Spurs.

Denver slipped to a 35-47 record during the 1995-1996 season and missed the playoffs altogether. Nuggets management allowed players like Mutombo and Jackson (now Mahmoud Abdul-Rauf) to leave as free agents. Denver entered another downward spiral that bottomed out with another historically bad team during the 1997-1998 season.

1990-1991 Denver Nuggets final statistics

Name	G	PPG	FG%	FT%	RPG	APG
Michael Adams	66	26.5	.394	.879	3.9	10.5
Orlando Woolridge	53	25.1	.498	.797	6.8	2.2
Walter Davis	39	18.7	.474	.915	3.2	2.2
Reggie Williams	51	16.1	.444	.840	4.8	1.7
Mahmoud Abdul-Rauf	67	14.1	.413	.857	1.8	3.1
Todd Lichti	29	14.0	.439	.855	3.9	2.5
Blair Rasmussen	70	12.5	.458	.677	9.7	1.0
Jim Farmer	25	10.0	.458	.730	2.5	1.5
Corey Gaines	10	8.3	.400	.846	1.4	9.1
Terry Mills	17	7.5	.467	.727	5.2	0.9
Jerome Lane	62	7.5	.438	.411	9.3	2.0
Joe Wolf	74	7.3	.451	.831	5.4	1.4
Marcus Liberty	76	6.7	.421	.630	2.9	0.8
Kenny Battle	40	6.1	.485	.781	3.1	1.2
Tim Legler	10	5.8	.347	.833	1.8	1.2
Anthony Cook	58	5.3	.417	.550	5.6	0.4
Cadillac Anderson	41	5.2	.440	.506	5.8	0.3
Craig Neal	10	4.4	.400	.591	1.6	3.7
Avery Johnson	21	3.8	.426	.656	1.0	3.7
Anthony Mason	3	3.3	.500	.750	1.7	0.0
T.R. Dunn	17	3.1	.447	.900	2.5	1.4
Team	82	119.9	.440	.763	49.4	24.5
Opponents	82	130.8	.512	.775	52.5	30.4

V. Team by Team

The good, the bad, and the interesting from every NBA franchise

Atlanta Hawks
1949-present
Also Tri-Cities Blackhawks (1949-1951), Milwaukee Hawks (1951-1955), and St. Louis Hawks (1955-1968)
Most dominant team: 1986-1987 Atlanta Hawks
Record: 57-25
Overall ranking: 48th, 7.014 points above average

The 1986-1987 Atlanta Hawks romped to a 57-25 record, the best record in franchise history (since matched by the 1993-1994 squad).

Dominique Wilkins (29.0 points per game) finished second in the league in scoring and served as the face of the franchise. Yet the Hawks won their games with defense. Atlanta allowed a league-low 102.8 points per game, 1.1 points better than the next-best team. The Hawks also posted an average point differential of +7.2 points per game, the best mark in franchise history.

The Hawks won the Central Division by five games over the Detroit Pistons, but Detroit upset Atlanta in five games in the Eastern Conference semifinals. The Pistons went on to become the NBA's dominant team of the late 1980s.

Least dominant team: 2004-2005 Atlanta Hawks
Record: 13-69
Overall ranking: 1,139th, 9.503 points below average

The Atlanta Hawks set the stage for the worst season in franchise history by trading away top scorers Jason Terry and Stephen Jackson after the 2003-2004 campaign. Atlanta got high-scoring forwards Antoine Walker and Al Harrington in return. The deals left the Hawks woefully short on players known for defensive intensity.

Walker and Harrington scored plenty of points as the 2004-2005 season unfolded. Atlanta allowed plenty more. The Hawks gave up 102.5 points per game, the second-worst figure in the league. They answered with just 92.7 points per game, resulting in a franchise-worst average point differential of -9.8 points per game.

The most exciting moments of Atlanta's season occurred when the Hawks traded Walker to the Boston Celtics in a deadline deal. Atlanta ostensibly received guard Gary Payton in return. Yet the Hawks quickly agreed to Payton's request for an unconditional release, allowing Payton to return to the Celtics. Thus, Atlanta managed to trade its leading scorer and receive nothing in return.

The Walker trade occurred in the middle of a 13-game losing streak. The Hawks followed up that skid with a 14-game losing streak, resulting in a stretch of 27 losses in 28 games.

Atlanta staggered home with a 13-69 record, the worst record in the league and the worst mark in franchise history. The ultimate ignominy: The Hawks finished with five fewer wins than the expansion Charlotte Bobcats.

Another team of note: 1967-1968 St. Louis Hawks
Record: 56-26
Overall ranking: 347th, 2.327 points above average

The last season for the Hawks franchise in St. Louis produced a team noteworthy for two reasons.

The team posted a 56-26 record, the best record of the franchise's St. Louis era and the most wins for any team in a season prior to a franchise relocation.

The Hawks won the Western Division title by four games over the more-heralded Los Angeles Lakers. St. Louis succeeded even though Lou Hudson, the team's leading scorer as a rookie during the 1966-1967 season, threatened to leave the team to play in the ABA and eventually had to leave the team anyway when drafted by the military.

The final St. Louis season ended with a disappointing Western Division semifinals loss against the San Francisco Warriors. Ben Kerner, who founded the Hawks as a National Basketball League team in Buffalo in 1946, sold his controlling interest in the franchise after the season. The new owners moved the team to Atlanta

Boston Celtics
1946-present
Most dominant team: 1985-1986 Boston Celtics
Record: 67-15
Overall ranking: 8th, 8.842 points above average

This season saw Boston's legendary frontcourt of Larry Bird, Kevin McHale, and Robert Parish (with Bill Walton in reserve) at the peak of its powers. Bird won his third consecutive Most Valuable Player award as the Celtics posted a 67-15 record.

This Boston team made its mark with a 40-1 home record. The Celtics' only home loss came December 6 against the Portland Trail Blazers. Boston went on to win its last 31 home games. The overall home winning streak would reach 38 early in the 1986-1987 season, a since-surpassed NBA record.

The Celtics also won all their home games during the playoffs en route to the franchise's 16th and most recent NBA title.

Read more about the 1985-1986 Boston Celtics in Chapter 1.

Least dominant team: 1996-1997 Boston Celtics
Record: 15-67
Overall ranking: 1,079th, 6.700 points below average

Boston's gradual decline during the 1990s culminated with a complete collapse during the 1996-1997 season.

A steady personnel drain left Boston bereft of talent by the 1996-1997 season. Players like Larry Bird and Kevin McHale retired. Potential successors like Len Bias and Reggie Lewis succumbed to untimely deaths.

The Celtics proceeded to break all of the unwanted Boston franchise records during the 1996-1997 season.

Worst record: 15-67.

Longest losing streak: 13, from February 5 to March 1 (a mark since broken).

A last-place finish, the franchise's first since the 1978-1979 season.

A franchise record-tying fourth consecutive losing season (the streak eventually would reach eight).

Boston also gave up more points than any team in the league (107.9 per game, a figure no team has approached since) and posted a league-worst 4-37 road record

Another team of note: 1968-1969 Boston Celtics
Record: 48-34
Overall ranking: 124th, 5.335 points above average

Boston legend tells how an aging, overmatched Celtics team somehow overcame all odds during Bill Russell's final season and won the franchise's 11th NBA title in 13 years.

Even a Boston Garden leprechaun, however, should admit Boston didn't need good fortune to win the 1968-1969 NBA title.

The Celtics did finish fourth in the Eastern Conference. Boston did play without home court advantage in any postseason series. The Celtics did show some signs of age.

Boston also showed signs of having the best team in the league. The Celtics led the league with an average point differential of +5.6 points per game. Boston also achieved the league's second-best POST rating, just a fraction behind the up-and-coming New York Knicks.

Accordingly, the Celtics clawed through the playoffs and won another championship. Boston rallied from a 3-2 deficit to topple the Los Angeles Lakers in the NBA Finals. The wonder is not how Boston won the title. The wonder is how the Celtics lost so many games during the regular season in the first place.

Charlotte Bobcats
2004-present
Most dominant team: 2005-2006 Charlotte Bobcats
Record: 26-56
Overall ranking: 941st, 3.850 points below average

The Charlotte Bobcats endured several tough breaks during the franchise's second season, but still made measurable progress.

Charlotte finished 26-56, eight wins better than the team's expansion season. The Bobcats posted an average point differential of -4.0 points per game, 1.9 points better than their average margin during the 2004-2005 season.

Charlotte improved even tough top scorer Gerald Wallace (rib) and reigning Rookie of the Year Emeka Okafor (ankle) combined to miss 83 games with injuries.

The Bobcats still had expansion-esque moments. Charlotte lost 13 consecutive games during one midseason stretch. The Bobcats shot just .433 from the field, the worst percentage in the league.

Charlotte got better because it went to the free throw line more frequently and made a greater percentage of those free throw attempts. The increase in points from the charity stripe helped the Bobcats score 2.6 more points per game than the franchise's first team.

Charlotte closed its second season on a high note. The Bobcats won their last four games, the longest winning streak in the franchise's short history.

Least dominant team: 2004-2005 Charlotte Bobcats
Record: 18-64
Overall ranking: 1,059th, 6.057 points below average

The Charlotte Bobcats exceeded most expectations in their inaugural season.

Charlotte did experience the usual expansion season growing pains. The Bobcats finished 18-64 with an average point differential of -5.9 points per game. Charlotte endured a pair of 10-game losing streaks. The Bobcats did not win their first road game until their 21st try, a February 1 victory in Utah.

Charlotte also succeeded in some ways. The Bobcats stayed reasonably competitive despite a salary cap just two-thirds the size of the cap allowed to the other 29 NBA teams. Charlotte also identified the league's Rookie of the Year with its first draft choice: Emeka Okafor, a double-double machine who averaged 15.1 points and 10.9 rebounds per game.

The Bobcats' biggest first-year triumphs came at the expense of the New Orleans Hornets, the franchise that left Charlotte in disgrace after the 2002 season.

The Bobcats defeated the Hornets in the teams' first head-to-head meeting. Charlotte also boasted a better overall record than the established New Orleans squad for most of the season. The two teams finished the campaign with identical 18-64 records.

Another team of note: 2006-2007 Charlotte Bobcats
Record: 33-49
Overall ranking: 945th, 3.889 points below average

The NBA's youngest franchise continued to take baby steps during its third season of existence.

Charlotte clearly made strides on the court. The Bobcats enjoyed a seven-win improvement and set a franchise record with 33 victories. Charlotte never won more than four in a row, but also never lost more than eight in a row. (The Bobcats suffered at least one double-digit losing streak during each of the franchise's first two seasons). Charlotte claimed 19 victories against playoff teams just two seasons after winning 18 games total.

The Bobcats' young core players (top scorer Gerald Wallace, forward Emeka Okafor, and point guard Raymond Felton) all improved their production. Shooting guard Matt Carroll enjoyed a breakthrough season. Critics panned top draft pick Adam Morrison as one of the league's least efficient players, but he did average 11.8 points per game as a rookie.

Charlotte also made some big moves off of the court. NBA icon Michael Jordan assumed control of the Bobcats' basketball operations before the season. Bernie Bickerstaff stepped down as Charlotte's coach after the season.

Chicago Bulls
1966-present
Most dominant team: 1995-1996 Chicago Bulls
Record: 72-10
Overall ranking: 2nd, 11.767 points above average

Michael Jordan best summed up the 1995-1996 Bulls' claim to greatness: "Anyone else go 72-10?"

More claims to greatness: Chicago boasted the league's scoring leader, Most Valuable Player and NBA Finals MVP (Jordan). The Bulls had the league's top rebounder (Dennis Rodman). Chicago had the league's Sixth Man of the Year

(Toni Kukoc). Bulls coach Phil Jackson won his only Coach of the Year award. Chicago general manager Jerry Krause won the league's Executive of the Year honor for pulling off the trade that brought Rodman to the Bulls.

Chicago also had Scottie Pippen, regarded by some as the league's best all-around player during Jordan's "retirement" during the 1993-1994 and 1994-1995 seasons.

The Bulls cemented their place in history with a romp to the NBA title. Read more about the 1995-1996 Chicago Bulls in Chapter 1.

Least dominant team: 1999-2000 Chicago Bulls
Record: 17-65
Overall ranking: 1,132nd, 9.144 points below average

Chicago spiraled into a swift, stunning decline after winning the last championship of the Michael Jordan era in 1998. The painful rebuilding process bottomed out with a disastrous 1999-2000 season.

The Bulls harbored no delusions of grandeur entering the 1999-2000 campaign. Only three players (Toni Kukoc, Randy Brown, and Dickey Simpkins) remained from the franchise's 1998 title team. The Bulls would trade Kukoc early in the season.

Chicago added future All-Stars Elton Brand and Ron Artest via the 1999 NBA draft, but they didn't help much during their rookie seasons. The Bulls staggered to a 17-65 record, just four more wins than a much-maligned 1998-1999 Chicago squad managed during a lockout-shortened 50-game season.

The Bulls ranked last in the league on offense for the second consecutive year and produced an average point differential of -9.4 points per game.

Chicago would give up on the 1999-2000 team's nucleus within one year. The Bulls traded away Brand, Artest, and others by the 2001 NBA draft. They tried re-rebuilding (in time, successfully) around high school big men Eddy Curry and Tyson Chandler.

Another team of note: 1966-1967 Chicago Bulls
Record: 33-48
Overall ranking: 911th, 3.334 points below average

The Chicago Bulls earned two distinctions during their expansion season.

The Bulls set a record for most wins in a season for a post-1960 expansion team with a 33-48 ledger.

Chicago also stands as the only post-1960 expansion team to qualify for the playoffs during its inaugural season.

The Bulls did benefit from two strokes of good fortune.

The NBA used an expanded playoff format that allowed eight of the league's 10 teams—a record 80 percent—to qualify for the postseason.

Chicago also got to play in a weak Western Division. The San Francisco Warriors won the division with a so-so 44-37 record. No other team in the division finished above .500. The Bulls qualified for the postseason by finishing ahead of a Detroit Pistons team that went 30-51.

Guy Rodgers averaged 18.0 points and led the league in assists to lead the Baby Bulls. Rodgers also led the league in assists with the San Francisco Warriors during the 1962-1963 season. He was the only guard other than Oscar Robertson to win an assist title during the 1960s.

Bulls coach Johnny "Red" Kerr received the league's Coach of the Year honor.

Cleveland Cavaliers
1970-present
Most dominant team: 1988-1989 Cleveland Cavaliers
Record: 57-25
Overall ranking: 28th, 7.752 points above average

Magic Johnson took one look at this Cleveland squad and declared the Cavaliers the "Team of the 1990s."

Cleveland looked the part during the 1988-1989 season. The Cavaliers set a franchise record for wins with a 57-25 season. Cleveland set another franchise record with 11 consecutive victories early in the season.

The Cavaliers excelled on both ends of the floor with a balanced lineup that included players like center Brad Daugherty and guards Mark Price and Ron Harper.

Only Cleveland and the Los Angeles Lakers shot over 50 percent from the field for the season. The Cavaliers also ranked third in the league in fewest points allowed (101.2 per game). They set a franchise record with an average point differential of +7.6 points per game.

Cleveland's ascent to greatness got derailed by Michael Jordan and the eventual team of the 1990s, the Chicago Bulls.

The Cavaliers went 6-0 against the Bulls during the 1988-1989 regular season, but Chicago stunned Cleveland in five games in the first round of the playoffs. Jordan hit his famous buzzer-beating floating jumper over Craig Ehlo to lift the Bulls to a 101-100 victory in the decisive Game 5. The Cavaliers never seemed to recover.

Least dominant team: 1970-1971 Cleveland Cavaliers
Record: 15-67
Overall ranking: 1,152nd, 11.790 points below average

The 1970-1971 Cleveland Cavaliers can thank the NBA schedule makers for helping them avoid a more prominent spot on the list of the least dominant teams in league history.

Cleveland did struggle mightily during its expansion season. The Cavaliers lost their first 15 games. Cleveland went on to a 15-67 record and produced an average point differential of -11.2 points per game, club records for futility that still stand today.

Now imagine how bad things could have gotten had the NBA not given its expansion teams a scheduling break during the 1970-1971 season. The league's three new teams (the Cavaliers, the Buffalo Braves, and the Portland Trail Blazers) got to play 24 games in their 82-game schedule against their expansion brethren. Cleveland went a reasonable 9-15 against Buffalo and Portland. The Cavaliers went 6-52 against everyone else, a pace that would have yielded an 8-74 record over a full season.

Read more about the 1970-1971 Cleveland Cavaliers in Chapter 4.

Another team of note: 1981-1982 Cleveland Cavaliers
Record: 15-67
Overall ranking: 1,109th, 7.857 points below average

This Cleveland team also avoided a more prominent spot on the list of the NBA's least dominant teams thanks to a fortuitous schedule. Or more precisely, thanks to a schedule that came to a merciful end.

The 1981-1982 Cavaliers did most of the work establishing the NBA record of 24 consecutive losses. Cleveland completed the 1981-1982 campaign with 19 consecutive defeats. The Cavs then opened the 1982-1983 campaign with five more losses.

The 1995-1996 Vancouver Grizzlies and 1997-1998 Denver Nuggets both lost 23 in a row within a single season, but fell "short" of Cleveland's somewhat obscure record.

Fortunately for the Cavaliers, consecutive game records spanning multiple seasons often get ignored. Media outlets often refer to the Vancouver and Denver losing streaks as the "official" NBA record.

The 1981-1982 Cavs represented the nadir of Ted Stepien's disastrous ownership tenure. Cleveland burrowed through four coaches and 23 players, all just to tie the franchise record for most losses in a season with a 15-67 record.

Dallas Mavericks
1980-present
Most dominant team: 2002-2003 Dallas Mavericks
Record: 60-22
Overall ranking: 26th, 7.762 points above average

This eventful season still stands as the Dallas franchise's best.

The Steve Nash-Michael Finley-Dirk Nowitzki Mavericks reached their apex during this campaign. Dallas jumped ahead of the NBA pack with a 14-0 start. The Mavericks finished with a then-franchise best 60-22 record. They led the league in scoring with 103 points per game. Dallas' most amazing stat: The Mavericks committed fewer turnovers than anyone in the league despite a run-and-gun philosophy.

Dallas made a lengthy run through a postseason gauntlet.

The Mavericks survived the Portland Trail Blazers in a best-of-seven first round series. Dallas had to win a seventh and decisive game after building a 3-0 series lead.

Dallas also needed seven games to win its West semifinal against the Sacramento Kings.

The Mavericks matched up against the San Antonio Spurs in the Western Conference finals. Both teams posted 60-22 marks during the regular season. The Spurs got home court advantage on a tiebreaker.

Home court advantage might not have made a difference for Dallas. The Mavericks won a pair of games in San Antonio, but lost all three West finals games they played at home. Dallas had a sizeable lead at home during Game 6 and a chance to force a decisive Game 7, but reserve guard Steve Kerr led a surprising San Antonio rally that ended the best season in Mavs history.

Least dominant team: 1992-1993 Dallas Mavericks
Record: 11-71
Overall ranking: 1,153rd, 14.575 points below average

The number 12.5 seems to mark a statistical limit for NBA teams. Every team in NBA history has an average point differential between +12.5 and -12.5.

Except one.

The 1992-1993 Dallas Mavericks finished with an average point differential of -15.2 points per game.

As records go, that is the equivalent of a baseball player hitting 89 home runs in a season. That is the equivalent of a football quarterback throwing 60 touchdown passes in one season. That is the equivalent of some future NBA team achieving a 40-game winning streak.

Proportionally, that is how bad the 1992-1993 Dallas Mavericks were compared to every other team in NBA history.

Read more about the 1992-1993 Dallas Mavericks in Chapter 4.

Another team of note: 2006-2007 Dallas Mavericks
Record: 67-15
Overall ranking: 43rd, 7.188 points above average

The 2006-2007 Dallas Mavericks looked like a clear candidate for post-NBA Finals disappointment hangover. Dallas lost the last four games of the 2005-2006 NBA Finals against the Miami Heat after holding a 2-0 series lead. The Mavericks then dropped the first four games of the 2006-2007 regular season.

Hangover? Nope. Dallas spent the rest of the 2006-2007 regular season giving headaches to the rest of the NBA.

The Mavericks bounced back from that 0-4 start with 12 consecutive victories. Dallas would become the first team in league history to produce three winning streaks of 12 games or more, including a franchise-record 17-game win streak during the second half of the season.

The victories added up to a 67-15 record, the best mark in the league and by far the most wins in franchise history. Dallas won its first outright division title since the 1986-1987 season. The Mavericks also earned home court advantage throughout the playoffs for the first time in team history.

Star forward Dirk Nowitzki averaged 24.6 points and 8.9 rebounds per game to earn his first Most Valuable Player award. Versatile wing Josh Howard produced a career-best 18.9 points and 6.8 rebounds per game, and made his first All-Star appearance.

Avery Johnson completed his second full season as Dallas' coach with a dizzying 143-39 record. Johnson's career winning percentage (.786) dwarfed that of legendary coaches like Phil Jackson (.700) and Red Auerbach (.662).

Johnson failed to join Jackson and Auerbach on the list of NBA champion coaches. The Mavericks drew a less-than-ideal first round playoff matchup against the No. 8 seed Golden State Warriors. Golden State won all three of its matchups against Dallas during the regular season. Warriors coach Don Nelson presumably knew the Mavericks' weaknesses better than anyone. Nelson assembled most of the Dallas roster during his time as the Mavericks' coach and groomed Johnson as his successor.

Teacher schooled the pupil during the postseason. Dallas lost the home court advantage it worked all season to earn when Golden State pulled away for a 97-85 victory in Game 1. The Warriors proceeded to build a 3-1 lead in the series. The Mavericks hoped for a momentum reversal when they rallied to win Game 5 in Dallas after trailing by nine points late in the fourth quarter. Golden State responded with a resounding 111-86 home win in Game 6 that clinched the first victory for a No. 8 seed against a No. 1 seed in a best-of-seven first round playoff series, a result left the Mavericks and their fans feeling sick.

Denver Nuggets
1976-present
Most dominant team: 1976-1977 Denver Nuggets
Record: 50-32
Overall ranking: 147th, 4.938 points above average

The Denver Nuggets' first season as an NBA franchise still ranks as their best.

The 1976-1977 Nuggets came over from the American Basketball Association—where they compiled a 60-24 record in the league's final season—and dominated the NBA's Midwest Division.

Denver finished with a 50-32 record (tied for second-best in the league) and won the division by six games. The Nuggets finished with an average point differential of +5.2 points per game, a number no Denver team has approached since.

High-flying Nuggets guard David Thompson had no trouble switching from ABA competition to NBA opposition. Thompson averaged 25.9 points per game and made the All-NBA first team. (How good was Thompson? Fellow former ABA legend Julius Erving made the All-NBA second team in his first NBA campaign).

Denver's feel-good initial NBA season ended on a down note. The Nuggets dropped their playoff opener 101-100 at home against the Portland Trail Blazers in the Western Conference semifinals. Portland defended its home court throughout the remainder of the series and eliminated Denver in six games en route to its eventual NBA title.

Least dominant team: 1997-1998 Denver Nuggets
Record: 11-71
Overall ranking: 1,151st, 11.579 points below average

They were the worst of both worlds: They were bad and they were boring.

The 1997-1998 Nuggets tied the NBA record for most consecutive losses within one season with 23. They finished with an 11-71 record, dangerously close to the 1972-1973 Philadelphia 76ers' 82-game low of nine wins. They managed to stay relatively anonymous throughout a train wreck of a season.

Denver never looked like a threat to finish with a win total worse than the 1972-1973 76ers' 9-73 mark. The team thus avoided the spotlight that would have accompanied a record "chase."

The Nuggets set franchise records for most losses (71), fewest points per game (89.0), average point differential (-11.8 points per game), and worst road record (2-39).

The 1998-1999 Denver squad, hardly world beaters by any standard, managed three more wins in 32 fewer games during a lockout shortened season.

Read more about the 1997-1998 Denver Nuggets in Chapter 4.

Other teams of note: 1981-1982 Denver Nuggets; 1993-1994 Denver Nuggets
Records: 46-36 (1981-1982); 42-40 (1993-1994)
Overall rankings: 572nd, 0.224 points above average (1981-1982); 435th, 1.510 points above average (1993-1994)

Two other Denver Nugget teams deserve recognition.

The 1981-1982 Denver Nuggets set NBA records for points scored *and* points allowed.

Denver scored 10,371 points and allowed 10,371 points during the 1981-1982 season, an average of 126.5 points scored and allowed per game. The 1981-1982 Nuggets are the only team to score 100 points in every game in a season. They were the first team to allow 100 points during every game in a season, a feat matched only once since.

The Nuggets managed a 46-36 record, but lost 2-1 against the Phoenix Suns in a three-game miniseries in the opening round of the playoffs.

The points scored record still stands. The points allowed record fell to another Denver Nuggets team. Then 1990-1991 Nuggets allowed 130.8 points per outing.

The 1993-1994 Denver Nuggets became the first No. 8 seed to upset a No. 1 seed in the playoffs under the current postseason format. Denver rallied from a 2-0 deficit to defeat the Seattle Supersonics in five games. Seattle had finished the regular season with a 63-19 record, best in the NBA by five games. Denver had finished 42-40. The Nuggets won the last two games of the series in overtime, including a 98-94 stunner in Seattle in the decisive fifth game.

Denver nearly went on to become the first NBA team to win a playoff series after trailing 3-0. The Nuggets forced a Game 7 in the Western Conference semifinals against the Utah Jazz, but Utah recovered and won the finale 91-81.

Detroit Pistons
1948-present
Also Fort Wayne Pistons (1948-1957)
Most dominant team: 2005-2006 Detroit Pistons
Record: 64-18
Overall ranking: 80th, 6.251 points above average

The Detroit Pistons played like a team on a mission during the 2005-2006 regular season.

Detroit started the year intent on proving it could continue the success it enjoyed under former coach Larry Brown. Brown led Pistons the 2003-2004 NBA title and the 2004-2005 NBA Finals before leaving to coach the New York Knicks.

Detroit welcomed new coach Flip Saunders with eight consecutive wins to start 2005-2006 season. The Pistons later reeled off 11 consecutive victories to run their record to 37-5 in late January.

Detroit would finish 64-18, setting a franchise record for wins in a season. Saunders' presence seemed to help the defensive-minded Pistons flourish on offense. Detroit scored 3.5 more points per game than it did during Brown's final season. The Pistons committed just 931 turnovers during the regular season, the only team in the league to finish with less than 1,000 giveaways.

Detroit also continued to play some of the toughest defense in the NBA. It added up to an average point differential of +6.6 points per game, the best mark in franchise history.

Shooting guard Richard Hamilton led Detroit's balanced offense with 20.1 points per game. Hamilton, point guard Chauncey Billups, forward Rasheed Wallace, and center Ben Wallace all represented the Pistons at the All-Star Game. Ben Wallace led the NBA in offensive rebounds and earned the league's Defensive Player of the Year award for the fourth time in five seasons.

The mission went awry during the playoffs.

Detroit won the first two games of its East semifinal against LeBron James and the Cleveland Cavaliers by a total of 33 points.

The Pistons suddenly lost their Motown mojo. The Cavaliers stunned Detroit by sweeping three consecutive games to take a 3-2 series lead. The Pistons would win the series with victories in Games 6 and 7, but they suddenly looked vulnerable.

Vulnerable they were. The Miami Heat went into Detroit and pounded the weary Pistons 95-78 in Game 1 of the Eastern Conference finals. Miami later won Games 3, 4, and 6 on its home court by a total of 43 points to win the series 4-2.

A mission accomplished, but not for Detroit. The Pistons instead tasted a bitter ending to the most dominant season in franchise history.

Least dominant team: 1979-1980 Detroit Pistons
Record: 16-66
Overall ranking: 1,104th, 7.579 points below average

The 1979-1980 Detroit Pistons accomplished two things. They compiled the worst record in franchise history (16-66) and they indirectly helped launch Dick Vitale's television career.

Vitale came to the Pistons prior to the 1978-1979 season after a successful run as head coach at the University of Detroit.

Vitale led the Pistons to a 30-52 mark during his first season. He expected better things in his second season. Detroit acquired high-scoring forward Bob McAdoo from the Boston Celtics during the offseason. Vitale also hoped center Bob Lanier could play a full season after missing 39 games during the 1978-1979 campaign.

Vitale never got a chance to coach McAdoo and Lanier in tandem.

McAdoo started the season on the injured list. Vitale got "the ziggy"—his own term for termination—after a 4-8 start. (Vitale soon landed on his feet as an analyst with a new all-sports cable television station. He has worked with ESPN ever since).

As it turned out, Vitale did the best coaching in Detroit during the 1979-1980 season. Richie Adubato took Vitale's place and coached the Pistons to a 12-56 finish.

The talent shortage got worse when Detroit traded away Lanier at midseason. The Pistons closed the worst season in franchise history with a team record 14-game losing streak.

Another team of note: 1954-1955 Fort Wayne Pistons
Record: 43-29
Overall ranking: 388th, 1.944 points above average

The 1954-1955 Pistons were the best team of the franchise's nine-year NBA run in Fort Wayne. Fort Wayne posted a 43-29 record, won the first of three consecutive division titles, and advanced to the NBA Finals for the first time in franchise history.

The Pistons lost a memorable championship series against the Syracuse Nationals. Fort Wayne lost the first two games in Syracuse, won the middle three games at home, but dropped the final two contests and the series back in Syracuse. The Nationals won Game 7 by one point on a late free throw and championship-clinching steal.

One last note: Fort Wayne played its three NBA Finals "home" games in Indianapolis, the only time a franchise has played home Finals games away from its base city. Fort Wayne's home arena booked a national bowling tournament during the NBA Finals and couldn't accommodate the Pistons.

Golden State Warriors
1946-present
Also Philadelphia Warriors (1946-1962) and San Francisco Warriors (1962-1971)
Most dominant team: 1975-1976 Golden State Warriors
Record: 59-23
Overall ranking: 84th, 6.199 points above average

The Golden State Warriors carried the momentum from their surprise 1974-1975 NBA title over to the 1975-1976 season.

Golden State rolled to a franchise-best 59-23 record, the best mark in the NBA.

The Rick Barry-led Warriors won their second consecutive Pacific Division title. (They haven't won a division title since).

Golden State led the league in points scored with 109.8 per game. The Warriors posted a franchise-best average point differential of +6.7 points per game, 4.2 points per game better than any other team in the league.

Golden State entered the playoffs as a prohibitive favorite to defend its title. Yet the Warriors' run ended with a seven-game loss against the Phoenix Suns in the Western Conference finals.

Golden State missed two golden opportunities to take control of the series. The Warriors lost in double overtime in Game 4. They dropped a one-point decision in Game 6. Finally, the most dominant season in Golden State history came to a premature end with a 94-86 loss in Game 7 in Oakland.

Least dominant team: 1997-1998 Golden State Warriors
Record: 19-63
Overall ranking: 1,131st, 9.050 points below average

The 1997-1998 Golden State Warriors choked away their chances at a competitive season.

The Warriors' year all but ended on December 1, when leading scorer Latrell Sprewell assaulted and choked coach P.J. Carlesimo during practice.

Golden State tried to "terminate" Sprewell's contract. The NBA tried to ban Sprewell for life. Both got overruled by an arbiter, who reinstated Sprewell's contract and reduced his suspension to the remainder of the 1997-1998 season.

The suspension rid the Warriors of Sprewell's presence, but also robbed them of his skills.

Without Sprewell's 21.4 points per game (his pre-suspension average), Golden State plummeted to the lowest points per game average in the league. The Warriors established a since-broken record for the shot clock era by failing to score at least 100 points in 27 consecutive games.

Golden State finished with a 19-63 record, but not in the cellar. The Warriors actually finished ahead of the 17-65 Los Angeles Clippers. Golden State also set a franchise record with an average point differential of -9.1 points per game.

Proof that talent sometimes matters more than character: Sprewell's playing career lasted until 2005. Carlesimo's career as a head coach went on hiatus when the Warriors fired him 27 games into the 1999-2000 season.

Another team of note: 1986-1987 Golden State Warriors
Record: 42-40
Overall ranking: 836th, 2.385 points below average

George Karl reached the peak of his coaching career when he led the Seattle Supersonics to the NBA Finals following the 1995-1996 season.

Karl might have done some of his finest coaching during an unheralded earlier stop with the Golden State Warriors.

Karl led Golden State to an unlikely 42-40 record during the 1986-1987 season. The POST formula recognizes the 1986-1987 Warriors as the least dominant team to finish with a winning record.

Karl coaxed a 12-win improvement out of the likes of Purvis Short, Joe Barry Carroll, and Eric "Sleepy" Floyd. The only difference in personnel between the 1985-1986 Warriors and the 1986-1987 edition: Short played 30 fewer games in 1986-1987.

Golden State tightened up its defense under Karl. The defensive improvement helped the Warriors win a majority of their games despite giving up more points per game than they allowed (an average point differential of -2.4 points per game).

Golden State upset the fourth-seeded Utah Jazz in five games in the first round of the playoffs before falling against the eventual champion Los Angeles Lakers in the Western Conference semifinals.

Houston Rockets
1967-present
Also San Diego Rockets (1967-1971)
Most dominant team: 2006-2007 Houston Rockets
Record: 52-30
Overall ranking: 145th, 4.952 points above average

Houston's pairing of high-scoring wing Tracy McGrady and 7-foot-6 center Yao Ming produced the most dominant teams in Rockets history.

McGrady and Yao provided a glimpse of what they could accomplish during the 2004-2005 season, when they led Houston to a 51-31 record during their first year together.

Injuries decimated the Rockets during the 2005-2006 campaign. Houston limped to a 34-48 finish as McGrady and Yao combined to sit out 60 games. The Rockets went 21-10 when both McGrady and Yao played. Houston went 13-38 when they didn't.

The Rockets roared back into the NBA's stratosphere during the 2006-2007 season. Houston went 52-30, the team's best record since the 1996-1997 season.

The Rockets produced an average point differential of +4.9 points per game, almost a half-point better than any other team in franchise history.

Injuries still plagued the team. McGrady missed 11 games with back spasms. Yao sat out 30 games, most of them because of a broken leg suffered at midseason. McGrady wouldn't let the injuries give Houston a problem. McGrady led the Rockets to a 20-10 mark in games he played without Yao.

When Houston had McGrady and Yao together? The Rockets went 30-11, a pace that would yield 60 wins over a full season.

Houston won with defense. The Rockets let their opponent make just 42.9 percent of their shots, the lowest mark in the league. Yao (25.0 points per game) and McGrady (24.6 points per game) provided Houston with enough scoring punch to outpoint most opponents.

Yet not enough to win a round in the playoffs.

McGrady and Yao did their part. The Rockets' stars combined for 50.4 points per game, almost a point more than their regular season average, during Houston's seven-game loss against the Utah Jazz in the first round of the postseason. The Rockets' supporting players averaged just 36.3 points per game against the Jazz, 11.1 points per game fewer than they scored during the regular season.

Houston led the series 2-0 and 3-2, but fell at home in Game 7. Utah built a big early lead and held on for a 103-99 win in the decisive contest. The Rockets got dominant performances from McGrady (29 points, 13 assists) and Yao (29 points), but not enough to extend the most dominant season in franchise history.

Also not enough for coach Jeff Van Gundy to keep his job. Houston cut ties with the man who coached the two most dominant teams in franchise history soon after the playoff loss against the Jazz.

Least dominant team: 1982-1983 Houston Rockets
Record: 14-68
Overall ranking: 1,149[th], 10.986 points below average

The concept of completely cleaning house and accepting a few seasons of absolute futility at the beginning of a rebuilding process became the norm by the late 1990s.

The Houston Rockets inadvertently pioneered the concept during the 1982-1983 season.

Houston had parted ways with Moses Malone, Robert Reid, and Rudy Tomjanovich, three key cogs in the team's surprise run to the 1981 NBA Finals, by the summer of 1982. Star centers Ralph Sampson and Akeem (later Hakeem) Olajuwon had not arrived yet.

The 1982-1983 Rockets staggered to a franchise-worst 14-68 record in the interim. Houston finished with an average point differential of -11.6 points per game, another unwanted franchise record. The Rockets tied a since-broken NBA record with 11 consecutive home losses to end the season.

Houston's "efforts" resulted in the No. 1 selection in the 1983 NBA draft and the rights to Sampson. The Rockets added Olajuwon one year later. They would win two NBA titles in three NBA Finals appearances over the next 11 years.

Read more about the 1982-1983 Houston Rockets in Chapter 4.

Other teams of note: 1993-1994 Houston Rockets; 2000-2001 Houston Rockets
Records: 58-24 (1993-1994); 45-37 (2000-2001)
Overall rankings: 185th, 4.154 points above average (1993-1994); 323rd, 2.568 points above average (2000-2001)

The 1993-1994 Houston Rockets tied the NBA record with 15 consecutive wins to start the season and never looked back.

The Rockets went on to a 58-24 record, a franchise best. Houston center Hakeem Olajuwon won the NBA's Most Valuable Player award. He also repeated as the league's Defensive Player of the Year.

Houston solidified its place in history by winning the city's first NBA title. The Rockets won Games 6 and 7 of the NBA Finals at home against the New York Knicks and claimed the first of two consecutive championships.

The 2000-2001 Houston Rockets managed two unusual feats in a season of transition from the Hakeem Olajuwon era to the brief Steve Francis era.

Houston compiled a perfect 16-0 record against foes from the Central Division. The Rockets became just the second team to go undefeated against an entire division since the NBA went to a four-division format for the 1970-1971 season. (The Los Angeles Lakers ran the table against the Central Division during the 1982-1983 season).

The Rockets also missed the playoffs despite a 45-37 record. Houston's consolation prize: the most wins for a lottery-bound team since the NBA expanded the postseason field to 16 teams starting with the 1983-1984 season.

Indiana Pacers
(1976-present)
Most dominant team: 1997-1998 Indiana Pacers
Record: 58-24
Overall ranking: 87th, 6.112 points above average

Doubts swirled around the Indiana Pacers prior to the 1997-1998 season. Indiana slumped to a 39-43 record during the 1996-1997 season, leading to the resignation of coach Larry Brown.

The Pacers brought in former Boston Celtics legend but coaching neophyte Larry Bird to replace Brown.

Bird proved a perfect fit for Reggie Miller and a veteran Indiana team. The Pacers won a then-club record 58 games and produced a franchise record average point differential of +6.1 points per game. Bird earned the right to coach the Eastern Conference at the All-Star Game. He also won the league's Coach of the Year award.

Indiana pushed Michael Jordan's final Chicago Bulls team to seven games in the Eastern Conference finals before succumbing. The Pacers held a lead in the fourth quarter of Game 7, but couldn't hold off the eventual NBA champions.

Least dominant team: 1984-1985 Indiana Pacers
Record: 22-60
Overall ranking: 1,034th, 5.550 points below average

Indiana fans in the mid-1980s pointed to career-halting injuries to players like forward Clark Kellogg and center Steve Stipanovich as a reason for the franchise's lack of progress at the time.

In truth, the Pacers didn't have much success with all of their players healthy.

All of Indiana's key players suited up for at least 70 games during the 1984-1985 season. The Pacers still managed just a 22-60 record, the third in a string of four consecutive last place finishes. Indiana posted an average point differential of -6.2 points per game, the worst mark in franchise history.

The Pacers sealed their spot in the Central Division basement by tying a team record with a 12 consecutive losses late in the season

Another team of note: 2004-2005 Indiana Pacers
Record: 44-38
Overall ranking: 533rd, 0.586 points above average

The 2004-2005 Indiana Pacers endured perhaps the wildest season in franchise history.

The Pacers started the year looking like the team that finished the 2003-2004 campaign with a league-best 61-21 record. A November 19 victory at defending NBA champion Detroit improved Indiana's record to 7-2, but also ruined the Pacers season.

All-Star forward Ron Artest charged into the stands after a fan hit him with a cup of beer late in Indiana's 97-82 win. The ensuing melee resulted in a season-long suspension for Artest, a 30-game suspension for guard Stephen Jackson, and a 25-game suspension (later reduced to 15 games) for leading scorer Jermaine O'Neal.

The Pacers later dealt with disruptions ranging from point guard Jamaal Tinsley's foot injury to O'Neal's shoulder injury to Reggie Miller's retirement announcement. Indiana took the floor for a game against the Orlando Magic one night after the brawl in Detroit with just six players in uniform.

The Pacers still managed a 44-38 record and a playoff spot. Indiana defeated the Boston Celtics in seven games in the first round of the playoffs. The Pacers beat the Celtics 97-70 in Game 7 in Boston, handing the Celtics their worst Game 7 loss in franchise history.

Indiana's season came full circle when the Pacers faced the Pistons in the Eastern Conference semifinals. Indiana took a 2-1 lead in the series, but Detroit imposed its will over the last three games and closed out the Pacers' season and Miller's career in six games.

Los Angeles Clippers
1970-present
Also Buffalo Braves (1970-1978) and San Diego Clippers (1978-1984)
Most dominant team: 1974-1975 Buffalo Braves
Record: 49-33
Overall ranking: 375th, 2.144 points above average

The often-rudderless Los Angeles Clippers franchise traces its roots to a respectable eight-year run as the Buffalo Braves between 1970-1978.

The Braves' era and the franchise's overall history crested during the 1974-1975 season. Buffalo finished with a 49-33 record, still the best in franchise history. The Braves finished with an average point differential of +2.2 points per game, also still the best in franchise history.

Bob McAdoo powered the Braves with a career-best 34.5 points per game. McAdoo won the second of three consecutive scoring titles. He also received the NBA's Most Valuable Player award.

Buffalo pushed the Washington Bullets to seven games in an Eastern Conference semifinal, but fell 115-96 in Game 7 in Washington.

Least dominant team: 1986-1987 Los Angeles Clippers
Record: 12-70
Overall ranking: 1,147th, 10.806 points below average

The first truly horrid Clippers team of Donald Sterling's ownership tenure still stands as the most horrid.

The Clippers' pattern of trading young players on the rise in exchange for bigger-name players on the decline resulted in a complete collapse during the 1986-1987 season.

Los Angeles struggled to score with a lineup led by Mike Woodson. The Clippers also let opponents make 51.8 percent of their shots, the most lax percentage in the league.

It all added up to a franchise-worst 12-70 record and a then-franchise worst average point differential of -11.4 points per game.

A sidebar regarding the Clippers' futility:

The Clippers have six 60-loss seasons since moving to Los Angeles for the 1984-1985 campaign. The Clippers' cross-town rivals, the Los Angeles Lakers, have six 60-win campaigns during the same span. Four of those seasons overlapped.

Read more about the 1986-1987 Los Angeles Clippers in Chapter 4.

Another team of note: 2005-2006 Los Angeles Clippers
Record: 47-35
Overall ranking: 413th, 1.723 points above average

Appropriately, a defeat served as the defining moment for the most successful season of the Los Angeles Clipper franchise's California history.

The Clippers lost 101-95 at Memphis in the next-to-last game of the 2005-2006 season. The win gave the Grizzlies a "reward" in the form of the No. 5 seed for the Western Conference playoffs and a first round playoff matchup against the powerful Dallas Mavericks. Memphis lost the series against the eventual Western Conference champions in four games.

Los Angeles "fell" to the No. 6 seed and a first round playoff matchup against the less-imposing Denver Nuggets. Denver held the No. 3 seed as the Northwest Division champion. The Clippers got home court advantage for the series because of a superior regular season record.

The Clippers used that home court advantage to beat the Nuggets in a pair of close games to start the postseason. Los Angeles went on to win the series in five games for the first playoff series victory in the franchise's California history.

The Clippers gave their long-suffering fans several other reasons to cheer during the 2005-2006 season.

Los Angeles won 47 games, the most in the franchise's West Coast history. The Clippers posted an average point differential of +1.6 points per game, the best mark of the team's time in California.

Power forward Elton Brand averaged a career-best 24.7 points per game and made the All-Star team. Veteran point guard Sam Cassell joined the Clippers as a free agent and provided the team a winning mindset, along with 17.2 points and 6.3 assists per game.

Los Angeles pushed the Phoenix Suns to seven games in the Western Conference semifinals. The season ended there with, as usual, a loss.

Los Angeles Lakers
1948-present
Also Minneapolis Lakers (1948-1960)
Most dominant team: 1971-1972 Los Angeles Lakers
Record: 69-13
Overall ranking: 3rd, 11.581 points above average

The 1971-1972 Los Angeles Lakers hold perhaps the most unassailable team milestone in the NBA. Jerry West, Wilt Chamberlain and company reeled off a 33-game winning streak.

The Lakers smashed the previous standard of 20 consecutive wins, set just one season earlier by the Milwaukee Bucks.

The 1999-2000 Los Angeles Lakers reeled off 19 consecutive wins, but few suggested they might threaten their predecessors' record.

The 1995-1996 Chicago Bulls posted a 72-10 overall record to surpass the 1971-1972 Lakers' single-season standard of 69-13, but never won more than 18 games in one stretch.

Los Angeles validated its season for the ages with a championship. The Lakers lost Game 1 of the NBA Finals against the New York Knicks, but roared back to win the next four games and the title.

Read more about the 1971-1972 Los Angeles Lakers in Chapter 1.

Least dominant team: 1957-1958 Minneapolis Lakers
Record: 19-53
Overall ranking: 1,039th, 5.678 points below average

The Minneapolis Lakers gradually declined when center George Mikan retired in 1954 after leading the Lakers to five titles in six seasons. The down cycle bottomed out with the 1957-1958 campaign.

Mikan had replaced John Kundla as Minneapolis' coach, but only Vern Mikkelsen remained on the active roster from the Lakers' glory years.

Mikan perhaps started the adage about how star players cannot succeed as coaches. Kundla had to come down from the Lakers' front office and replace Mikan as coach after a 9-30 start. Kundla's return had little impact. Minneapolis finished with a 19-53 record and an average point differential of -6.4 points per game, both franchise worsts.

The Lakers finished last in the West Division. They had finished first or second in their division every year since joining the Basketball Association of America (forerunner to the NBA) for the 1948-1949 season

Other teams of note: 1958-1959 and 1959-1960 Minneapolis Lakers
Records: 33-39 (1958-1959); 25-50 (1959-1960)
Overall rankings: 741st, 1.435 points below average (1958-1959); 951st, 3.955 points below average (1959-1960)

The Lakers' disastrous 1957-1958 season did produce one positive: Minneapolis got star forward Elgin Baylor with the first overall pick in the 1958 NBA draft.

The Lakers managed just a 58-89 overall record during Baylor's first two seasons. Yet Baylor did help Minneapolis achieve postseason distinctions.

The 1958-1959 Minneapolis squad finished with a 33-39 record, good enough to return to the playoffs. The Lakers stunned the West Division champion St. Louis Hawks in six games in the Western Division finals—winning the last two games by a total of three points—to reach the NBA Finals. The POST formula ranks the 1957-1958 Minneapolis Lakers as the least dominant team to reach the Finals.

The 1959-1960 Lakers fared even worse during the regular season, checking in with a 25-50 mark. Minneapolis still made the postseason. The Lakers finished ahead of a horrid Cincinnati Royals team for the final playoff spot in the West Division.

Once in the postseason, the Lakers swept an equally unimposing Detroit Pistons team (30-45 record) a best-of-three first round series. The POST formula designates the final Minneapolis Lakers team (the franchise relocated to Los Angeles after the 1959-1960 season) as the least dominant team to win a playoff series.

The 1960 Detroit-Minneapolis playoff pairing ranks as perhaps the worst postseason matchup in NBA history. The teams combined for a 55-95 regular season record. They compiled nearly identical POST ratings. Had the Pistons defeated the Lakers in the 1960 Western Division semifinals, *they* would hold the distinction as the least dominant team to win a playoff series.

Memphis Grizzlies
1995-present
Also Vancouver Grizzlies (1995-2001)
Most dominant team: 2005-2006 Memphis Grizzlies
Record: 49-33
Overall ranking: 215th, 3.704 points above average

Jerry West validated his greatness as an NBA executive when he transformed the Memphis Grizzlies into a successful team.

The Memphis-Vancouver franchise averaged 19 wins per year during its first six full seasons (along with an 8-42 mark during the lockout-shortened 1998-1999 campaign) before West took over as the team's general manager in 2002.

West put a competitive team on the floor by the 2003-2004 season. The Grizzlies achieved the franchise's first winning record and first playoff berth

A coaching shuffle caused Memphis to take a small step back during the 2004-2005 campaign. Reigning NBA Coach of the Year Hubie Brown left the Grizzlies' bench early in the season because of health concerns. Mike Fratello stepped in as coach.

The franchise took another great leap forward during Fratello's first (and only) full season. Memphis finished the 2005-2006 campaign with a 49-33 record. The Grizzlies posted an average point differential of +3.7 points per game, the best mark in franchise history by over a point.

Memphis' defense allowed just 88.5 points per game, the lowest figure in the league. The Grizzlies also finished second in the league in points allowed per possession.

Memphis played its best basketball down the stretch. The Grizzlies started a 15-4 closing kick with a seven-game winning streak. Memphis later won eight of its last nine games. The Grizzlies earned the No. 5 seed for the Western Conference playoffs, the best postseason seeding in franchise history.

Pau Gasol averaged 20.4 points per game, one of seven Memphis players to average double figures in scoring. Gasol became the first player from the Grizzlies franchise to play in the All-Star Game. Memphis guard Mike Miller won the league's Sixth Man of the Year award.

The most dominant season in franchise history ended on a sour note.

The Dallas Mavericks swept Memphis in four games in the first round of the playoffs. The defeat gave the Grizzlies three 4-0 first round defeats in three playoff appearances. Memphis' 0-12 franchise playoff ledger set an NBA record for most consecutive postseason games lost.

Least dominant team: 1996-1997 Vancouver Grizzlies
Record: 14-68
Overall ranking: 1,142nd, 10.040 points below average

The Vancouver Grizzlies endured a worse-than-usual expansion season in 1995-1996, featuring a single-season NBA record 23-game losing streak.

Things got even worse in 1996-1997.

Most of the Grizzlies franchise's unwanted milestones occurred during the 1996-1997 campaign. Vancouver added standout rookie forward Shareef Abdur-

Rahim, but the Grizzlies still set still-standing club records for worst record (14-68) and worst average point differential (-10.2).

Another team of note: 1995-1996 Vancouver Grizzlies
Record: 15-67
Overall ranking: 1,140th, 9.517 points below average

Vancouver put together a historic expansion season in 1995-1996, but not for the reasons the Grizzlies hoped.

The Grizzlies lost 23 consecutive games between February 16 and April 2, setting a since-tied record for consecutive losses within a single season. Two other historically bad teams (the 1972-1973 Philadelphia 76ers and the 1992-1993 Dallas Mavericks) shared the previous single-season standard for consecutive losses with 20.

Vancouver completed its expansion season with a 15-67 record and started a stretch of six last-place finishes during the franchise's first seven years.

Miami Heat
(1988-present)
Most dominant team: 2004-2005 Miami Heat
Record: 59-23
Overall ranking: 99th, 5.823 points above average

The Miami Heat gleefully snapped up Shaquille O'Neal when the Los Angeles Lakers put the dominant big man on the trading block after the 2003-2004 season.

Miami's investment immediately paid off with the most dominant season in franchise history.

The 2004-2005 Heat finished with a 59-23 record, the best in the Eastern Conference. Miami set a franchise record with 14 consecutive wins between December 6 and January 1. The Heat later won 12 in a row.

Miami finished with an average point differential of +6.5 points per game, a full point better than any other team in franchise history.

O'Neal lived up to the super-sized expectations. He averaged 22.9 points and 10.4 rebounds per game. He finished second in the league's Most Valuable Player voting.

O'Neal's new sidekick, second-year guard Dwyane Wade, emerged as a superstar. Wade elevated his scoring average from 16.2 points per game to 24.1 points per game.

Players like center Alonzo Mourning, forward Udonis Haslem, and guards Eddie Jones and Damon Jones performed well in supporting roles.

The Heat ran out of gas in the Eastern Conference finals against the Detroit Pistons. O'Neal played with a painful thigh bruise. Wade injured a rib in Game 5. Miami pushed Detroit to a seventh game, but lost the finale at home.

The most dominant season in Heat history served as the prelude to the team's run to the franchise's first NBA title one season later.

Least dominant team: 1988-1989 Miami Heat
Record: 15-67
Overall ranking: 1,148th, 10.913 points below average

No franchise began its existence on more of a sour note than the 1988-1989 Miami Heat.

Miami started its expansion season with 17 consecutive losses, setting a since-tied NBA record for most losses at the start of a season. The skid still stands as the longest in club history.

Things never got much better for the Heat during the 1988-1989 campaign.

Miami averaged just 97.8 points per game, 5.7 points fewer than any other team in the league. The Heat finished with a 15-67 mark, still the worst record in club history. Miami finished with an average point differential of -11.2 points per game, still the worst margin in club history.

Read more about the 1988-1989 Miami Heat in Chapter 4.

Another team of note: 1998-1999 Miami Heat
Record: 33-17
Overall ranking: 152nd, 4.780 points above average

The 1998-1999 Miami Heat are the Eastern Conference's answer to the 1993-1994 Seattle Supersonics.

The 1998-1999 Heat became the first Eastern Conference No. 1 seed to lose in the first round of the playoffs since the NBA went to its current 16-team post-season format during the 1983-1984 season.

Miami's postseason collapse comes with a couple of asterisks.

The Heat achieved the No. 1 seed in a lockout-shortened season.

Miami faced an atypical No. 8 seed—the New York Knicks—in the first round of the playoffs. The Knicks knocked better-seeded Heat teams out of the playoffs three consecutive times between 1998 and 2000

New York won the 1999 playoff series when Allan Houston's running jumper at the buzzer gave the Knicks a 78-77 victory in the decisive Game 5. New York went on to become the only No. 8 seed to reach the NBA Finals.

Milwaukee Bucks
(1968-present)
Most dominant team: 1970-1971 Milwaukee Bucks
Record: 66-16
Overall ranking: 1st, 11.817 points above average

The Big A (Lew Alcindor, later Kareem Abdul-Jabbar) and the Big O (Oscar Robertson) led the 1970-1971 Milwaukee Bucks to the franchise's biggest season.

The pairing of second-year center Abdul-Jabbar and freshly acquired veteran point guard Robertson clicked better than anyone in Milwaukee could have imagined. The Bucks posted a 66-16 regular season record and an average point differential of +12.2 points per game, both club records by a large margin. Milwaukee also set a league record with 20 consecutive wins late in the season. (The Los Angeles Lakers shattered the Bucks' record with 33 consecutive wins one season later).

The Bucks won the NBA title in one of the most dominant postseason runs in league history. Milwaukee won 12 of 14 playoff games. Eleven of those wins came by double figures. The Bucks capped their season with a sweep of the Baltimore Bullets in the NBA Finals.

Milwaukee won its only NBA title during the franchise's third season. No other modern expansion franchise in North America's major professional sports leagues has won a title more quickly.

Read more about the 1970-1971 Milwaukee Bucks in Chapter 1.

Least dominant team: 1993-1994 Milwaukee Bucks
Record: 20-62
Overall ranking: 1,062th, 6.197 points below average

The Milwaukee Bucks kick-started a much-needed rebuilding process into high gear during the 1993-1994 season. Unfortunately for Milwaukee fans, the Bucks also played like a team in transition.

Milwaukee had rookie Vin Baker as the cornerstone of its building process. The roster otherwise consisted of has-beens and never-weres.

The Bucks finished with a franchise-worst 20-64 record. They finished with a franchise worst average point differential of -6.4 points per game.

Another team of note: 1999-2000 Milwaukee Bucks
Record: 42-40
Overall ranking: 591st, 0.007 points above average

The 1999-2000 Milwaukee Bucks' POST rating comes closer to zero than that of any other NBA team, thus making the Bucks the "most average" team in league history.

Milwaukee performed like a below-average team for the first half of the season. The Bucks then played like an above-average team down the stretch. They finished with a 42-40 record and grabbed the final playoff spot in the Eastern Conference.

Milwaukee very nearly went down in history as the third No. 8 seed to win a first round playoff series. Ray Allen, Glenn Robinson, and Sam Cassell helped the Bucks push the top-seeded Indiana Pacers to the absolute limit. Travis Best's 3-pointer late in the fourth quarter of Game 5 allowed Indiana to escape with a 96-95 victory in the decisive game of the best-of-five series. The Bucks outscored the Pacers by nine points over the course of the series.

Minnesota Timberwolves
(1989-present)
Most dominant team: 2003-2004 Minnesota Timberwolves
Record: 58-24
Overall ranking: 106th, 5.686 points above average

The Minnesota Timberwolves rolled the dice before the 2003-2004 season. Minnesota acquired high-priced veteran guards Sam Cassell and Latrell Sprewell as the supporting cast for star forward Kevin Garnett.

For one season, the gamble paid off.

Garnett averaged 24.2 points and 13.9 rebounds per game and won the Most Valuable Player award. Cassell enjoyed a fine season and earned a spot on the All-Star team for the first time in his career. Sprewell blended in as the team's No. 2 scorer.

The trio powered the Timberwolves to a 58-24 record, the best record in the Western Conference. Minnesota set franchise records for wins and average point differential (+5.4 points per game).

The Timberwolves won the franchise's first division title. They also won a playoff series for the first time after seven consecutive first round exits.

Minnesota got to the Western Conference finals before falling against the Los Angeles Lakers in six games.

(Neither team returned to the playoffs in 2004-2005, marking the first time both teams in an NBA conference finals pairing missed the postseason the following year).

Least dominant team: 1994-1995 Minnesota Timberwolves
Record: 21-61
Overall ranking: 1,118th, 8.256 points below average

The 1994-1995 Minnesota Timberwolves typified the franchise's fortunes during its first seven seasons. The Timberwolves won just 21 games, the sixth of seven consecutive sub-30 win seasons at the beginning of the franchise's existence. Minnesota produced a franchise record average point differential of -9.0 points per game. Talks swirled about a potential move to New Orleans. The Timberwolves seemed to have no hope in sight.

Things changed in the summer of 1995, when Minnesota drafted a forward named Kevin Garnett directly out of high school.

Another team of note: 1996-1997 Minnesota Timberwolves
Record: 40-42
Overall ranking: 770th, 1.711 points below average

The 1996-1997 Minnesota Timberwolves elevated the franchise from laughingstock to contender.

Second-year forward Kevin Garnett emerged as a force, averaging 17.0 points and 8.0 rebounds when he should have been a sophomore in college. Rookie point guard Stephon Marbury averaged 15.8 points and 7.8 assists when *he* should have been a sophomore in college. Veteran forward Tom Gugliotta led the team in scoring with 20.6 points per game.

The Timberwolves went 40-42, a 14-game improvement and then the best mark in franchise history. (Minnesota went on to finish .500 or better for the next eight seasons).

Minnesota also made the playoffs for the first time in playoff history.

The Timberwolves would lose both Gugliotta and Marbury by the 1998-1999 season, but the duo's efforts for the 1996-1997 squad put the club on course to make eight consecutive playoff appearances and solidified Minnesota's place as a legitimate NBA franchise.

New Jersey Nets
1976-present
Also New York Nets (1976-1977)
Most dominant team: 2002-2003 New Jersey Nets
Record: 49-33
Overall ranking: 163rd, 4.516 points above average

The New Jersey Nets' sad-sack NBA history abruptly turned around when the team acquired point guard Jason Kidd prior to the 2001-2002 season.

Kidd led the Nets to an NBA franchise best 52-30 record and an NBA Finals appearance during his first year in the Meadowlands. He led a more dominant New Jersey team during the 2002-2003 season.

The Nets' 2002-2003 record slipped slightly, to 49-33, but New Jersey posted the best average point differential in franchise history at +5.3 points per game.

Popular opinion described the Nets as a run-and-gun team with Kidd as the catalyst. In truth, New Jersey enjoyed success because of defense. The Nets ranked second in the NBA in points allowed during the 2002-2003 season. They ranked first in points allowed per possession.

New Jersey's dominance showed clearly during the Eastern Conference playoffs. The Nets won 10 consecutive playoff games, including sweeps of the Boston Celtics and top-seeded Detroit Pistons, to make a return trip to the NBA Finals.

New Jersey fought to a 2-2 deadlock with the San Antonio Spurs through four games in the NBA Finals, but finally succumbed in six games.

Least dominant team: 1989-1990 New Jersey Nets
Record: 17-65
Overall ranking: 1,105th, 7.667 points below average

Bill Fitch successfully executed one of his patented franchise revivals during his three-year coaching tenure in New Jersey, but things did get worse before they got better.

Fitch's stay with the Nets began with a franchise-worst 17-65 record during the 1989-1990 campaign.

New Jersey went 26-56 the year prior to Fitch's arrival. The Nets then traded their most valuable asset (center Buck Williams) to the Portland Trail Blazers in exchange for Sam Bowie. With predictable results.

Another team of note: 1983-1984 New Jersey Nets
Record: 45-37
Overall ranking: 466th, 1.172 points above average

New Jersey enjoyed a brief spurt as a reasonably competitive team during the early 1980s.

Larry Brown led the Nets to a 20-win improvement and a 44-38 record during the 1981-1982 season. New Jersey had a 47-29 mark late in the 1982-1983 season when Brown resigned abruptly, even by his standards, to take over the program at the University of Kansas.

The highlight of the Nets' early 1980s run of success came during the 1984 playoffs. New Jersey finished the 1983-1984 regular season with a 45-37 record under first-year coach Stan Albeck. Still, few thought the Nets had a chance of beating the defending NBA champion Philadelphia 76ers in the first round of the postseason.

Surprise! New Jersey opened the best-of-five series with a pair of convincing wins in Philadelphia. The 76ers squared the series with a pair of taut wins in New

Jersey. The Nets never wavered. They completed the shocking upset with a 101-98 victory in Philadelphia in the decisive Game 5.

No other team would eliminate a reigning NBA champion in the first round of the postseason until the Phoenix Suns defeated the San Antonio Spurs in the opening round of the 2000 playoffs.

New Orleans Hornets
1988-present
Also Charlotte Hornets (1988-2002)
Most dominant team: 1994-1995 Charlotte Hornets
Record: 50-32
Overall ranking: 283rd, 2.907 points above average

The Charlotte Hornets' gradual building process reached its peak during the 1994-1995 season.

The Hornets added useful players like forward Larry Johnson and center Alonzo Mourning via the draft during the early 1990s. The run of solid picks had Charlotte poised for a breakthrough season during the franchise's lucky seventh year.

The 1994-1995 Hornets reached the 50-win plateau for the first time in team history. Charlotte enjoyed an average point differential of +3.3 points per game, still the best in franchise history.

The Hornets' strong season ended unfulfilled thanks to a pair of Charlotte's Central Division rivals. The Indiana Pacers denied the Hornets the division title by two games. The Chicago Bulls and newly un-retired Michael Jordan eliminated Charlotte in four games in the first round of the postseason.

Least dominant team: 1988-1989 Charlotte Hornets
Record: 20-62
Overall ranking: 1,110th, 7.873 points below average

The Hornet franchise's first season still ranks as its worst.

Charlotte made its NBA debut with a 20-62 record during the 1988-1989 season. The Hornets' expansion season average point differential of -8.5 points per game still stands as the worst in team history.

Fans at the time regarded the season as a relative on-court success since Charlotte finished with five more wins than fellow expansion team Miami Heat. In retrospect, the Hornets franchise endured its worst on-court moments during the 1988-1989 campaign.

Other teams of note: 1992-1993 Charlotte Hornets; 2004-2005 New Orleans Hornets
Records: 44-38 (1992-1993); 18-64 (2004-2005)
Overall rankings: 596th, 0.068 points below average (1992-1993); 1,069th, 6.363 points below average (2004-2005)

The 1992-1993 Charlotte Hornets accomplished a dual distinction. Charlotte became the first of the NBA's four late-1980s expansion teams to win a playoff series. The Hornets also become the first post-1960 expansion team to win its first playoff series against the Boston Celtics.

Center Alonzo Mourning, acquired with the No. 2 overall pick in the 1992 NBA draft, led Charlotte to a 44-38 record during his rookie season. The Hornets' first winning record also resulted in the team's first playoff berth.

Charlotte took control of its first round postseason matchup against Boston with a 99-98 double-overtime victory in Boston Garden in Game 2 of the best-of-five series. Mourning won the series for the Hornets when he sank a 20-foot jumper in the final seconds to lift Charlotte to a 104-103 victory in Game 4.

The Hornets were the first late-1980s expansion team to win a playoff series, but they never have advanced past the second round. The three other expansion teams of the era (the Miami Heat, Orlando Magic, and Minnesota Timberwolves) all took longer to win their first playoff series, but all have advanced farther than the Hornets' deepest run.

The 2004-2005 New Orleans Hornets set an NBA record for biggest win decline in the season of a conference switch.

The Hornets made 12 postseason appearances during their last 15 years in the Eastern Conference, including five in a row from 2000-2004.

The Hornets moved from the Eastern Conference to the Western Conference as part of the NBA's realignment for the 2004-2005 season. New Orleans' fortunes in its new conference illustrated the West's superiority over the East at the time.

The Hornets entered the West with largely the same cast they employed during the 2003-2004 season. Their record changed dramatically, from 41-41 and in the playoffs to 18-64 and in the lottery.

New York Knickerbockers
1946-present
Most dominant team: 1969-1970 New York Knickerbockers
Record: 60-22
Overall ranking: 15th, 8.363 points above average

New York legend tells of an underdog Knicks team that overcame the odds, a Willis Reed injury and the mighty Los Angeles Lakers to win the franchise's first NBA title.

In reality, New York thoroughly owned the 1969-1970 NBA season.

The Knicks set the tone for their magical year with a then-league record 18-game winning streak early in the season. New York went on to post a league-best 60-22 record, a mark only one other Knicks team has matched. New York enjoyed an average point differential of +9.1 points per game, far and away the best in franchise history.

This Knicks team inspired its fans to invent the "DE-fense" chant. New York led the league in defense at 105.9 points allowed per game. Every other team in the NBA gave up at least 111.8 points per game.

New York's championship season ended with a dramatic victory over the Los Angeles Lakers in the NBA Finals. Reed missed Game 6 of the series with an injury. Yet he hobbled out of the Madison Square Garden entrance tunnel before the decisive Game 7 and started the contest. Reed then scored the game's first two baskets to inspire his team to a runaway 113-99 triumph.

Reed became the first player to win Most Valuable Player honors for the regular season, All-Star Game and NBA Finals in the same season.

Read more about the 1969-1970 New York Knickerbockers in Chapter 1.

Least dominant team: 2005-2006 New York Knickerbockers
Record: 23-59
Overall ranking: 1,064th, 6.251 points below average

The 2005-2006 New York Knicks produced the most expensive failure in NBA history.

The Knicks' $128.8 million payroll bought just 23 victories. New York had to win its season finale to avoid the first 60-loss season in franchise history.

The Knicks' roster featured notable names like high-scoring point guard Stephon Marbury, talented shooting guard Jamal Crawford, 3-point specialist Quentin Richardson, and skilled young frontliners Eddy Curry and Channing Frye. Versatile players like Steve Francis and Jalen Rose came to New York via midseason trades.

Knicks general manager Isiah Thomas lured Larry Brown to New York to coach this collection of talent. Brown came to the Knicks after leading the Detroit Pistons to a pair of NBA Finals appearances, including the 2003-2004 league title.

Brown's tenure in the Big Apple would last just one year.

The impressive list of names never meshed on the basketball court. New York tipped off the season with five consecutive losses. The Knicks gave their fans some signs of hope with six consecutive wins at the beginning of January. They followed that hot stretch with seven consecutive losses, the start of a stretch of 22 defeats in 24 games.

The team's disharmony showed in its turnover numbers. New York finished the season with 1,449 turnovers, 90 more than any other squad in the league.

The Knicks finished the campaign with an average point differential of -6.4 points per game, the third-worst mark in team history. New York had to pay $5.6 million per victory despite playing a majority of its games against teams from a poor Eastern Conference. Only five East teams managed a winning record during the 2005-2006 season.

Another team of note: 1998-1999 New York Knickerbockers
Record: 27-23
Overall ranking: 472nd, 1.119 points above average

The 1998-1999 New York Knicks made the NBA's ultimate Cinderella run.

The Knicks are the only No. 8 seed to reach the NBA Finals since the league went to a 16-team postseason format for the 1983-1984 season.

New York finished the lockout-shortened 1998-1999 season with a nondescript 26-24 record. The Knicks edged the Charlotte Hornets by one game for the final Eastern Conference playoff spot. Most assumed New York coach Jeff Van Gundy would lose his job after an inevitable one-and-done postseason.

New York showed it planned to stick around during the playoffs with a 95-75 victory in Game 1 of its best-of-five first round series against the top-seeded Miami Heat. The Knicks would win the series when Allan Houston hit a running jumper at the buzzer in Game 5 to lift New York to a 78-77 victory.

The revived Knicks swept the Atlanta Hawks in the Eastern Conference semifinals as chants of "Jeff Van Gundy" echoed through Madison Square Garden.

New York took its final step with a 4-2 victory over the Indiana Pacers in the Eastern Conference finals. Larry Johnson converted a four-point play in the waning seconds of Game 3 to propel the Knicks to a momentum-swinging 92-91 win. New York also overcame a 14-point deficit to win Game 5 in Indiana and take a 3-2 series lead.

The Knicks played the last four games of the East finals without franchise icon Patrick Ewing, who injured his hand during the final seconds of Game 2. New York still overcame the Pacers, thanks to inspired play from guard Latrell Sprewell and fill-in center Marcus Camby.

Sprewell came to the Knicks from the Golden State Warriors before the season as a villain in the aftermath of his infamous choke of Warriors coach P.J. Carlesimo. By the end of the Eastern Conference finals, television commercials joyfully promoted Sprewell as "The American Dream."

The clock struck midnight on the Cinderella Knicks in the NBA Finals. Ewing-less New York proved no match for the San Antonio Spurs' twin towers, David Robinson and Tim Duncan. San Antonio won the series in five games.

Orlando Magic
1989-present
Most dominant team: 1994-1995 Orlando Magic
Record: 57-25
Overall ranking: 70th, 6.477 points above average

The Orlando Magic headed into the 1994-1995 NBA Finals poised to win the franchise's first championship.

Orlando had added power forward Horace Grant (from the Chicago Bulls' first three-peat of the 1990s) to a young nucleus led by center Shaquille O'Neal and guard Anfernee Hardaway. The Magic jumped from 50 wins during the 1993-1994 season to a 57-25 mark during the 1994-1995 campaign. Orlando finished with the best record in the Eastern Conference.

The Magic completed the season with an average point differential of +7.1 points per game, best in franchise history. Orlando also won 39 of its 41 home games.

The Magic followed up their regular season success with an impressive playoff run. Orlando defeated the Chicago Bulls and newly un-retired Michael Jordan in six games in the Eastern Conference semifinals. The Magic outlasted the Indiana Pacers in seven games in the Eastern Conference finals.

Orlando headed into the NBA Finals against the defending champion Houston Rockets as a heavy favorite. The tide turned against the Magic at the end of Game 1.

Orlando blew a 20-point first half lead before the end of the third quarter. The Magic still had a chance to wrap up the game late in regulation, but Orlando guard Nick Anderson missed four consecutive free throws with the Magic ahead by three. Houston guard Kenny Smith then drilled a 3-pointer at the buzzer to force overtime. The Rockets went on to a stunning 120-118 win.

The game set the tone for the series. Orlando's breakthrough season ended with a heartbreaking sweep at the hands of Houston.

Least dominant team: 1989-1990 Orlando Magic
Record: 18-64
Overall ranking: 1,124th, 8.580 points below average

Unlike many recent expansion teams, the Orlando Magic did not attempt to play slow-tempo basketball in their inaugural season.

The strategy kept fans entertained, but didn't result in a successful year.

Orlando finished the 1989-1990 campaign with an 18-64 record, the worst in franchise history. The Magic scored 110.9 points per game during their first season, considerably more than the other expansion teams of the late 1980s. They also allowed 119.8 points per game, the worst mark in the NBA. It all added up to an average point differential of -8.9 points per game, the worst margin in team history.

Another team of note: 1999-2000 Orlando Magic
Record: 41-41
Overall ranking: 543rd, 0.494 points above average

See if you can keep this straight:

Team is expected to fail in the present, but to succeed in the future. Team somehow achieves reasonable success in the present. Team's coach and general manager receive accolades, based on reasonable success in present and expected success in future. Team then fails to achieve expected future success, making some long for the team that was expected to fail.

That, in a nutshell, tells the bizarre story of the 1999-2000 Orlando Magic.

The Magic brain trust assembled its 1999-2000 roster with a collection of relative unknowns. Orlando expected to struggle during the 1999-2000 season. The franchise also expected to upgrade the talent base after the season with space created under the team's salary cap.

The Magic nonetheless stayed competitive throughout the 1999-2000 campaign. Guard Darrell Armstrong led Orlando to a 41-41 record. The Magic missed out on a playoff spot by just one game. First-year coach Doc Rivers received the league's Coach of the Year award for getting the most out of his collection of no-names. Orlando general manager John Gabriel won the league's Executive of the Year honor for maintaining a competitive roster while building for the future.

As expected, the Magic made a big splash in the free agent market following the 1999-2000 season. Orlando signed up-and-coming shooting guard Tracy McGrady away from the Toronto Raptors. The Magic also pried versatile forward Grant Hill away from the Detroit Pistons in a sign-and-trade deal. Orlando gave Detroit a one-dimensional forward named Ben Wallace in the transaction.

The much-ballyhooed plan never panned out. Hill spent most of his time in central Florida battling injuries. McGrady emerged as a superstar, but couldn't get the Magic past the first round of the playoffs.

(That one-dimensional forward named Wallace would go on to win four Defensive Player of the Year awards).

The grand plan collapsed completely during the 2003-2004 season.

Orlando won its season opener, but then lost its next 19 games. Rivers and Gabriel both lost their jobs by the end of the campaign. McGrady demanded and received a trade after the season. The one-dimensional forward named Wallace led the Pistons to the NBA title. Orlando finished with a 21-61 record, worst in the NBA and 20 games worse than the 1999-2000 Magic team that was expected to fail miserably.

Got that straight?

Philadelphia 76ers
1949-present
Also Syracuse Nationals (1949-1963)
Most dominant team: 1966-1967 Philadelphia 76ers
Record: 68-13
Overall ranking: 14th, 8.395 points above average

The Philadelphia 76ers left nothing to chance during the 1966-1967 season after two years of near-misses in the Eastern Division finals against the reigning NBA champion Boston Celtics.

Philadelphia stormed to an astounding 68-13 record. The 76ers smashed the existing NBA record for wins in a season by six games. They also set a new league record for single-season winning percentage. Philadelphia completed the season with an average of point differential of +9.4 points per game, the best in the NBA since the Washington Capitols posted a +9.9 average point differential during the 1946-1947 campaign

Philadelphia center Wilt Chamberlain failed to win the league scoring title for the first time in his career, but he did receive the league Most Valuable Player honor. Chamberlain led the league in rebounds. He finished third in the scoring and assist races.

The 76ers ended Boston's eight-year reign as NBA champion with a 4-1 triumph in the Eastern Conference finals. Philadelphia fans took up the chant "Boston is dead!" during the series-clinching victory.

The 76ers concluded their resounding season with a 4-2 victory over the San Francisco Warriors in the NBA Finals. Philadelphia coach Alex Hannum, who also led the 1957-1958 St. Louis Hawks to a championship, cemented his place in history as the only opposing coach to win an NBA title during Bill Russell's career in Boston.

Read more about the 1966-1967 Philadelphia 76ers in Chapter 1.

Least dominant team: 1972-1973 Philadelphia 76ers
Record: 9-73
Overall ranking: 1,150th, 11.418 points below average

The Philadelphia 76ers held every major NBA record for single-season futility by the end of the 1972-1973 campaign.

Worst record in a single season: 9-73.
Worst single-season winning percentage: .110.
Worst average point differential: -12.1.
Longest losing streak: 20 games.

Other teams have surpassed the losing streak and point differential records. The 76ers still hold the one milestone all talent-poor teams try to avoid: the 9-73 final record.

Read more about the 1972-1973 Philadelphia 76ers in Chapter 4.

Another team of note: 1958-1959 Syracuse Nationals
Record: 35-37
Overall ranking: 217th, 3.692 points above average

The 1958-1959 Syracuse Nationals rank as the most hard-luck team in NBA history by this standard: the POST formula tabs these Nats as the most dominant team to finish with a losing record.

Syracuse finished the 1958-1959 season with an average point differential of +4.0 points per game, but somehow posted s 35-37 overall record. By comparison, the Nationals' 1954-1955 NBA championship team had an average point differential of +1.4 points per game.

Syracuse struggled in close games and also had the misfortune of playing in the tougher Eastern Division. East teams had four of the top six records in the eight-team NBA. The East finished the season with an aggregate record 30 games better than the West.

Past and future seasons further exposed the Nationals' losing record during the 1958-1959 campaign as a fluke. Syracuse went 41-31 during the 1957-1958 season and 45-30 during the 1959-1960 campaign with far less impressive average point differential numbers.

Phoenix Suns
(1968-present)
Most dominant team: 2006-2007 Phoenix Suns
Record: 61-21
Overall ranking: 44th, 7.174 points above average

The 2006-2007 Phoenix Suns scorched their competition with a fast-paced style not seen in the NBA since the early 1990s

Phoenix set the stage for the most dominant years in franchise history with two key moves after the team posted a 29-53 record during the 2003-2004 season.

The Suns signed free agent point guard Steve Nash away from the Dallas Mavericks. Phoenix then retained Mike D'Antoni as its coach.

D'Antoni implemented a frenetic offense designed to accentuate the talents of players like Nash and blossoming forwards Amare Stoudemire and Shawn Marion.

The new approach worked instantly. Phoenix improved by 33 victories during the 2004-2005 season and tied a franchise record with 62 wins. The Suns reached the Western Conference finals.

Nash repeated as MVP one season later when he led Phoenix back to the Western Conference finals even though Stoudemire missed all but three games recovering from a knee injury.

Stoudemire returned to full-time action at the start of the 2006-2007 season, but the Suns began the year with five losses in six games. Observers wondered if Phoenix would struggle to fit Stoudemire back into the fold.

The Suns got their act together in a hurry. Phoenix followed up the slow start with a 37-3 tear. The Suns established a franchise record with a 15-game winning streak and soon topped it with 17 consecutive victories. Phoenix's three losses during its scorching run came by 10 total points.

The Suns stayed hot and finished the regular season with a 61-21 record, the third 60-win year in franchise history. Phoenix led the NBA in most major offensive categories: points per game, field goal percentage, 3-point percentage, and free throw percentage. The Suns enjoyed an average point differential of +7.3 points per game, the best mark in franchise history.

Nash produced another MVP-worthy season. He averaged 18.6 points per game. He led the league in assists for the third consecutive season with a career-high 11.6 per game. He also finished second in the league in 3-point percentage.

Stoudemire flashed his pre-injury form with 20.4 points and a career-best 9.6 rebounds per game. Marion contributed 17.5 points per game and led the team in rebounds, steals, and blocks. NBA Sixth Man of the Year Leandro Barbosa (18.1 points per game) allowed Phoenix to play its free-flowing style when Nash needed a rest.

A Texas-sized roadblock denied the Suns in the playoffs. The San Antonio Spurs eliminated Phoenix in a controversial West semifinal. The Spurs ended a dominant Suns season for the second time in three years.

Least dominant team: 1968-1969 Phoenix Suns
Record: 16-66
Overall ranking: 1,117th, 8.222 points below average

The Phoenix Suns have emerged as one of the most consistent franchises in the NBA. The Suns rarely set for long. They often rebound from subpar seasons in spectacular fashion

As a result, Phoenix's 1968-1969 expansion season still stands as the least dominant campaign in franchise history. The Suns went 16-66 during their inaugural season. They finished with an average point differential of -8.8 points per game.

Phoenix has won at least 28 games every season since.

Another team of note: 1971-1972 Phoenix Suns
Record: 49-33
Overall ranking: 111th, 5.574 points above average

The Phoenix Suns also have emerged as one of the hard-luck franchises in the NBA. They lost a coin flip against the Milwaukee Bucks for the rights to center Lew Alcindor (later Kareem Abdul-Jabbar) after the 1968-1969 season. Their two appearances in the NBA Finals ended with heartbreaking six-game losses.

Fortune also failed to favor Phoenix during the 1971-1972 season. The Suns posted a 49-33 record, at the time the best in franchise history, only to fail to qualify for the postseason.

Phoenix set a record for most wins for a non-playoff team. The POST formula also identifies the 1971-1972 Suns as the most dominant team to miss the postseason.

Phoenix boasted an exciting team led by Connie Hawkins, but couldn't crack the postseason lineup in the brutal Western Conference. The top four teams in each conference qualified for the playoffs. The West included the eventual NBA champion Los Angeles Lakers (NBA record 69-13 season), the defending NBA champion Milwaukee Bucks (63-19), the underrated Chicago Bulls (57-25), and the future NBA champion Golden State Warriors (51-31).

Had Phoenix played in the Eastern Conference, the Suns would have qualified for the postseason as a No. 2 seed.

Portland Trail Blazers
(1970-present)
Most dominant team: 1990-1991 Portland Trail Blazers
Record: 63-19
Overall ranking: 12th, 8.421 points above average

"The dynasty that never was" peaked with the 1990-1991 season.

Portland averaged 60.3 wins per season between the 1989-1990 and 1991-1992 campaigns, but failed to win a championship.

The Trail Blazers had their best chance during the 1990-1991 season. Portland set a club record with a 63-19 ledger. The Trail Blazers posted an average point differential of +8.7 points per game, another team record. Guard Clyde Drexler led a lineup with six players who averaged in double figures. A seventh double-figure scorer (Walter Davis) arrived in a midseason trade.

Portland also seemed to peak at the right time. The Trail Blazers reeled off a franchise record 16 consecutive wins late in the regular season. They earned the overall No. 1 seed and home court advantage for the playoffs.

The positive momentum didn't carry over to the postseason.

The first signs of trouble popped up when the No. 8 seed Seattle Supersonics pushed Portland to the full five games in the first round of the playoffs.

The Trail Blazers' season ended, literally, at the hands of Magic Johnson and the Los Angeles Lakers in the Western Conference finals.

Los Angeles stole Game 1 in Portland and later won three games at home to clinch the series in six games. Johnson alertly grabbed a loose ball and flipped it to the empty end of the court to eat up the final seconds of the Lakers' 91-90 Game 6 victory.

More than a few observers think the Trail Blazers could have beaten Michael Jordan and the Chicago Bulls in the 1991 NBA Finals. They never got the chance.

Read more about the 1990-1991 Portland Trail Blazers in Chapter 2.

Least dominant team: 2005-2006 Portland Trail Blazers
Record: 21-61
Overall ranking: 1,129th, 8.926 points below average

The Portland Trail Blazers started the 2000s with a mildly successful but wildly unpopular roster. Portland began the century with four consecutive playoff appearances, including a trip to the Western Conference finals in 2000. The Trail Blazers also alienated their once-loyal fan base. Pundits gave the team the moniker "Jail Blazers" because of a propensity for off-the-court troubles.

The Portland front office began to disassemble the squad following the resignation of general manager Bob Whitsitt after the 2003 season. The Trail Blazers succeeded in putting together a new team that proved both unpopular and unsuccessful.

Things bottomed out with the 2005-2006 season. First-year coach Nate McMillan led the team to a better-than-expected 17-28 start. The Trail Blazers then collapsed down the stretch.

Portland lost 33 of its last 37 games to finish with a 21-61 record, the worst mark in the NBA. The late-season fade included an 11-game losing streak and then an eight-game skid to conclude the season.

The Trail Blazers' core players like flashy point guard Sebastian Telfair and high-scoring forwards Zach Randolph and Darius Miles failed to change the team's fortunes, both on the court and off.

Randolph and Miles led Portland in scoring, but frequently clashed with McMillan. The Trail Blazers fined and suspended Telfair in February after he carried a handgun onto a team flight.

The Trail Blazers produced an average point differential of -9.5 points per game, over three points worse than any other team in the league.

Portland lost its games because it couldn't get enough rebounds and because it couldn't score when it did have the ball.

The Trail Blazers grabbed fewer rebounds than any team in the league and got outrebounded by an average of five boards per game. Portland averaged just 88.8 points per game, the lowest figure in the league.

Another team of note: 1976-1977 Portland Trail Blazers
Record: 49-33
Overall ranking: 119th, 5.383 points above average

NBA legend holds up the 1976-1977 Portland Trail Blazers as the epitome of team play. As an example of how teamwork can allow a squad of overachievers to reach the greatest heights.

As Portland star center Bill Walton might say in his current role as a television analyst, "Gag me with a spoon."

Portland and Walton did display brilliant team play during their run to the 1976-1977 NBA title. They didn't overachieve.

The Trail Blazers produced the NBA's best average point differential (+5.5 points per game) and the highest POST rating during the 1976-1977 season.

Portland entered the playoffs as an underdog because of its 49-33 record (tied for fourth-best in the league) and because it never had reached the postseason before.

The Trail Blazers defeated a pair of division champions to reach the NBA Finals. Portland took out the Denver Nuggets in six games. The Trail Blazers then swept the Los Angeles Lakers in the Western Conference Finals. Walton outdueled Kareem Abdul-Jabbar in a matchup of legendary former UCLA centers.

Portland sustained its underdog status when it fell behind the Philadelphia 76ers and star forward Julius Erving 2-0 in the NBA Finals. The Trail Blazers then roared back to win the next four games to claim the franchise's first and only NBA title.

Portland became the first team to win an NBA championship in its first post-season appearance. The Trail Blazers also became the first team to win four consecutive NBA Finals games after falling behind 2-0.

Sacramento Kings
1948-present
Also Rochester Royals (1948-1957), Cincinnati Royals (1957-1972), Kansas City/Omaha Kings (1972-1975), and Kansas City Kings (1975-1985)
Most dominant team: 2001-2002 Sacramento Kings
Record: 61-21
Overall ranking: 33rd, 7.501 points above average

The most dominant season of the Sacramento Kings' long and winding history ended with heartbreak.

The 2001-2002 Sacramento Kings finished with a 61-21 record, the most wins in the NBA and the most wins in franchise history. Sacramento won the Pacific Division, ending a 50-year division title drought dating to the franchise's days as the Rochester Royals.

The Kings enjoyed a 12-game winning streak at midseason, the longest spurt of the franchise's time in Sacramento. The Kings posted an average point differential of +7.6 points per game, tops in the NBA and again a record for the franchise's California era.

Chris Webber, Mike Bibby and company accomplished all but one thing. They couldn't dethrone the Los Angeles Lakers as NBA champions.

The Kings grabbed a 2-1 lead over the Lakers in the Western Conference finals. Sacramento missed a golden opportunity to take a chokehold on the series when Los Angeles' Robert Horry sank a 3-pointer at the buzzer of Game 4 to lift the Lakers to a 100 99 win.

Sacramento got to host the decisive Game 7, but saw its memorable season end with a 112-106 overtime defeat.

Least dominant team: 1958-1959 Cincinnati Royals
Record: 19-53
Overall ranking: 1,100th, 7.488 points below average

The Cincinnati Royals endured a truly tragic 1958-1959 season.

The Royals posted a respectable 33-39 record and earned a playoff appearance during the 1957-1958 campaign, the franchise's first in Cincinnati. But late in the season the career of promising power forward Maurice Stokes came to a sudden and frightening end. Stokes became incapacitated because of encephalitis a few days after taking a hard fall during a game. He would not play basketball again.

The Royals staggered through the 1958-1959 season haunted by the past and shadowed by future. Stokes' absence represented the past. The expected arrival of University of Cincinnati star Oscar Robertson starting with the 1960-1961 season (the Royals could guarantee themselves the rights to Robertson with a territorial draft pick) represented the future.

Cincinnati finished the 1958-1959 campaign with a 19-53 mark, still a franchise record for fewest wins in season. The Royals also had the league's worst offense and defense, resulting in a franchise-worst average point differential of -8.9 points per game.

Another team of note: 1990-1991 Sacramento Kings
Record: 25-57
Overall ranking: 1,067th, 6.289 points below average

Two patterns emerged during the first 15 years of the Kings' existence in Sacramento after the franchise moved from Kansas City following the 1984-1985 season.

The Kings generally played lousy basketball, but they got unwavering support from their fans.

Both trends showed up to an extreme during the 1990-1991 season.

Sacramento posted a respectable 24-17 record in front of its home fans. Yet the Kings finished the season with a 25-57 overall record because of a 1-40 record in away games.

Sacramento's 1-40 road ledger established a new low for fewest road wins in a season under the NBA's modern 82-game schedule. The Kings lost their last 37 road games of the 1990-1991 season and six more to start the 1991-1992 campaign, establishing another league record with 43 consecutive road defeats.

San Antonio Spurs
1976-present
Most dominant team: 2006-2007 San Antonio Spurs
Record: 58-24
Overall ranking: 17th, 8.246 points above average

The San Antonio Spurs of the Tim Duncan era keep getting better with age.

Duncan marked his 10th NBA season by leading San Antonio to the most dominant year in franchise history.

The Spurs finished the 2006-2007 season with a 58-24 record, matching the franchise's average win total during Duncan's career. San Antonio set a team record with an average point differential of +8.4 points per game. The Spurs led the NBA in defense, yielding just 90.1 points per game. Duncan and point guard Tony Parker played in the All-Star Game. Duncan and forward Bruce Bowen made the All-Defense team.

San Antonio rode under the radar until the postseason. The Spurs did not emerge as the playoff favorite until they beat the Phoenix Suns in a controversial six-game West semifinal that amounted to a de facto league championship series. San Antonio went on to defeat the Utah Jazz in the Western Conference finals and the Cleveland Cavaliers in the NBA Finals to claim its fourth championship in nine years.

Read more about the 2006-2007 San Antonio Spurs in Chapter 1.

Least dominant team: 1996-1997 San Antonio Spurs
Record: 20-62
Overall ranking: 1,133rd, 9.205 points below average

The San Antonio Spurs' 1996-1997 season ended before it got started when David Robinson could play just six games because of a back injury.

The Spurs slumped from a 59-23 record during the 1995-1996 season to a franchise-worst 20-62 record in 1996-1997. San Antonio's 39-win decline set a league record for biggest single-season downturn in league history.

Gregg Popovich replaced Bob Hill as the Spurs' coach after a 3-15 start, but couldn't right this listing ship. San Antonio acquired Dominique Wilkins to pick up some of the scoring slack, but the Spurs still produced a franchise-worst average point differential of -7.9 points per game.

Another team of note: 1997-1998 San Antonio Spurs
Record: 56-26
Overall ranking: 238th, 3.420 points above average

The San Antonio Spurs' stormy 1996-1997 season produced the ultimate silver lining: San Antonio received the rights to the No. 1 overall selection in the 1997 NBA draft.

The Spurs used the choice to select franchise forward Tim Duncan out of Wake Forest.

The arrival of Duncan and the return of David Robinson helped San Antonio make an immediate turnaround.

The Spurs went 56-26 during the 1997-1998 season. San Antonio set an NBA record for biggest single-season improvement with a 36-win jump. Duncan claimed Rookie of the Year honors. The season laid the foundation for the Spurs' future NBA titles.

The Spurs broke the record for biggest single-season improvement set by the 1989-1990 San Antonio squad under remarkably similar circumstances. The Spurs suffered through a then-franchise-worst 21-61 season during the 1988-1989 campaign. Robinson, the No. 1 overall selection in the 1987 draft, spent the year completing his Naval Academy obligations.

Robinson made his debut during the 1989-1990 season and helped San Antonio to a 56-26 record.

Seattle Supersonics
1967-present
Most dominant team: 1993-1994 Seattle Supersonics
Record: 63-19
Overall ranking: 9th, 8.615 points above average

The 1993-1994 Seattle Supersonics probably stand as the most-remembered team in franchise history, but not for the reasons they expected when the 1994 postseason began.

Seattle ran its opposition ragged during the 1993-1994 regular season. The combination of guard Gary Payton and forward Shawn Kemp led the Supersonics to a 63-19 record, best in the NBA by five games and a franchise record at the time.

Seattle could score. It had the third-best shooting team in the league. The Sonics could defend. They forced over 200 more turnovers than any other team. Seattle could win. It posted an average point differential of +9.0, two full points better than any other team in the league.

Seattle entered the postseason as the No. 1 seed in the Western Conference. The Sonics had home court advantage in a postseason made wide open by Michael Jordan's retirement from the three-time defending champion Chicago Bulls.

Seattle showed no signs of trouble during the first two games of its best-of-five first round series against the No. 8 seed Denver Nuggets. The Sonics won both games by double figures. Kemp talked about the need to close out the series as soon as possible to gain some rest before the conference semifinals.

Denver had other ideas. The Nuggets evened the series with a pair of home wins, including an overtime triumph in Game 4.

Seattle still didn't worry too much. Two No. 8 seeds had pushed No. 1 seeds to the full five games since the NBA expanded the postseason to 16 teams starting with the 1984 playoffs, but no No. 8 seed had won a series.

History changed in 1994. Denver concluded its stunning upset with a 98-94 overtime victory in Seattle in Game 5. The most dominant team in Supersonics history gets remembered as the first No. 1 seed to lose against a No. 8 seed in the first round of the playoffs.

Read more about the 1993-1994 Seattle Supersonics in Chapter 2.

Least dominant team: 1967-1968 Seattle Supersonics
Record: 23-59
Overall ranking: 1,052nd, 5.960 points below average

The Seattle Supersonics got their worst season out of the way in their first season.

Seattle went 23-59 as an expansion team during the 1967-1968 season, a respectable first-year record but the franchise low for wins in a season nonetheless. The Supersonics posted an average point differential of -6.4 points per game, also respectable for an expansion team but also a franchise low.

Another team of note: 1978-1979 Seattle Supersonics
Record: 52-30
Overall ranking: 306th, 2.696 points above average

The 1978-1979 Seattle Supersonics achieved a place in history when they defeated the Washington Bullets in five games in the NBA Finals to win the franchise's first and only championship.

The 1978-1979 Sonics since have settled into another niche in history: They are the only team to win an NBA championship without a Hall of Fame player or a likely Hall of Fame player on the roster.

Seattle coach Lenny Wilkens has earned Hall of Fame enshrinement as a player and as a coach. None of the Sonics' top players (Gus Williams, Dennis Johnson, and Jack Sikma) have gained induction. Most likely, none ever will.

Of the NBA's recent champions, only the 2003-2004 Detroit Pistons appear to have a chance to match the 1978-1979 Sonics' "accomplishment."

Toronto Raptors
1995-present
Most dominant team: 2000-2001 Toronto Raptors
Record: 47-35
Overall ranking: 402nd, 1.809 points above average

The "Air Canada" era in Toronto reached its ceiling during the 2000-2001 season.

The arrival of Vince Carter during the 1998-1999 campaign revived the Raptors' franchise. Carter averaged 18.3 points per game and won the league's Rookie of the Year award. He acquired the nickname "Air Canada" because of some similarities he shared with Michael "Air" Jordan. Both played college basketball at North Carolina. Both had shaved heads. Both excited fans with high-flying, high-scoring games.

Carter helped Toronto reach the playoffs during the 1999-2000 season. He then led the Raptors to the franchise's best season in 2000-2001.

Toronto posted a club-best 47-35 record. The Raptors enjoyed an average point differential of +2.3 points per game, the only team to post a positive average point differential in the franchise's first 11 years.

Carter led Toronto to the only playoff series win in franchise history. The Raptors rallied from a 2-0 deficit against the New York Knicks and won the first round series in five games.

Carter then engaged in an exciting shootout against league Most Valuable Player Allen Iverson and the top-seeded Philadelphia 76ers in the Eastern Conference semifinals. Carter sank an NBA playoff record nine 3-pointers and scored 50 points during Toronto's Game 3 victory. Carter scored 39 points in Game 6 to help his team force a seventh game.

The Raptors' rise ended on May 20, 2001. Carter elected to spend the morning of Game 7 participating in graduation exercises at North Carolina. He received nationwide criticism for the decision. He ended the afternoon by missing a potential game-winning shot at the buzzer of Toronto's 88-87 loss.

The Raptors of the Carter era would not reach such heights thereafter.

Least dominant team: 1997-1998 Toronto Raptors
Record: 16-66
Overall ranking: 1,120th, 8.418 points below average

The Toronto Raptors took small steps forward during their first two seasons.

They fell apart completely during Season Three.

Toronto posted an acceptable 21-61 record as an expansion team during the 1995-1996 season, led by Rookie of the Year Damon Stoudamire. The Raptors added center Marcus Camby before their second season and improved to 30-52.

Toronto expected further progress in Season Three. The Raptors now had experience. They also boasted another rookie phenom in fresh-from-high-school Tracy McGrady.

Toronto's building process instead collapsed amidst organizational infighting. A 17-game losing streak in November and December put the Raptors in an early hole. General manager Isiah Thomas departed after a squabble with ownership.

New general manager Glen Grunwald replaced coach Darrell Walker with Butch Carter after a 11-38 start. Things got worse under Carter. The Raptors won just five of their last 33 games.

Toronto concluded the season back at square one. The Raptors finished 16-66, the worst record in franchise history. Toronto posted an average point differential of -9.3 points per game, also the worst mark in club history.

Another team of note: 2006-2007 Toronto Raptors
Record: 47-35
Overall ranking: 525th, 0.682 points above average

The 2006-2007 Toronto Raptors crawled off of the endangered species list and clawed their way to the first division title in franchise history.

Toronto seemed destined to extend a string of four consecutive losing seasons when it lost eight of its first 10 games.

Fortunately for the Raptors, they played in the putrid Atlantic Division. All five teams in the division possessed losing records for most of the first half of the season. Toronto quickly climbed into contention for the division lead.

The Raptors moved above the .500 mark for good with a five-game winning streak that started January 31. The first victory in the surge, against the Washington Wizards, gave Toronto the division lead for keeps. The Raptors finished 47-35 and won the division by six games.

First-year general manager Bryan Colangelo, who built the Phoenix Suns into a high-scoring powerhouse, engineered Toronto's 20-win improvement. Seventeen players suited up for the Raptors during the 2006-2007 season. Only six of those players remained from Toronto's 2005-2006 roster.

Observers referred to the Raptors as Phoenix North because of the Colangelo connection. In truth, Toronto got better because it tightened up its defense. The Raptors allowed 98.5 points per game, way down from the 104.0 points per game they yielded during the 2005-2006 season. Toronto scored 99.5 points per game for an average point differential of +1.0 points per game, just the second positive point differential in franchise history.

All-Star forward Chris Bosh proved worth his offseason contract extension by averaging 22.6 points and a career-high 10.7 rebounds per game. Raptors coach Sam Mitchell received the league's Coach of the Year award. Colangelo won the Executive of the Year honor.

The player many Toronto fans blamed for the four losing seasons preceding the division title run brought the Raptors' bounce-back year to an end. Vince Carter led Toronto to three postseason berths at the start of the decade. Carter's popularity dwindled as his scoring average plummeted from 27.6 points per game during the 2000-2001 season to 15.9 points per game during the first half of the 2004-2005 season, resulting in a trade to the New Jersey Nets.

Carter promptly raised his game to its former heights when he joined the Nets, raising the ire of the Raptors' fans. Their anger did not dissipate after Toronto's series against New Jersey in the first round of the 2006-2007 postseason. Carter averaged 25.0 points per game as the Nets upset the Raptors in six games.

Utah Jazz
1974-present
Also New Orleans Jazz (1974-1979)
Most dominant team: 1996-1997 Utah Jazz
Record: 64-18
Overall ranking: 19th, 8.056 points above average

The 1997-1998 Utah Jazz probably had a better chance to win the NBA title, but the 1996-1997 Jazz produced the more dominant season.

Forward Karl Malone and point guard John Stockton finally broke through to the NBA Finals after a record-setting season. Utah posted a 64-18 record, the best in club history and the start of a string of four consecutive division titles. The Jazz set a team record with 15 consecutive wins early in the season and then matched the streak during the season's final month. Utah posted a franchise-best average point differential of +8.8 points per game. Malone received his first Most Valuable Player award.

Utah reached the NBA Finals for the first time when Stockton drilled a long 3-pointer at the buzzer to lift the Jazz to a 103-100 victory over the Houston Rockets in Game 6 of the Western Conference finals.

Utah had chances to win five of the six games during the 1997 NBA Finals against the Chicago Bulls, but Michael Jordan led the Bulls to a 4-2 triumph.

Utah fans know the stories all too well.

Jordan made the game-winning jumper at the buzzer in Game 1, moments after Malone missed a pair of free throws with the score tied.

Jordan scored 38 points with flu-like symptoms, including a key 3-pointer, during Chicago's pivotal Game 5 victory in Utah.

Finally, Jordan set up reserve Steve Kerr for the go-ahead shot during the Bulls' championship-clinching 90-86 victory in Game 6.

Read more about the 1996-1997 Utah Jazz in Chapter 2.

Least dominant team: 1974-1975 New Orleans Jazz
Record: 23-59
Overall ranking: 1,092nd, 7.236 points below average

The New Orleans Jazz tried to do things the right way when they came into existence for the 1974-1975 season.

The Jazz acquired a star player and excited their fan base in one fell swoop when they traded for star guard Pete Maravich before their inaugural season. Maravich, a crowd-pleasing guard from nearby Louisiana State University, finished second in the league in scoring during the 1973-1974 season.

Just one problem: The Maravich deal left New Orleans without the resources to fill out the rest of the roster.

Maravich did his part. He averaged 21.5 points per game, but the Jazz went through 21 other players trying to assemble a supporting cast.

The roster merry-go-round had predictable results.

New Orleans' first coach, Scotty Robertson, lost his job after a 1-14 start. The Jazz finished 23-59, the worst record in the league and the worst record in franchise history. New Orleans fielded the worst defense in the league with 109.3 points allowed per game, 2.1 more points than any other team in the league.

The Jazz hit especially sour notes on the road, with a 3-38 record in away games. They finished the season with an average point differential of -7.8 points per game, 3.8 points worse than any other team in the league and the worst mark in team history.

Another team of note: 1987-1988 Utah Jazz
Record: 47-35
Overall ranking: 263rd, 3.163 points above average

The 1987-1988 season marks the point when John Stockton and Karl Malone truly emerged as household names.

Stockton, in his fourth season out of Gonzaga, finally supplanted Rickey Green as Utah's starting point guard. He promptly won the first of his nine consecutive league assist titles with 13.8 per game.

Malone, in his third season out of Louisiana Tech, enjoyed his true breakthrough season. He upped his scoring average from 21.7 points per game to 27.7 points per outing.

Stockton and Malone led Utah to a 47-35 mark, at the time a club record for wins. (The Jazz would match or surpass that winning percentage every year for the next 13 years).

Stockton and Malone burst into national consciousness when they pushed the defending NBA champion Los Angeles Lakers to seven games in the Western

Conference semifinals. The Jazz led the series 2-1. They lost by just two points in the series' pivotal fifth game.

Stockton and Malone had arrived.

Washington Wizards
1961-present
Also Chicago Packers (1961-1962), Chicago Zephyrs (1962-1963), Baltimore Bullets (1963-1973), Capital Bullets (1973-1974), and Washington Bullets (1974-1997)
Most dominant team: 1974-1975 Washington Bullets
Record: 60-22
Overall ranking: 68th, 6.488 points above average

The Washington Bullets dominated their competition throughout the 1974-1975 regular season. Yet they got dominated in stunning fashion at the climax of the campaign.

Washington established most of its club records during the 1974-1975 regular season. Elvin Hayes and Wes Unseld led the Bullets to a 60-22 record, the best mark in team history. Washington enjoyed a franchise-best average point differential of +7.2 points per game. Unseld led the league in rebounds. Point guard Kevin Porter led the league in assists.

The Bullets cleared what most regarded as their biggest postseason hurdle when they eliminated the defending champion Boston Celtics in six games in the Eastern Conference finals. Boston matched Washington with 60 wins during the regular season.

The NBA Finals shaped up as a mismatch. The Bullets' opponent, the Golden State Warriors, managed just a 48-34 record during the regular season.

Sure enough, the Finals ended in a sweep—in Golden State's favor. All four games were close, decided by a grand total of 16 points, but the Warriors won all four games. Washington became the first team to get swept in an NBA Finals by a team with an inferior regular season record. It has happened only once since.

Least dominant team: 1961-1962 Chicago Packers
Record: 18-62
Overall ranking: 1,098th, 7.416 points below average

The Washington Wizards franchise does hold at least one distinction. The team now known as the Wizards holds the "record" for most franchise nicknames.

The Wizards started life as the Chicago Packers, the NBA's first expansion team since the BAA-NBL merger before the 1949-1950 season.

The Packers met the same fate as almost every expansion team to follow. They struggled mightily during their first season.

Chicago finished with an 18-62 record. The Packers finished with 11 fewer wins than every other team in the league. They established a franchise record for fewest wins. Chicago posted another club low with an average point differential of -8.5 points per game.

The Packers struggled on offense despite the presence of No. 1 overall draft pick and Rookie of the Year Walt Bellamy, who averaged 31.6 points per game. Chicago scored 110.9 points per game, 3.9 points fewer than every other team in the league.

Another team of note: 1977-1978 Washington Bullets
Record: 44-38
Overall ranking: 510th, 0.818 points above average

The Bullets enjoyed success throughout the 1970s, but they rose up and claimed the franchise's only NBA title when most expected it least.

Washington won the 1977-1978 NBA championship despite a 44-38 record during the regular season. The Bullets still hold the "record" for worst regular season winning percentage for an NBA champion.

Washington needed time to gel because of injuries and new personnel. The Bullets started to find their range just in time for the postseason.

Washington cruised through the Eastern Conference playoffs. The Bullets won all three of their pre-Finals series without facing an elimination game. They rallied from a 3-2 deficit to win the NBA Finals in seven games over the Seattle Supersonics.

Read more about the 1977-1978 Washington Bullets in Chapter 3.

DEFUNCT FRANCHISES
Anderson Packers
1949-1950
Most dominant, least dominant, and only team of note: 1949-1950 Anderson Packers
Record: 37-27
Overall ranking: 303rd, 2.728 points above average

Don't dismiss the credentials of this one-time NBA locale. Anderson, Indiana, currently boasts a 9,000-seat high school gymnasium. The Anderson High School boys basketball team might outdraw an NBA team or two on a given Friday evening.

Anderson hosted a respectable team during the city's lone NBA campaign after the BAA-NBL merger. The Packers finished with a 37-27 record, good for second place in the Western Division. Anderson won a pair of playoff series before falling in the NBA semifinals against George Mikan and the eventual champion Minneapolis Lakers.

The Packers elected to return to the (briefly) revived National Basketball League after the 1949-1950 campaign. Anderson thus became the only team to drop out of the NBA after a season that included a victory in a playoff series.

Baltimore Bullets
1947-1954
Most dominant team: 1947-1948 Baltimore Bullets
Record: 28-20
Overall ranking: 219th, 3.673 points above average

Imagine the NBA adding a team from the Continental Basketball Association just before the season and then seeing that team win the NBA title.

That's essentially what the Baltimore Bullets did during the 1947-1948 season.

The Bullets jumped from the American Basketball League to the second-year Basketball Association of America just before the 1947-1948 season.

Player/coach Buddy Jeannette led Baltimore to a 28-20 record. The Bullets finished in a three-way tie for the second-best record in the league.

Those same three teams all finished behind the St. Louis Bombers and in a three-way tie for the last two playoff spots available in the Western Division. The Bullets had to win a "tiebreaker" game against the Chicago Stags just to earn a spot in the six-team BAA postseason.

Baltimore beat the Eastern Division runner-up New York Knicks in the BAA quarterfinals. The Bullets advanced to the BAA Finals with two more victories against Chicago in a best-of-three BAA semifinal.

Baltimore matched up against the defending champion Philadelphia Warriors and star guard Joe Fulks in the BAA Finals. Philadelphia won the first game, but the Bullets took control of the series with three consecutive wins (by a grand total of eight points). Baltimore sealed its place in history as the pro basketball's most accidental champion with a series-clinching 88-73 victory in Game 6.

Least dominant team: 1951-1952 Baltimore Bullets
Record: 20-46
Overall ranking: 1,070th, 6.455 points below average

The Baltimore Bullets franchise disintegrated quickly after the 1947-1948 championship season.

The team's least dominant year came during the 1951-1952 campaign. The next two Bullets teams (and last two Bullets teams) would win fewer games. The 1951-1952 squad otherwise had inferior numbers.

Baltimore had no players left from its 1947-1948 BAA championship squad by the time the 1951-1952 season started. The Bullets posted an average point differential of -7.5 points per game, the worst in the franchise's brief history. Baltimore allowed 89.0 points per game, at the time the second-worst defensive season in the NBA's seven-year history.

Another team of note: 1954 Baltimore Bullets
Record: 3-11
Overall ranking: N/A

The original Baltimore Bullets franchise folded 14 games into the 1954-1955 season. Baltimore became just the second NBA franchise to fold during a season. No NBA team has folded since. The 14 games the Bullets played at the beginning of the 1954-1955 season were erased from the record books.

Coincidentally, the NBA's next expansion franchise (the 1961-1962 Chicago Packers) eventually would become the Baltimore Bullets.

One last note from the 1954 Bullets: The team disbanded on November 27. The NBA then assigned the Baltimore players to other teams. Only four Bullets players did not get a chance to play with another club. One of them embarked on a fairly successful coaching career. His name: Al McGuire.

Chicago Stags
1946-1950
Most dominant team: 1948-1949 Chicago Stags
Record: 38-22
Overall ranking: 214th, 3.707 points above average

Other Chicago Stags teams achieved more victories and postseason success, but the 1948-1949 squad enjoyed the franchise's most dominant season.

Chicago went 38-22, behind just the powerful Rochester Royals and eventual BAA champion Minneapolis Lakers in the Western Division.

Star guard Max Zaslofsky helped the Stags post an average point differential of +4.0 points per game, the best margin in franchise history.

Chicago matched Minneapolis and Rochester for the top scoring average in the league at 84.0 points per game. The Stags couldn't match their rivals' defensive prowess. Minneapolis and star center George Mikan swept Chicago out of the playoffs, winning a best-of-three Western Division semifinal in two easy games.

Least dominant team: 1949-1950 Chicago Stags
Record: 40-28
Overall ranking: 404th, 1.797 points above average

The Chicago Stags are, by far, the best NBA franchise ever to go out of business.

The Stags folded after the 1949-1950 season, when they went 40-28 with an average point differential of +1.6 points per game. The Chicago franchise ended its four-year run with an aggregate record of 145-92, good for a .612 winning percentage. (Perspective: The Boston Celtics franchise has an overall winning percentage of .587).

The addition of the Minneapolis Lakers and Rochester Royals to the BAA starting with the 1948-1949 season sealed the Stags' doom. Chicago posted the third-best record in the BAA/NBA over the 1948-1949 and 1949-1950 seasons, but didn't come close to finishing ahead of the Lakers or Royals in the division race. The Stags' existence ended with a second consecutive sweep loss against Minneapolis in a best two-of-three division semifinal.

Another team of note: 1946-1947 Chicago Stags
Record: 39-22
Overall ranking: 250th, 3.342 points above average

The 1946-1947 Chicago Stags pulled the NBA's first great playoff upset, only to suffer the NBA's first case of post-upset letdown.

Chicago won the Western Division during the BAA's inaugural season with a 39-22 record. But the first-year league's bizarre playoff format—first-place teams played first-place teams; second-place teams played second-place teams; and so on—penalized the Stags. Chicago got "rewarded" with a playoff semifinal matchup against the Washington Capitols. Washington boasted a 49-11 record, the best in the league.

The Stags matched up favorably with the Capitols, thanks to the presence of guards Max Zaslofsky and Don Carlson, plus then-monstrous 6-foot-9 center Chuck Halbert.

Chicago proceeded to dominate Washington. The Stags won the first three games of the best-of-seven series. They closed out the series in six games.

Chicago went into the first BAA Finals on a high note, but saw its fortunes reverse against the Philadelphia Warriors. The Stags fell behind 3-0. They lost the series in five games.

Cleveland Rebels
1946-1947

Most dominant, least dominant, and only team of note: 1946-1947 Cleveland Rebels

Record: 30-30
Overall ranking: 682nd, 0.880 points below average

The Cleveland Rebels broke even on the court during the 1946-1947 season. They didn't break even in the ledger books and folded after one campaign.

Cleveland finished the inaugural BAA season with a 30-30 record, good for third place in the Western Division. The Rebels qualified for the playoffs, but lost a best-of-three BAA quarterfinal series against the New York Knicks in three games.

The moderate success did not merit a second season. The Cleveland Rebels faded into history as the most successful of the four teams to fold after the BAA's first season.

Denver Nuggets
1949-1950
Most dominant, least dominant, and only team of note: 1949-1950 Denver Nuggets
Record: 11-51
Overall ranking: 1,146th, 10.771 points below average

The Denver Nuggets struggled in the National Basketball League during the winter of 1948-1949. Things only got worse when the Nuggets joined the newly merged NBA for the 1949-1950 season.

Denver started the 1949-1950 season with an 15-game losing streak. The Nuggets never came close to recovering. Denver finished with an 11-51 mark, eight wins fewer than any other team in the league. The Nuggets went 1-26 in road games and 1-10 in games played on neutral courts, numbers that were somewhat understandable since the NBA had no other teams west of Minneapolis and St. Louis.

Denver posted an average point differential of -11.4 points per game, a number no team would approach for two decades. The Nuggets allowed 89.1 points per game, a number that would stand as the worst in the NBA's pre-shot clock era.

Read more about the 1949-1950 Denver Nuggets in Chapter 4.

Detroit Falcons
1946-1947
Most dominant, least dominant, and only team of note: 1946-1947 Detroit Falcons
Record: 20-40
Overall ranking: 783rd, 1.810 points below average

If nothing else, the 1946-1947 Detroit Falcons established a tradition of defense-oriented teams in the Motor City.

Detroit played the second lowest-scoring games of the first BAA season. A typical Falcons game ended with a 65.3-63.3 final score.

The Falcons finished their only season with a 20-40 record, good for fourth place in the Western Division.

Indianapolis Jets
1948-1949
Most dominant, least dominant, and only team of note: 1948-1949 Indianapolis Jets
Record: 18-42
Overall ranking: 961st, 4.138 points below average

The Indianapolis Jets went through 25 players and two coaches during their only BAA season, only to get shoved out of existence in favor of another Indianapolis franchise.

The multitude of off-court moves didn't help the Jets much on the court. Indianapolis finished the season with an 18-42 record, last in the Western Division and the second-worst record in the league.

The most notable name on the team: Bruce Hale, who later would coach Rick Barry at the University of Miami.

The BAA replaced the Jets after one season with a franchise called the Indianapolis Olympians in the newly merged NBA.

Indianapolis Olympians
1949-1953
Most dominant team: 1949-1950 Indianapolis Olympians
Record: 39-25
Overall ranking: 280th, 2.946 points above average

Perhaps no new team has entered the NBA better stocked than the Indianapolis Olympians.

The newly merged National Basketball Association had the brainstorm to stock a professional team with stars from the University of Kentucky. The Wildcats won the 1948 and 1949 NCAA titles. The UK players also formed the core of the United States' gold-medal winning basketball team at the 1948 Summer Olympics. Hence, the "Olympians" nickname.

The Olympians lived up to expectations during their first NBA season. Indianapolis won the Western Division with a 39-25 record. The Olympians enjoyed an average point differential of +3.7 points per game. Alex Groza, one of the former Kentucky stars, finished second in the league in scoring at 23.4 points per game.

Things never again would be so good for Indianapolis. The Olympians' first season ended with a two-point loss against the Anderson Packers in the third and decisive game of the best-of-three Western Division finals. Things went straight downhill from there.

Least dominant team: 1952-1953 Indianapolis Olympians
Record: 28-43
Overall ranking: 820th, 2.274 points below average

The Olympians were a shell of their original selves by the 1952-1953 season.

The team's top two scorers and marquee players, Alex Groza and Ralph Beard, received lifetime suspensions from the NBA after the 1950-1951 season because of their involvement with a point-shaving scandal when they played in college.

The Indianapolis franchise never recovered. The Olympians lasted two more seasons, bottoming out with the 1952-1953 season. Indianapolis posted a 28-43 record, the worst in franchise history. The Olympians managed a 19-14 home record, but went 4-23 in road games.

Indianapolis coach Herman Schaefer perhaps pioneered the concept of playing at a slow pace with a team with inferior talent. The Olympians led the league in fewest points allowed at 77.4 points per game, but finished last in the league in offense with just 74.6 points per game.

The Indianapolis Olympians folded after the 1952-1953 season, doomed to a place in history as the NBA's answer to baseball's 1919 Chicago Black Sox.

Another team of note: 1951-1952 Indianapolis Olympians
Record: 34-32
Overall ranking: 586th, 0.082 points above average

The 2004-2005 Indiana Pacers, a team that made the playoffs despite a multitude of suspensions and injuries, could have looked back to one of their city's early NBA teams for a model on overcoming adversity.

The Indianapolis Olympians' 1951-1952 season all but ended before it began. Indianapolis' top two scorers, Alex Groza and Ralph Beard, received lifetime suspensions from the NBA because of their involvement with a point-shaving scandal when they played in college. Groza and Beard had combined for 38.5 points per game during the 1950-1951 season. Indianapolis managed just a 31-37 record *with* Groza and Beard. The Olympians appeared doomed without them.

Indianapolis rallied around newcomer Joe Graboski and new coach Herman Schaefer. Graboski topped the team with 13.7 points per game. Schaefer would have won Coach of the Year honors had the award existed at the time. He coaxed a 34-32 record out of a group that had just five players who would continue their NBA careers (none with distinction) after the Olympians folded one year later.

Indianapolis qualified for the playoffs. The Olympians' near-miraculous season ended with a sweep defeat at the hands of the eventual league champion Minneapolis Lakers in the first round of the postseason.

Pittsburgh Ironmen
1946-1947
Most dominant, least dominant, and only team of note: 1946-1947 Pittsburgh Ironmen
Record: 15-45
Overall ranking: 1,044th, 5.755 points below average
  Perhaps no city has a professional basketball history worse than Pittsburgh's
  No fewer than three franchises in three major leagues have failed in Pittsburgh. The only Pittsburgh pro basketball team to achieve any kind of success: The Pittsburgh Pisces in the forgettable movie, *The Fish That Saved Pittsburgh.*
  The Steel City's ignoble basketball tradition began with the Pittsburgh Ironmen during the 1946-1947 season. The Ironmen posted a 15-45 record during the inaugural BAA season, the worst mark in the league by five games. Pittsburgh posted an average point differential of -6.4 points per game, also worst in the league. The franchise was the worst of the four to fold after the BAA's first season.
  The most notable name on the Pittsburgh roster: Press Maravich, who later would gain fame coaching his son, Pete Maravich, at Louisiana State University.

Providence Steamrollers
1946-1949
Most dominant team: 1946-1947 Providence Steamrollers
Record: 28-32
Overall ranking: 750th, 1.510 points below average
  The Providence Steamrollers would finish their three-year existence as basketball's answer to baseball's Cleveland Spiders: An awful team mercifully shoved out of existence before the sport began its modern era.
  Providence did put together a respectable year during the BAA's first season. The Steamrollers went 28-32, the best record they ever would have. Providence finished in fourth place in the Eastern Division, just one spot out of a playoff berth.
  Yet signs of trouble already existed.
  The Steamrollers finished last in the league on defense, allowing 74.2 points per game.
  Providence then used its No. 1 draft pick on Walt Dropo of the University of Connecticut. Dropo would play Major League Baseball, but he would not play one second for the Steamrollers.

The defensive and personnel troubles soon would send the Providence franchise tumbling into oblivion.

Least dominant team: 1947-1948 Providence Steamrollers
Record: 6-42
Overall ranking: 1,143rd, 10.096 points below average

Providence came back to the BAA after a moderately successful inaugural year. It promptly produced one of the worst seasons in professional basketball history.

The Steamrollers went 6-42, probably an unbreakable record for fewest victories in a season. (The 1972-1973 Philadelphia 76ers, who went 9-73, generally get "credit" for fewest victories in a full NBA season).

Providence posted a winning percentage of .125, the second-worst percentage in league history. Only the 1972-1973 Philadelphia 76ers did worse. The Steamrollers' victory rate would have played out to a 10-72 record over a modern 82-game schedule.

Providence posted an average point differential of -11.0 points per game. The Steamrollers became the first team to crack the -11.0 "barrier."

The Steamrollers enjoyed relative stability during their first season. The roster turned into a merry-go-round as their second season disintegrated. Providence went through 21 players and a pair of coaches. (The Washington Capitols, the most stable team in the league during the 1947-1948 season, used just 10 players). The one constant: Shoddy defense. The Steamrollers allowed 80.1 points per game, a whopping 6.9 more points per game than any other team in the league.

Another team of note: 1948-1949 Providence Steamrollers
Record: 12-48
Overall ranking: 1,119th, 8.327 points below average

The Providence merry-go-round finally spun to a halt following the 1948-1949 season, after the Steamrollers "improved" to 12-48 in their final campaign.

Providence again struggled on defense. The Steamrollers allowed a league-worst 87.1 points per game, 3.7 points per game more than any other team in the league.

Kenny Sailors led Providence in scoring during the franchise's final season. His destination after he escaped the Steamrollers when the franchise folded? The Denver Nuggets, who proceeded to fold after one 11-51 season.

St. Louis Bombers
1946-1950
Most dominant team: 1946-1947 St. Louis Bombers
Record: 38-23
Overall ranking: 350th, 2.312 points above average

The St. Louis Bombers franchise might not have succeeded—it folded after four seasons—but it didn't truly fail, either.

St. Louis' first franchise in the league that would become the NBA posted respectable results throughout its existence, most notably during the 1946-1947 season.

The Bombers finished with a 38-23 record, just one game behind the Chicago Stags and good for second place in the Western Division. The Bombers, Stags, and Washington Capitols were the only teams to earn winning records at home and on the road during the BAA's inaugural season.

St. Louis ended its season by setting a precedent for an inexplicable franchise tradition: a tendency to get blown out in key playoff games.

The Bombers' first season concluded with a 75-59 loss against the eventual champion Philadelphia Warriors in the third and decisive game of a best-of-three BAA quarterfinals series. One year later, St. Louis' best playoff run would end with consecutive losses, by an average of 31.0 points per game, in Games 6 and 7 of a best-of-seven BAA semifinal against Philadelphia.

Least dominant team: 1948-1949 St. Louis Bombers
Record: 29-31
Overall ranking: 896th, 3.163 points below average

The BAA convinced the four strongest NBL teams (the Minneapolis Lakers, the Rochester Royals, the Fort Wayne Pistons, and the Indianapolis Jets) to jump leagues for the 1948-1949 season.

The new teams ensured the eventual triumph of the BAA over the NBL, but also triggered the demise of the St. Louis Bombers.

The BAA placed all four of the former NBL teams in St. Louis' Western Division. The Bombers proved inferior to Minneapolis and Rochester in particular. St. Louis dropped from first in the division during the 1947-1948 season to fourth in the division one year later, despite no significant personnel changes.

Another blowout playoff defeat, a 93-64 loss against Rochester in both teams' postseason opener, paved the way for the Royals' 2-0 series victory against the Bombers in a best-of-three Western Division semifinal. St. Louis would not return to the postseason again.

Another team of note: 1949-1950 St. Louis Bombers
Record: 26-42
Overall ranking: 817th, 2.239 points below average

The St. Louis franchise seemed to possess all the elements it would need to thrive in the newly merged NBA. Instead, the Bombers folded after their first and only season under the NBA banner.

St. Louis had quality personnel in hometown hero Ed Macauley and center Red Rocha. Macauley would lead the Bombers in scoring as a rookie during the 1949-1950 season.

St. Louis nonetheless nosedived to a franchise-worst 26-42 record and last place in the Central Division. Every other team in the division finished with a 40-28 record or better.

The decline meant the end of the road for the St. Louis Bombers franchise.

Sheboygan Redskins
1949-1950
Most dominant, least dominant, and only team of note: 1949-1950 Sheboygan Redskins
Record: 22-40
Overall ranking: 1,026th, 5.420 points below average

The Sheboygan Redskins were one of six NBL teams to join the new NBA when the NBL and BAA merged for the 1949-1950 season.

The NBA put five of the six former NBL teams in the same division, meaning Sheboygan played 35 of its 62 games against familiar former NBL teams.

The relatively cozy arrangement didn't benefit the former NBL teams much. Just two of the six Western Division teams managed a winning record. The Redskins finished fourth in the division with a 22-40 record. They lost against the division champion Indianapolis Olympians in the first round of the playoffs.

Six franchises, including four of the first-year former NBL teams, dropped out of the NBA after the 1949-1950 season. The Sheboygan NBA squad perished in the purge.

Toronto Huskies
1946-1947
Most dominant, least dominant, and only team of note: 1946-1947 Toronto Huskies
Record: 22-38
Overall ranking: 953rd, 3.970 points below average

Look up the famous "firsts" in NBA history and the Toronto Huskies franchise pops up frequently.

Toronto hosted the first game in the history of the league now known as the NBA. The Huskies hosted the New York Knicks on November 1, 1946. (The Knicks, however, scored the BAA's first basket and earned the league's first victory).

Toronto became the first BAA team to change coaches when it traded player-coach Ed Sadowski after 12 games. The Huskies also made the second and third coaching changes in BAA history before settling on Robert Rolfe for the balance of the year.

Toronto finished its lone NBA season with a 22-38 record, tied for last place in the Eastern Division.

If nothing else, the Huskies' existence provided the future Toronto Raptors franchise with a legitimate reason to wear "throwback jerseys" when retro gear became the fad of the early 2000s.

Washington Capitols
1946-1951
Most dominant team: 1946-1947 Washington Capitols
Record: 49-11
Overall ranking: 7th, 8.885 points above average

The Washington Capitols probably had the most star-crossed franchise of the early days of the BAA and NBA.

Washington put together one of the most dominant seasons in BAA/NBA history during the 1946-1947 campaign, but didn't get a championship to show for its efforts.

The Capitols finished the inaugural BAA season with a 49-11 record, 10 games better than any other team in the league. Washington's pace would have yielded a 67-15 record over a modern 82-game schedule.

Coach Arnold "Red" Auerbach's team won its first 27 home games. The Capitols finished the regular season with a 29-1 home record. Washington became the first of five teams to finish a season with just one home loss.

No team surpassed Washington's .817 winning percentage until the 1966-1967 Philadelphia 76ers. No team surpassed the Capitols' average point differential of +9.9 points per game until the 1970-1971 Milwaukee Bucks. No team will surpass Washington's pre-shot clock record of 63.9 points allowed per game.

Unfortunately for Washington, the Chicago Stags surpassed the Capitols during the 1946-1947 postseason.

The BAA's bizarre postseason format matched the league's two division champions in the league semifinals. Western Division champion Chicago finished 10 wins behind Washington during the regular season, but the Stags matched up favorably against the Capitols in a head-to-head setting.

Chicago won the first two games of the best-of-seven series in Washington. The Stags went on to close out the series in six games. The POST formula recognizes the Capitols as the most dominant team not to win a league title.

Read more about the 1946-1947 Washington Capitols in Chapter 2.

Least dominant team: 1950-1951 Washington Capitols
Record: 10-25
Overall ranking: 988th, 4.597 points below average

The Washington Capitols collapsed with astonishing speed after coach Red Auerbach cut ties with the franchise because of a contract dispute following the 1948-1949 season.

Washington folded 35 games into the 1950-1951 season, already well on pace to the worst season in the franchise's brief history. The Capitols bowed out with a 10-25 record, the worst winning percentage in the league during the 1950-1951 season.

Washington had the league's lowest-scoring team at 81.3 points per game.

Just four players from Auerbach's last Capitols team remained with the squad when the franchise disbanded. Only one other team in NBA history has folded at midseason.

Another team of note: 1948-1949 Washington Capitols
Record: 38-22
Overall ranking: 380th, 2.083 points above average

The 1948-1949 Washington Capitols established almost as many NBA/BAA records as the 1946-1947 squad.

Red Auerbach still had the nucleus from his 1946-1947 team. He added Kleggie Hermsen to the mix before the 1948-1949 season. Hermsen led the BAA champion Baltimore Bullets in scoring during the 1947-1948 campaign.

Washington started its year with 15 consecutive wins, still a record for most consecutive wins at the start of a season. The 15-game winning streak, combined with the Capitols' five consecutive victories at the end of the 1947-1948 season, established a record of 20 consecutive wins. The milestone stood until the Los Angeles Lakers won 33 in a row during the 1971-1972 season.

Washington cooled off as the season went on. The Capitols would finish the season with a relatively unimpressive average point differential of +2.4 points per game. Washington still cruised to the Eastern Division title with a 38-22 record.

The Capitols made their way to the BAA Finals, but proved no match for big George Mikan and the Minneapolis Lakers. Minneapolis won the in the best-of-seven series in six games.

Auerbach left the franchise after the Finals and took over the Tri-Cities Blackhawks. The Capitols would fold within a season-and-a-half.

Waterloo Hawks
1949-1950
Most dominant, least dominant, and only team of note: 1949-1950 Waterloo Hawks
Record: 19-43
Overall ranking: 1,033rd, 5.535 points below average

First, a clarification. The Waterloo Hawks have no connection to today's Atlanta Hawks. The Atlanta Hawks trace their origins to the Tri-Cities Blackhawks, who also began their NBA existence during the 1949-1950 season.

The Waterloo Hawks dropped out of the NBA after one season and a 19-43 record. Waterloo finished fifth in the watered-down Western Division, ahead of only the historically bad Denver Nuggets.

The Hawks' road record led to their proverbial Waterloo. The Hawks went 1-22 in road games and 1-6 in games played in neutral settings.

The most notable name on Waterloo's roster: Johnny Orr, who would go on to a successful college coaching career.

VI. The NBA From Top to Bottom

A complete ranking of every team in NBA history, from No. 1 through No. 1,153

Rank	Year	Team	POST	W-L	Playoffs
1	1970-71	Milwaukee Bucks	11.817	66-16	NBA champion

The Big A (center Lew Alcindor, later Kareem Abdul-Jabbar) and the Big O (point guard Oscar Robertson) combined for the NBA's biggest season

2	1995-96	Chicago Bulls	11.767	72-10	NBA champion

First and only NBA team to win 70 games in a season romped to title during Michael Jordan's first full season after his first comeback

3	1971-72	Los Angeles Lakers	11.581	69-13	NBA champion

Lakers' 69-13 record stood as NBA's best for 24 years; 33-game winning streak still stands as record

4	1971-72	Milwaukee Bucks	10.646	63-19	West finals

Scored more total points than eventual champion Lakers during West finals, but lost series 4-2

5	1996-97	Chicago Bulls	10.570	69-13	NBA champion

Blockbuster sequel to previous season's epic 72-10 campaign

6	1991-92	Chicago Bulls	10.023	67-15	NBA champion

Michael Jordan's memorable 35-point first half and shrug during Game 1 of NBA Finals highlighted Bulls' second title run

7	1946-47	Washington Capitols	8.885	49-11	BAA semifinals

Quick playoff ouster only black mark on coach Red Auerbach's career postseason resume

8	1985-86	Boston Celtics	8.842	67-15	NBA champion

Last of Celtics' 16 championship teams also franchise's most dominant

9	1993-94	Seattle Supersonics	8.615	63-19	West first round

First No. 1 seed to lose in first round of playoffs under current postseason format

10	1990-91	Chicago Bulls	8.572	61-21	NBA champion

Bulls' first championship run also was easiest, with just two playoff losses

11	1985-86	Milwaukee Bucks	8.473	57-25	East finals

Bucks' most dominant team of decade swept by Celtics in East finals

12	1990-91	Portland Trail Blazers	8.421	63-19	West finals

Set franchise record for wins, but upset by Lakers in six games in West finals

13 1986-87   Los Angeles Lakers   8.409   65-17   NBA champion
NBA Finals victory against Celtics gave Laker guard Magic Johnson 2-1 advantage over Boston icon Larry Bird in head-to-head Finals matchups

14 1966-67   Philadelphia 76ers   8.395   68-13   NBA champion
Wilt Chamberlain's record run of seven consecutive scoring titles ended, but he won his first NBA championship

15 1969-70   New York Knickerbockers   8.363   60-22   NBA champion
Star center Willis Reed was MVP of regular season, playoffs, and All-Star game

16 1999-00   Los Angeles Lakers   8.327   67-15   NBA champion
The one season everything truly clicked for big center Shaquille O'Neal, guard Kobe Bryant and coach Phil Jackson

17 2006-07   San Antonio Spurs   8.246   58-24   NBA champion
Most dominant team in franchise history won fourth title in nine seasons

18 1972-73   Los Angeles Lakers   8.110   60-22   NBA finalist
Lakers limited to less than 100 points in last four games of 4-1 NBA Finals loss against Knicks

19 1996-97   Utah Jazz   8.056   64-18   NBA finalist
John Stockton's 3-pointer at buzzer of Game 6 of West finals against Rockets sent Jazz to first NBA Finals

20 1961-62   Boston Celtics   8.054   60-20   NBA champion
Most dominant Celtics team of Bill Russell era needed overtime in Game 7 of NBA Finals against Lakers to win title

21 1949-50   Minneapolis Lakers   7.952   51-17   NBA champion
Best record and most dominant of any George Mikan era Lakers team

22 1967-68   Philadelphia 76ers   7.896   62-20   East finals
Wilt Chamberlain became only center to lead league in assists, but 76ers blew 3-1 lead in East finals against Celtics

23 1971-72   Chicago Bulls   7.849   57-25   West semifinals
Led league in defense, but stuck behind Lakers and Bucks in the Western Conference

24 1994-95   Seattle Supersonics   7.809   57-25   West first round
Stunned in first round of playoffs for second consecutive year; this time by no-name Lakers outfit

25 2000-01   San Antonio Spurs   7.765   58-24   West finals
Had league's best record, but swept away by eventual champion Lakers in West finals

26   2002-03   Dallas Mavericks   7.762   60-22   West finals
Set then-franchise record for wins in a season, but lost against eventual NBA champion Spurs in all-Texas West finals

27   1972-73   Milwaukee Bucks   7.762   60-22   West semifinals
Third consecutive 60-win season, a feat matched only by Celtics, Lakers, and Bulls, ended with upset loss against Warriors in West semifinals

28   1988-89   Cleveland Cavaliers   7.752   57-25   East first round
First round playoff loss against Bulls on Michael Jordan's series-winning shot in decisive Game 5 derailed franchise's progress toward title contention

29   2004-05   San Antonio Spurs   7.729   59-23   NBA champion
Robert Horry's game-winning 3-pointer at end of Game 5 the key moment in Spurs' seven-game triumph over defending champion Pistons in NBA Finals

30   1980-81   Philadelphia 76ers   7.727   62-20   East finals
Couldn't hold 3-1 series lead in East finals against Celtics; lost last three games by total of five points

31   1994-95   Utah Jazz   7.651   60-22   West first round
John Stockton became league's all-time assist leader during season, but Jazz surprised by eventual champion Rockets in first round of playoffs

32   1973-74   Milwaukee Bucks   7.555   59-23   NBA finalist
Hall of Fame guard Oscar Robertson retired after tough seven-game loss against Celtics in NBA Finals

33   2001-02   Sacramento Kings   7.501   61-21   West finals
Set franchise record for wins, but suffered devastating seven-game loss against Lakers in West finals

34   1959-60   Boston Celtics   7.449   59-16   NBA champion
Bob Cousy won last of eight consecutive assist titles as Celtics defended NBA title

35   1982-83   Philadelphia 76ers 7.417   65-17   NBA champion
"Fo, fo, fo": 76ers fulfilled championship prediction of center Moses Malone, the team's key offseason acquisition

36   1949-50   Rochester Royals   7.415   51-17   Central semifinals
Tied for best record in NBA and set franchise record with 15 consecutive wins, but lost all three of its postseason games

37   1998-99   San Antonio Spurs   7.388   37-13   NBA champion
Strong finish and 15-2 playoff run made Spurs first former ABA team to win the NBA title

38 1995-96 Seattle Supersonics 7.385 64-18 NBA finalist
Posted best record in franchise history and broke through to NBA Finals, but no match for Bulls in championship round

39 1964-65 Boston Celtics 7.361 62-18 NBA champion
John Havlicek stole the ball in the final seconds to clinch Game 7 of East finals against 76ers and keep Celtics on course to seventh consecutive title

40 2003-04 San Antonio Spurs 7.334 57-25 West semifinals
Lost pivotal Game 5 of West semifinals against Lakers on Derek Fisher buzzer-beater

41 1972-73 Boston Celtics 7.326 68-14 East finals
Set franchise record for wins in a season, but lost a playoff Game 7 at home for first time in team history

42 1979-80 Boston Celtics 7.284 61-21 East finals
Larry Bird's Rookie of the Year season ended with loss against 76ers in East finals

43 2006-07 Dallas Mavericks 7.188 67-15 West first round
Set a franchise record for wins, but made history of a different kind by becoming first No. 1 seed to lose against a No. 8 seed in the first round of the playoffs under the best-of-seven format

44 2006-07 Phoenix Suns 7.174 61-21 West semifinals
Most dominant season in Suns history derailed by controversial six-game loss against Spurs in West semifinals

45 1966-67 Boston Celtics 7.155 60-21 East finals
Record string of eight consecutive championships ended in East finals against 76ers

46 1997-98 Chicago Bulls 7.105 62-20 NBA champion
Michael Jordan ended his Bulls career with series-winning shot in Game 6 of NBA Finals against Jazz

47 2001-02 Los Angeles Lakers 7.037 58-24 NBA champion
First of Lakers' 14 championship teams to win NBA Finals in a sweep

48 1986-87 Atlanta Hawks 7.014 57-25 East semifinals
Established franchise record for wins in a season

49 1996-97 Seattle Supersonics 7.001 57-25 West semifinals
Sonics traded away frontcourt star Shawn Kemp after season despite division title

50 1997-98 Los Angeles Lakers 6.993 61-21 West finals
Lakers' first division title since 1990, but team swept by Jazz in West finals

51 2004-05 Phoenix Suns 6.964 62-20 West finals
New point guard Steve Nash won MVP award for guiding Suns to 33-win improvement, but Phoenix fell against Spurs in West finals

52 1989-90 Phoenix Suns 6.956 54-28 West finals
Ran top-seeded Lakers out of playoffs in West semifinals, but lost competitive West final against Portland

53 1988-89 Phoenix Suns 6.954 55-27 West finals
Coach of the Year Cotton Fitzsimmons, newly acquired gunner Tom Chambers helped team improve by 27 wins

54 1980-81 Milwaukee Bucks 6.944 60-22 East semifinals
Switch from Western Conference to Eastern Conference no trouble for Bucks

55 1991-92 Portland Trail Blazers 6.942 57-25 NBA finalist
Michael Jordan explosion in Game 1, rally by Bulls reserves in Game 6 resulted in Blazers' six-game loss against Chicago in NBA Finals

56 1985-86 Los Angeles Lakers 6.940 62-20 West finals
Stunned by Rockets in five games in West finals

57 1963-64 Boston Celtics 6.867 59-21 NBA champion
Easiest of Celtics' 16 championship runs: 8-2 postseason record, never tied or behind in two series

58 1949-50 Syracuse Nationals 6.772 51-13 NBA finalist
Eastern Division team played a Western Division schedule, but proved worthy of division championship during first NBA season by making league Finals

59 1948-49 Minneapolis Lakers 6.752 44-16 BAA champion
1948 NBL champion Lakers jumped leagues and won BAA title

60 1990-91 Los Angeles Lakers 6.698 58-24 NBA finalist
Lost against Bulls in "Magic vs. Michael" NBA Finals to conclude guard Magic Johnson's final full season

61 1992-93 Seattle Supersonics 6.691 55-27 West finals
Pushed top-seeded Suns to seven games in West finals

62 2005-06 San Antonio Spurs 6.643 63-19 West semifinals
Set franchise record for victories in a season, but bid for repeat title derailed by overtime loss in Game 7 of West semifinal against Mavericks

63 1989-90 Los Angeles Lakers 6.601 63-19 West semifinals
Surprised by Suns in West semifinals after posting NBA's best record during Pat Riley's final season as Lakers coach

64 1984-85 Los Angeles Lakers 6.558 62-20 NBA champion
First team to wrap up an NBA championship with a win in Boston Garden

65 2002-03 Sacramento Kings 6.544 59-23 West semifinals
Run at championship derailed by standout forward Chris Webber's late-season knee injury

66 1984-85 Milwaukee Bucks 6.530 59-23 East semifinals
Acquisition of high-scoring forward Terry Cummings gave defensive-minded Bucks a boost

67 1988-89 Los Angeles Lakers 6.507 57-25 NBA finalist
Injury to star guard Magic Johnson resulted in sweep loss against Pistons in NBA Finals, concluding center Kareem Abdul-Jabbar's final season

68 1974-75 Washington Bullets 6.488 60-22 NBA finalist
Set franchise record for wins in a season during first season as "Washington" Bullets, but stunned by Warriors in NBA Finals

69 1993-94 New York Knickerbockers 6.485 57-25 NBA finalist
Held 3-2 lead in NBA Finals, but dropped Games 6 and 7 in Houston to lose series

70 1994-95 Orlando Magic 6.477 57-25 NBA finalist
Cagey veteran center Hakeem Olajuwon schooled young Orlando center Shaquille O'Neal during Rockets' sweep of Magic in NBA Finals

71 1990-91 Phoenix Suns 6.453 55-27 West first round
Averaged 114 points per game during regular season, but limited to 102 points or less in all four games of first round playoff loss against Jazz

72 1997-98 Seattle Supersonics 6.448 61-21 West semifinals
Coach George Karl pushed out of job after third consecutive division title

73 1986-87 Boston Celtics 6.398 59-23 NBA finalist
Franchise's most recent NBA Finals appearance spoiled by Magic Johnson's game-winning shot for Lakers in pivotal Game 4 of Los Angeles' six-game triumph

74 1989-90 Portland Trail Blazers 6.365 59-23 NBA finalist
Made 20-win improvement and returned to NBA Finals for first time since 1977

75 1983-84 Boston Celtics 6.306 62-20 NBA champion
First of star forward Larry Bird's three consecutive MVP seasons; Home court advantage proved decisive for Celtics during seven-game victories against Knicks in East semifinals and against Lakers in NBA Finals

76   1992-93   Phoenix Suns   6.301   62-20   NBA finalist
Reached NBA Finals during star forward Charles Barkley's first season in Phoenix, but went 0-3 at home during six-game Finals loss against Bulls
77   1984-85   Boston Celtics   6.297   63-19   NBA finalist
Lost NBA Finals against Lakers in six games despite home court advantage, 148-114 win in Game 1
78   1999-00   Portland Trail Blazers 6.285 59-23   West finals
Lost double-digit lead in Game 7 of West finals against Lakers to conclude veteran forward Scottie Pippen's first season in Portland
79   1962-63   Boston Celtics   6.260   58-22   NBA champion
Celtics "win one for the Couz" during retiring guard Bob Cousy's final season
80   2005-06   Detroit Pistons   6.251   64-18   East finals
Most dominant team in franchise history set club record for wins, but lost its Motown mojo during six-game loss against eventual league champion Heat in East finals
81   1995-96   Utah Jazz   6.236   55-27   West finals
John Stockton completed stretch of nine consecutive seasons as league's assist leader; also became NBA record holder in career steals
82   1992-93   Cleveland Cavaliers 6.235   54-28   East semifinals
Sweep loss against Bulls in East semifinals ended Lenny Wilkens' coaching tenure in Cleveland
83   1981-82   Boston Celtics   6.218   63-19   East finals
Couldn't repeat previous season's comeback from 3-1 deficit against 76ers in East finals; lost Game 7 120-106
84   1975-76   Golden State   6.199   59-23   West finals
          Warriors
Franchise's finest regular season and bid for repeat title spoiled by loss against Suns in West finals
85   2001-02   San Antonio Spurs   6.167   58-24   West semifinals
Star forward Tim Duncan won his first MVP award, but Spurs stomped by Lakers in West semifinals
86   1992-93   Chicago Bulls   6.131   57-25   NBA champion
John Paxson's game-winning 3-pointer in Game 6 of NBA Finals against Suns completed Bulls' first three-peat
87   1997-98   Indiana Pacers   6.112   58-24   East finals
Larry Bird named Coach of the Year as Pacers pushed eventual champion Bulls to seven games in East finals
88   1948-49   Rochester Royals   6.077   45-15   West finals
Jumped to BAA from NBL and won a division title

89   1972-73   New York   6.060   57-25   NBA champion
               Knickerbockers
Only NBA champion to complete title run with series wins against Celtics and Lakers

90   1988-89   Detroit Pistons   6.050   63-19   NBA champion
Leading scorer: Adrian Dantley, who finished season with Mavericks after late season trade for forward Mark Aguirre

91   1998-99   Portland Trail Blazers 5.983   35-15   West finals
Blazers deflated after Sean Elliott's "Memorial Day Miracle" 3-pointer completed Spurs' comeback win in Game 2 of West finals, leading to eventual sweep

92   1995-96   San Antonio Spurs   5.970   59-23   West semifinals
Won second consecutive Midwest Division title, but humbled by division rival Jazz in West semifinals

93   2000-01   Sacramento Kings   5.920   55-27   West semifinals
Won a playoff series for first time in franchise's California history

94   2005-06   Dallas Mavericks   5.915   60-22   NBA finalist
Broke through to franchise's first NBA Finals appearance, but lost four consecutive games in Finals against Heat after leading series 2-0 and holding 13-point lead midway through fourth quarter of Game 3

95   1977-78   Portland Trail Blazers 5.906   58-24   West semifinals
Had 50-10 record when league MVP Bill Walton went out for the season with foot injury; Blazers lost in West semifinals against Sonics

96   1987-88   Boston Celtics   5.886   57-25   East finals
Posted best record in East for fifth consecutive year, but defeated by Pistons in East finals

97   1997-98   Utah Jazz   5.845   62-20   NBA finalist
Jazz's championship window of opportunity closed with second consecutive six-game loss against Bulls in NBA Finals

98   1999-00   San Antonio Spurs   5.844   53-29   West first round
First defending champion since 1983 to lose in opening round of playoffs

99   2004-05   Miami Heat   5.823   59-23   East finals
First season together for center Shaquille O'Neal and flashy guard Dwyane Wade ended with seven-game loss against Pistons in East finals

100 1994-95   San Antonio Spurs   5.811   62-20   West finals
MVP David Robinson led Spurs to NBA's best record, but San Antonio humbled by Rockets and Hakeem Olajuwon in West finals

101	1992-93	New York Knickerbockers	5.793	60-22	East finals

Blew 2-0 series lead, multiple game-winning layup attempts late in pivotal Game 5 of six-game East finals loss against Bulls

102	1998-99	Utah Jazz	5.790	37-13	West semifinals

Late-season slump cost Jazz No. 1 seed for playoffs, leading to early post-season exit

103	2004-05	Dallas Mavericks	5.748	58-24	West semifinals

Mavericks went 16-2 after Avery Johnson replaced Don Nelson as coach, but Dallas fell against former teammate Steve Nash and Suns in West semifinals

104	1958-59	Boston Celtics	5.729	52-20	NBA champion

Regained NBA title in first Celtics-Lakers Finals matchup

105	1991-92	Phoenix Suns	5.693	53-29	West semifinals

Cotton Fitzsimmons stepped down as coach after leading Suns to four consecutive 50-win seasons

106	2003-04	Minnesota Timberwolves	5.686	58-24	West finals

Earned No. 1 seed in Western Conference and won franchise's first playoff series during forward Kevin Garnett's MVP season

107	1991-92	Utah Jazz	5.686	55-27	West finals

Franchise's first appearance in West finals

108	1980-81	Boston Celtics	5.682	62-20	NBA champion

Celtics' first championship of Larry Bird era keyed by comeback from 3-1 deficit against 76ers in East finals

109	1986-87	Dallas Mavericks	5.651	55-27	West first round

Franchise's first division title spoiled by loss against No. 7 seed Sonics in first round of playoffs

110	1981-82	Philadelphia 76ers	5.608	58-24	NBA finalist

Lost in NBA Finals for third time in six years

111	1971-72	Phoenix Suns	5.574	49-33	

Most dominant team to miss postseason

112	2002-03	San Antonio Spurs	5.512	60-22	NBA champion

Franchise icon David Robinson got to retire as a champion

113	1989-90	Detroit Pistons	5.505	59-23	NBA champion

Pistons went 5-0 in NBA Finals road games during back-to-back championship seasons

114 1996-97   Miami Heat   5.439   61-21   East finals
Rallied from 3-1 deficit against Knicks in East semifinals to become first team in franchise history to reach conference finals
115 2005-06   Phoenix Suns   5.435   54-28   West finals
Steve Nash repeated as league MVP after leading Suns back to West finals even though star forward Amare Stoudemire missed all but three games with a knee injury
116 1970-71   Chicago Bulls   5.416   51-31   West semifinals
Dick Motta named Coach of the Year for directing 12-win improvement
117 1979-80   Los Angeles Lakers 5.409   60-22   NBA champion
Rookie Magic Johnson scored 42 points and grabbed 15 rebounds as Lakers clinched title with NBA Finals Game 6 win at Philadelphia without injured center Kareem Abdul-Jabbar
118 1996-97   Atlanta Hawks   5.395   56-26   East semifinals
Newly acquired center Dikembe Mutombo won Defensive Player of the Year honors, led Hawks to 10-win improvement
119 1976-77   Portland Trail Blazers 5.383 49-33   NBA champion
Season of firsts: Blazers' first winning season, first playoff appearance, and first NBA title during coach Jack Ramsay's first season
120 1995-96   Orlando Magic   5.377   60-22   East finals
Best record in franchise history, but season marred by sweep loss against Bulls in East finals
121 1968-69   New York Knickerbockers 5.354 54-28 East finals
Won a playoff series for the first time since 1953, but fell against veteran Celtics in East finals
122 1974-75   Boston Celtics   5.347   60-22   East finals
Standout center Dave Cowens' injury troubles began, but Celtics still won 60 games and reached East finals
123 1996-97   Detroit Pistons   5.337   54-28   East first round
Non-traditional new teal uniforms and departure of free agent guard Allan Houston didn't prevent eight-win improvement
124 1968-69   Boston Celtics   5.335   48-34   NBA champion
Bill Russell retired after winning 11th championship in 13 seasons
125 1991-92   Cleveland Cavaliers 5.311   57-25   East finals
Matched franchise record for wins in a season, but again denied by Bulls in postseason

126 1982-83   Boston Celtics   5.238   56-26   East semifinals
K.C. Jones replaced Bill Fitch as Celtics' coach after Bucks swept Boston in East semifinals

127 1981-82   Milwaukee Bucks   5.236   55-27   East semifinals
Defended division title despite injury-plagued season for most of Bucks regulars

128 2003-04   Sacramento Kings   5.234   55-27   West semifinals
Eliminated in a seven-game series for third consecutive season, this time by No. 1 seed Timberwolves in West semifinals

129 1990-91   Boston Celtics   5.216   56-26   East semifinals
Started 29-5, but injuries resulted in rough finish, six-game loss against Pistons in East semifinals

130 1987-88   Detroit Pistons   5.200   54-28   NBA finalist
Lost Games 6 and 7 of NBA Finals against Lakers by total of four points as star guard Isiah Thomas played through an ankle injury

131 1951-52   Minneapolis Lakers   5.185   40-26   NBA champion
George Mikan relinquished league scoring crown for first time as the NBA widened the three-second lane, but Lakers nonetheless regained the league title

132 2003-04   Detroit Pistons   5.177   54-28   NBA champion
Clinched championship in five games by becoming first team to win three middle games at home since return to 2-3-2 NBA Finals format in 1985

133 1999-00   Phoenix Suns   5.160   53-29   West semifinals
Finest hour for "Backcourt 2000"; Guards Jason Kidd and Anfernee Hardaway helped Suns eliminate defending champion Spurs in first round of playoffs

134 1982-83   Los Angeles Lakers   5.125   58-24   NBA finalist
Hobbled Lakers no match for 76ers in NBA Finals

135 2003-04   Indiana Pacers   5.071   61-21   East finals
Set franchise record for wins with league-best record, but ran out of gas against eventual champion Pistons in East finals

136 1988-89   Atlanta Hawks   5.051   52-30   East first round
Added veteran center Moses Malone and won 50 games for fourth consecutive year, but upset by Bucks in five games in first round of playoffs

137 1993-94   San Antonio Spurs   5.003   55-27   West first round
Defensive-minded forward Dennis Rodman started to earn reputation as an oddball when he clotheslined Utah guard John Stockton during Spurs' first round playoff loss against Jazz

138 1987-88   Los Angeles Lakers   4.998   62-20   NBA champion
Won seven-game series in last three rounds of playoffs to fulfill coach Pat Riley's repeat title "guarantee"

139 1952-53   Minneapolis Lakers   4.990   48-22   NBA champion
First time team with league's best regular season record went on to win NBA title

140 1970-71   New York Knickerbockers   4.980   52-30   East finals
Had 4-1 regular season record against eventual champion Bucks, but Knicks upset by Bullets in East finals before they could get a shot at Milwaukee

141 1980-81   Phoenix Suns   4.971   57-25   West semifinals
Acquisition of guard Dennis Johnson helped franchise win its first division title, but season spoiled by upset loss against Kings in West semifinals

142 1978-79   San Antonio Spurs   4.963   48-34   East finals
Lost 3-1 series lead during East finals against Bullets; lost last three games by total of 14 points

143 1993-94   Atlanta Hawks   4.956   57-25   East semifinals
Feel-good season and surprise No. 1 seed spoiled by loss against Pacers in East semifinals during Lenny Wilkens' first year as Hawks' coach

144 1997-98   Miami Heat   4.954   55-27   East first round
Star center Alonzo Mourning was suspended for deciding Game 5 loss against Knicks in first round of playoffs

145 2006-07   Houston Rockets   4.952   52-30   West first round
Most dominant team in franchise history unable to win a round in the postseason; Rockets blew 2-0 lead in first round playoff series against Jazz

146 1957-58   Boston Celtics   4.948   49-23   NBA finalist
Bill Russell's ankle injury doomed Celtics during NBA Finals loss against Hawks

147 1976-77   Denver Nuggets   4.938   50-32   West semifinals
Won a division title during first season after moving from ABA to NBA

148 1967-68   Los Angeles Lakers   4.925   52-30   NBA finalist
Lakers started string of three consecutive losses in NBA Finals; just the second team to be so snake-bitten

149 1977-78   Philadelphia 76ers   4.857   55-27   East finals
Coaching change after 2-4 start (Billy Cunningham replaced Gene Shue) sparked 76ers to best record since 1969

150 2000-01   Utah Jazz   4.853   53-29   West first round
Lost first round playoff series against Mavericks after holding 2-0 lead

151 1960-61   Boston Celtics   4.816   57-22   NBA champion
Celtics had a record eight Hall of Famers; seven players, plus coach Red Auerbach

152 1998-99   Miami Heat   4.780   33-17   East first round
Became first No. 1 seed in Eastern Conference to lose in first round against a No. 8 seed with five-game defeat at hands of Knicks

153 1968-69   Philadelphia 76ers   4.765   55-27   East semifinals
Celtics eliminated 76ers from playoffs for fourth time in six years during first season after Philadelphia traded away center Wilt Chamberlain

154 1978-79   Washington Bullets   4.731   54-28   NBA finalist
Won pair of seven-game playoff series to defend conference title, but lost rematch against Sonics in NBA Finals

155 1956-57   Boston Celtics   4.692   44-28   NBA champion
Won franchise's first NBA title with double-overtime win in Game 7 of NBA Finals against Hawks

156 2003-04   Dallas Mavericks   4.689   52-30   West first round
Led league in scoring for third consecutive year, but bounced by Kings in first round of playoffs

157 1989-90   Utah Jazz   4.688   55-27   West first round
Set then-franchise record for wins during forward Karl Malone's finest season (31.0 points per game), but lost in first round of playoffs for third time in four years

158 1950-51   Minneapolis Lakers 4.688   44-24   West finals
George Mikan's finest individual season (28.4 points per game), but Lakers lost against Royals in West finals

159 1982-83   Phoenix Suns   4.673   53-29   West first round
Bounce-back season for Suns and breakthrough season for forward Larry Nance (16.7 points per game) ended with overtime loss in decisive third game of first round playoff series against Nuggets

160 1993-94   Phoenix Suns   4.630   56-26   West semifinals
Lost West semifinal against eventual champion Rockets in seven games after winning first two games in Houston

161 2006-07   Chicago Bulls   4.589   49-33   East semifinals
Swept reigning NBA champion Heat in first round of the postseason for the franchise's first playoff series win since Michael Jordan's final championship season (1998)

162 1997-98   Phoenix Suns   4.557   56-26   West first round
Sixth Man of the Year Danny Manning and newly signed forward Antonio McDyess led Phoenix to 16-win improvement, but Suns no match for Spurs in first round of playoffs

163 2002-03 New Jersey Nets 4.516 49-33 NBA finalist
Romped through East playoffs to repeat as conference champion and pushed Spurs to six games in NBA Finals

164 2000-01 Dallas Mavericks 4.459 53-29 West semifinals
Rallied from 2-0 deficit against Jazz in first round of playoffs to win franchise's first playoff series since 1988

165 1981-82 Los Angeles Lakers 4.456 57-25 NBA champion
Pat Riley took over as coach and led Lakers to title after star guard Magic Johnson demanded ouster of Paul Westhead

166 1999-00 Utah Jazz 4.441 55-27 West semifinals
Repeat of 1999 season; Jazz won division, got pushed to limit in first round of playoffs and had nothing left against Blazers in West semifinals

167 2000-01 Portland Trail Blazers 4.377 50-32 West first round
Blazers collapsed down stretch, resulting in No. 7 playoff seed and sweep loss against eventual champion Lakers in first round of playoffs

168 1971-72 Boston Celtics 4.374 56-26 East finals
Returned to playoffs after two-season absence; started string of five consecutive division titles

169 1994-95 Chicago Bulls 4.350 47-35 East semifinals
Michael Jordan ended his first retirement late in the season and helped Bulls reach East semifinals

170 1963-64 Cincinnati Royals 4.337 55-25 East finals
Star guard Oscar Robertson won his only MVP award after leading Royals to best record of franchise's Cincinnati era

171 1989-90 Philadelphia 76ers 4.328 53-29 East semifinals
Big season from forward Charles Barkley and healthy season for point guard Johnny Dawkins propelled 76ers to their only division title of the 1990s

172 1963-64 San Francisco Warriors 4.317 48-32 NBA finalist
Coach Alex Hannum pushed Warriors to 17-win improvement, division title, and NBA Finals appearance during his first season with team

173 2001-02 Dallas Mavericks 4.311 57-25 West semifinals
Amazing stat: Led league in most points and fewest turnovers

174 1952-53 New York Knickerbockers 4.284 47-23 NBA finalist
Unwanted distinction: First team to lose three consecutive NBA Finals

175   1965-66   Boston Celtics   4.277   54-26   NBA champion
Red Auerbach ended his coaching career after leading Celtics to eighth consecutive title

176   1979-80   Seattle Supersonics   4.256   56-26   West finals
Had better record than franchise's NBA finalist teams of previous two seasons, but ousted by Lakers in five games in West finals

177   1990-91   San Antonio Spurs   4.249   55-27   West first round
Spurs won division championship, but surprised by No. 7 seed Warriors in first round of playoffs

178   1969-70   Milwaukee Bucks   4.215   56-26   East finals
Franchise made 29-win improvement and reached East finals during rookie season for center Lew Alcindor (later Kareem Abdul-Jabbar)

179   1999-00   Indiana Pacers   4.210   56-26   NBA finalist
Broke through to franchise's first Finals appearance during final season for center Rik Smits, coach Larry Bird

180   1995-96   Los Angeles Lakers   4.206   53-29   West first round
Los Angeles icon Magic Johnson made a brief comeback late in the season, but couldn't get Lakers past first round of playoffs

181   1982-83   Milwaukee Bucks   4.203   51-31   East finals
Swept Boston in East semifinals, but no match for eventual champion 76ers in East finals

182   2003-04   Los Angeles Lakers   4.178   56-26   NBA finalist
"Dream Team" of center Shaquille O'Neal, shooting guard Kobe Bryant, point guard Gary Payton, and forward Karl Malone saw season end with nightmare five-game loss in NBA Finals against Pistons

183   1953-54   Syracuse Nationals   4.171   42-30   NBA finalist
Pushed Lakers to toughest of their five George Mikan era league finals triumphs; Nationals succumbed by seven points in Game 7

184   2004-05   Houston Rockets   4.167   51-31   West first round
First season together for guard Tracy McGrady and center Yao Ming was franchise's first 50-win year since 1996-1997 season, but ended in first round of playoffs

185   1993-94   Houston Rockets   4.154   58-24   NBA champion
Matched NBA record with 15 consecutive wins to start the season and never looked back en route to franchise's first NBA title

186   1988-89   Utah Jazz   4.153   51-31   West first round
Jerry Sloan took over as coach for ailing Frank Layden and Jazz didn't miss a beat

| 187 | 1965-66 | Philadelphia 76ers | 4.091 | 55-25 | East finals |

Won division title to end Celtics' nine-year run of division championships, but couldn't beat Boston in the playoffs

| 188 | 1993-94 | Utah Jazz | 4.064 | 53-29 | West finals |

Traded for efficient shooting guard Jeff Hornacek at midseason, providing ideal complementary player for John Stockton and Karl Malone

| 189 | 1968-69 | Baltimore Bullets | 4.030 | 57-25 | East semifinals |

Wes Unseld became first rookie to earn MVP honors after boosting Bullets from worst to first in East

| 190 | 1984-85 | Philadelphia 76ers | 4.029 | 58-24 | East finals |

Reached East finals during future star Charles Barkley's rookie season; would not return until 2001

| 191 | 1973-74 | Detroit Pistons | 4.005 | 52-30 | West semifinals |

Ray Scott named Coach of the Year for leading Pistons to 12-win improvement and first playoff berth since 1968

| 192 | 1979-80 | Philadelphia 76ers | 3.972 | 59-23 | NBA finalist |

Julius Erving made all-time highlight reel with memorable reverse layup during NBA Finals, but Lakers won the series 4-2

| 193 | 1996-97 | Houston Rockets | 3.950 | 57-25 | West finals |

Added Charles Barkley to lineup that included fellow Hall of Famers Hakeem Olajuwon and Clyde Drexler, but bowed out in West finals

| 194 | 1988-89 | Milwaukee Bucks | 3.919 | 49-33 | East semifinals |

Time of transition: Bucks moved into new Bradley Center, but bid farewell to stalwart guard Sidney Moncrief after season

| 195 | 1983-84 | Milwaukee Bucks | 3.910 | 50-32 | East finals |

Sidney Moncrief won second consecutive Defensive Player of the Year award in second season for the honor

| 196 | 1986-87 | Milwaukee Bucks | 3.880 | 50-32 | East semifinals |

Coach Don Nelson departed after Celtics eliminated Bucks from playoffs for third time in four years

| 197 | 1951-52 | Syracuse Nationals | 3.870 | 40-26 | East finals |

Frontliner Red Rocha and guard Paul Seymour emerged as star forward Dolph Schayes' supporting cast and helped defensive-minded Nationals to eight-win improvement

| 198 | 1967-68 | Boston Celtics | 3.847 | 54-28 | NBA champion |

Rallied from 3-1 deficit against 76ers in East finals and went on to regain NBA title

199   1968-69   Los Angeles Lakers   3.817   55-27   NBA finalist
Combination of Wilt Chamberlain, Jerry West, and Elgin Baylor couldn't win the NBA title

200   1987-88   Dallas Mavericks   3.796   53-29   West finals
Pushed eventual champion Lakers to seven games in West finals

201   1991-92   Golden State Warriors   3.781   55-27   West first round
First round playoff loss against No. 6 seed Sonics spoiled best season of Don Nelson's coaching tenure with Warriors

202   1981-82   Seattle Supersonics   3.778   52-30   West semifinals
Shooting guard Gus Williams returned to average 23.4 points per game after missing previous season because of contract dispute, helping Sonics to 18-win improvement

203   1987-88   Portland Trail Blazers   3.778   53-29   West first round
Breakthrough season for guard Clyde Drexler (27.0 points per game)

204   1976-77   Philadelphia 76ers   3.776   50-32   NBA finalist
Julius Erving led 76ers to NBA Finals during his first NBA season, but Philadelphia became first team to lose four consecutive games in Finals after winning first two

205   1987-88   Atlanta Hawks   3.772   50-32   East semifinals
Couldn't close out Celtics in East semifinals after leading 3-2; Atlanta star Dominique Wilkins and Boston icon Larry Bird staged memorable shootout in fourth quarter of Game 7

206   1994-95   Phoenix Suns   3.767   59-23   West semifinals
Lost West semifinal against eventual champion Rockets after holding 3-1 lead in series and double-digit lead in Game 7

207   2006-07   Detroit Pistons   3.754   53-29   East finals
Surged after midseason acquisition of hometown product Chris Webber, but lost in East Finals as a No. 1 seed for the third time in five years

208   1996-97   Los Angeles Lakers   3.753   56-26   West semifinals
First season in Los Angeles for newly signed center Shaquille O'Neal and rookie guard Kobe Bryant

209   2000-01   Philadelphia 76ers   3.751   56-26   NBA finalist
76ers started 10-0 and went on to first NBA Finals appearance since 1983 during star guard Allen Iverson's MVP season

210   2001-02   New Jersey Nets   3.747   52-30   NBA finalist
Preseason trade for point guard Jason Kidd resulted in surprise run to franchise's first NBA Finals appearance

211 1955-56 Philadelphia Warriors 3.741 45-27 NBA champion
Versatile rookie forward Tom Gola from nearby LaSalle final piece in Warriors' championship puzzle

212 1997-98 Atlanta Hawks 3.727 50-32 East first round
Veteran center Dikembe Mutombo repeated as Defensive Player of the Year and speedy guard Mookie Blaylock repeated as league steals leader

213 1994-95 Portland Trail Blazers 3.710 44-38 West first round
Midseason trade of franchise icon Clyde Drexler signaled the end of an era

214 1948-49 Chicago Stags 3.707 38-22 West semifinals
Added George Mikan's younger brother Ed, but fell against George's Lakers in West semifinals

215 2005-06 Memphis Grizzlies 3.704 49-33 West first round
Most dominant season in franchise history spoiled by third consecutive 4-0 loss in first round of postseason

216 1993-94 Orlando Magic 3.702 50-32 East first round
Addition of rookie guard Anfernee Hardaway resulted in franchise's first 50-win season, first playoff appearance

217 1958-59 Syracuse Nationals 3.692 35-37 East finals
Most dominant team to finish with a losing record

218 1998-99 Detroit Pistons 3.676 29-21 East first round
Standout guard Joe Dumars ended a stellar playing career and started a successful front office career after season

219 1947-48 Baltimore Bullets 3.673 28-20 BAA champion
Jumped to BAA from American Basketball League and won league title

220 1983-84 New York Knickerbockers 3.672 47-35 East semifinals
Pushed eventual champion Celtics to seven games in East semifinals

221 1996-97 Portland Trail Blazers 3.660 49-33 West first round
Arrival of problem children (talented but troubled guard Isaiah Rider and moody forward Rasheed Wallace) did result in five-win improvement

222 1993-94 Cleveland Cavaliers 3.640 47-35 East first round
Injury-plagued Cavaliers declined by seven wins during center Brad Daugherty's final season

223 1991-92 New York Knickerbockers 3.629 51-31 East semifinals
Pushed eventual champion Bulls to seven games in East semifinals during Pat Riley's first year as coach

224 2005-06   Miami Heat   3.621   52-30   NBA champion
Dwyane Wade led Heat to first league title in franchise history as Miami became first team since 1977 to win four consecutive NBA Finals games after falling behind 2-0

225 2000-01   Los Angeles Lakers   3.600   56-26   NBA champion
Set NBA record with 15-1 mark during postseason

226 1992-93   Houston Rockets   3.593   55-27   West semifinals
Star center Hakeem Olajuwon won first of two consecutive Defensive Player of the Year awards as Rockets improved by 13 wins and won a playoff series for first time since 1987

227 1979-80   Milwaukee Bucks   3.590   49-33   West semifinals
First of seven consecutive division titles

228 1952-53   Syracuse Nationals   3.541   47-24   East semifinals
Season ended with four-overtime loss against Boston, the longest playoff game ever

229 1978-79   Phoenix Suns   3.540   50-32   West finals
Had 3-2 series lead in West finals against eventual league champion Sonics; lost last two games by total of five points

230 1951-52   Boston Celtics   3.530   39-27   East semifinals
Only team in pre-shot clock era to average over 90 points per game

231 1987-88   Denver Nuggets   3.525   54-28   West semifinals
Established NBA franchise record for wins in a season

232 1998-99   Indiana Pacers   3.523   33-17   East finals
No. 8 seed Knicks handed Pacers fourth East finals loss in six years

233 1987-88   Chicago Bulls   3.496   50-32   East semifinals
Michael Jordan won first of his five MVP awards, along with Defensive Player of the Year honor

234 1977-78   Phoenix Suns   3.481   49-33   West first round
Rookie of the Year guard Walter Davis key to 15-win improvement

235 2001-02   Minnesota   3.476   50-32   West first round
            Timberwolves
Promising point guard Terrell Brandon's career derailed by injury

236 1989-90   San Antonio Spurs   3.445   56-26   West semifinals
Rookie of the Year center David Robinson led Spurs to 35-win improvement

237 1980-81   Los Angeles Lakers   3.422   54-28   West first round
Injury-plagued season for young point guard Magic Johnson spoiled title defense

238 1997-98   San Antonio Spurs   3.420   56-26   West semifinals
Spurs improved by 36 wins thanks to center David Robinson's return from injury, addition of rookie forward Tim Duncan

239 1988-89   New York Knickerbockers   3.410   52-30   East semifinals
Coach Rick Pitino left for the University of Kentucky after leading Knicks to first division title since 1971

240 1983-84   Detroit Pistons   3.405   49-33   East first round
Start of nine-year run of playoff appearances coincided with Chuck Daly's first year as coach

241 1973-74   Boston Celtics   3.403   56-26   NBA champion
Boston center Dave Cowens outscored Bucks center Kareem Abdul-Jabbar 28-26 during Celtics' 102-87 triumph in Game 7 of NBA Finals

242 1994-95   Indiana Pacers   3.401   52-30   East finals
Won franchise's first NBA division title and reached Game 7 of East finals for second consecutive year

243 2006-07   Cleveland Cavaliers   3.397   50-32   NBA finalist
LeBron James scored 48 points in pivotal Game 5 of East finals against Pistons to propel Cavaliers to their first NBA Finals appearance

244 1983-84   Los Angeles Lakers   3.388   54-28   NBA finalist
Should have swept NBA Finals; lost Games 2 and 4 in overtime during seven-game loss against Celtics

245 2004-05   Detroit Pistons   3.385   54-28   NBA finalist
Loss in Game 7 of NBA Finals against Spurs ended strings of five consecutive wins in elimination games and 11 consecutive wins in potential series-clinching games

246 1991-92   Boston Celtics   3.377   51-31   East semifinals
Boston icon Larry Bird retired during the summer after Celtics lost in seven games against Cavaliers in East semifinals

247 1972-73   Chicago Bulls   3.376   51-31   West semifinals
Eliminated from playoffs by Lakers in West semifinals for third consecutive season

248 1950-51   Philadelphia Warriors   3.346   40-26   East semifinals
Rookie forward Paul Arizin contributed to 14-win improvement

249 1962-63   Syracuse Nationals   3.345   48-32   East semifinals
Franchise improved by seven wins during standout forward Chet Walker's rookie season and then moved to Philadelphia

250 1946-47   Chicago Stags   3.342   39-22   BAA finalist
Surprised favored Capitols in league semifinals, but surprised by Warriors in league finals

251 1986-87   Detroit Pistons   3.342   52-30   East finals
Botched inbounds pass late in Game 5 of East finals against Celtics probably kept Pistons out of NBA Finals

252 1969-70   Philadelphia 76ers 3.322   42-40   East semifinals
Unraveling of 76ers continued with departure of starting forward Chet Walker and 13-win decline

253 1989-90   Boston Celtics   3.319   52-30   East first round
First round playoff loss against Knicks made these Celtics the first team in franchise history to lose a postseason series after winning the first two games at home

254 1993-94   Indiana Pacers   3.286   47-35   East finals
Reggie Miller's 25-point fourth quarter during Game 5 of East finals versus superfan Spike Lee and Knicks gave Pacers 3-2 series lead, but Indiana couldn't close the deal

255 1979-80   Phoenix Suns   3.273   55-27   West semifinals
First of five times Lakers would eliminate Suns from the playoffs during the 1980s

256 2000-01   Milwaukee Bucks   3.242   52-30   East finals
Won first division title since 1986, but gave up big lead in pivotal Game 5 of seven-game East finals loss against 76ers

257 1990-91   Houston Rockets   3.217   52-30   West first round
Don Chaney named league's Coach of the Year for guiding team to 11-win improvement despite injury-plagued season for center Hakeem Olajuwon, but Rockets lost in first round of playoffs for fourth consecutive year

258 1970-71   Los Angeles Lakers 3.200   48-34   West finals
Injuries limited high-flying forward Elgin Baylor to two games; he would retire early in following season

259 1983-84   Portland Trail Blazers 3.196 48-34 West first round
Blazers got a boost from rookie guard Clyde Drexler, but lost decisive Game 5 at home to conclude first round playoff series against Suns

260 1977-78   San Antonio Spurs 3.195   52-30   East semifinals
Smooth shooting guard George Gervin won first of four scoring titles to lead Spurs to first division title

261 1996-97 New York Knickerbockers 3.195 57-25 East semifinals
Knick suspensions resulted in loss of 3-1 lead and series in East semifinals against Heat

262 1973-74 Chicago Bulls 3.170 54-28 West finals
Won a playoff series for first time in franchise history, but swept by Lakers in West finals

263 1987-88 Utah Jazz 3.163 47-35 West semifinals
Karl Malone and John Stockton burst into national prominence as Jazz pushed eventual champion Lakers to seven games in West semifinals

264 1982-83 San Antonio Spurs 3.154 53-29 West finals
Addition of center Artis Gilmore boosted Spurs to then-franchise record for wins in a season

265 1981-82 Phoenix Suns 3.145 46-36 West semifinals
Preseason elbow injury to starting guard Walter Davis contributed to offensive struggles and 11-win decline, but Suns recovered to win a series during the postseason

266 2001-02 Seattle Supersonics 3.140 45-37 West first round
Pushed No. 2 seed Spurs to full five games in first round of playoffs

267 1990-91 Utah Jazz 3.132 54-28 West semifinals
John Stockton set single-season record for total assists with 1,164

268 1946-47 Philadelphia Warriors 3.125 35-25 BAA champion
"Jumping" Joe Fulks led league in scoring, led Warriors to first BAA championship

269 2001-02 Portland Trail Blazers 3.105 49-33 West first round
Eliminated from playoffs by Lakers for fifth time in six years

270 1990-91 Detroit Pistons 3.098 50-32 East finals
Two-time defending champions ended reign by refusing to shake hands with Bulls after Chicago sweep in East finals

271 1976-77 Golden State Warriors 3.097 46-36 West semifinals
Warriors would not return to postseason until 1987 after seven-game loss against Lakers in West semifinals

272 1995-96 Indiana Pacers 3.083 52-30 East first round
Eye socket injury to leading scorer Reggie Miller contributed to loss against Hawks in first round of playoffs

273 1972-73 Golden State Warriors 3.079 47-35 West finals
Warriors won four fewer games despite high-scoring forward Rick Barry's return from the ABA, but team did upset Bucks in first round of playoffs

274 2002-03   Detroit Pistons   3.077   50-32   East finals
Coach Rick Carlisle fired after a pair of 50-win seasons and division titles
275 1998-99   Los Angeles Lakers   3.002   31-19   West semifinals
Wild season included three coaches, a Dennis Rodman appearance, and a sweep loss against eventual champion Spurs in West semifinals
276 2006-07   Utah Jazz   2.974   51-31   West finals
Franchise-best 12-1 start set the tone for season that featured Utah's first playoff appearance since 2003, first division title since 2000, and first appearance in the West final since 1998
277 1992-93   Portland Trail Blazers 2.969 51-31   West first round
Star guard Clyde Drexler limited to 49 games because of injuries, resulting in end of Blazers' reign as top team in Western Conference
278 1999-00   Sacramento Kings   2.967   44-38   West first round
Pushed No. 1 seed Lakers to full five games in first round of playoffs
279 1982-83   Seattle Supersonics 2.955   48-34   West first round
Seattle general manager Zollie Volchok named NBA's Executive of the Year for getting one last productive season from rapidly declining forward David Thompson and overseeing 12-0 start
280 1949-50   Indianapolis   2.946   39-25   West finals
             Olympians
University of Kentucky and 1948 U.S. Olympic stars Alex Groza and Ralph Beard had success during their first NBA seasons
281 1978-79   Los Angeles Lakers   2.941   47-35   West semifinals
Franchise underwent facelift after season; Jerry Buss took over as owner, Jerry West moved from coach to general manager, and Lakers took guard Magic Johnson with No. 1 overall pick in draft
282 1997-98   Cleveland Cavaliers 2.934   47-35   East first round
Standout forward Shawn Kemp's first season in Cleveland was his most successful
283 1994-95   Charlotte Hornets   2.907   50-32   East first round
Franchise's first 50-win season spoiled by playoff loss against Bulls and newly un-retired Michael Jordan
284 1953-54   Minneapolis Lakers   2.901   46-26   NBA champion
Hall of Fame center George Mikan retired after leading Lakers to fifth title in six seasons
285 1984-85   Portland Trail Blazers 2.896 42-40   West semifinals
Rookie center Sam Bowie, taken with No. 2 overall draft pick, contributed 10.0 points per game; No. 3 pick was Michael Jordan

286 2002-03 Indiana Pacers 2.891 48-34 East first round
Coach Isiah Thomas coached East in All-Star Game, but was dismissed after Pacers staggered down stretch and lost against Celtics in first round of playoffs

287 1993-94 Chicago Bulls 2.890 55-27 East semifinals
Bulls pushed eventual conference champion Knicks to seven games in East semifinals during first season after Michael Jordan's first retirement

288 1960-61 St. Louis Hawks 2.883 51-28 NBA finalist
Rookie point guard Lenny Wilkens helped Hawks win fifth consecutive division title and make franchise's most recent NBA Finals appearance

289 1951-52 Rochester Royals 2.856 41-25 West finals
Won third division title in four BAA/NBA seasons; would not win another until the 2001-2002 season

290 1974-75 Chicago Bulls 2.852 47-35 West finals
Had 3-2 lead in West finals against eventual champion Warriors

291 1974-75 Golden State Warriors 2.849 48-34 NBA champion
Warriors won only title of franchise's West Coast era with most surprising sweep in NBA Finals history; Finals victim Bullets had 12 more wins during regular season

292 1989-90 Chicago Bulls 2.849 55-27 East finals
Star forward Scottie Pippen's migraine headache derailed Bulls in Game 7 loss against Pistons in East finals

293 1972-73 Baltimore Bullets 2.847 52-30 East semifinals
Acquisition of high-scoring forward Elvin Hayes triggered Bullets' 14-win improvement during franchise's final season in Baltimore

294 2002-03 Portland Trail Blazers 2.844 50-32 West first round
Pushed Mavericks to seven games in first round of playoffs after falling behind 3-0

295 1979-80 Kansas City Kings 2.844 47-35 West first round
Winning record gave franchise consecutive winning seasons for first time since 1966; it wouldn't happen again until 2000

296 1994-95 New York Knickerbockers 2.839 55-27 East semifinals
Patrick Ewing missed potential tying layup at buzzer of Game 7 to end East semifinals loss against Pacers

297 1998-99 Orlando Magic 2.826 33-17 East first round
Coach Chuck Daly squeezed solid season out of veteran group; Magic then disassembled team for salary cap purposes

298   1991-92   San Antonio Spurs   2.810   47-35   West first round
Coach Larry Brown departed at midseason to take new job with Clippers
299   1999-00   Miami Heat   2.808   52-30   East semifinals
Knicks eliminated Heat from playoffs for third consecutive year, this time in seven games in East semifinals
300   2003-04   Memphis Grizzlies   2.786   50-32   West first round
Coach of the Year Hubie Brown led Grizzlies to franchise's first winning record, first playoff berth
301   1979-80   Atlanta Hawks   2.763   50-32   East semifinals
League-best defense helped Hawks win division title
302   1958-59   St. Louis Hawks   2.755   49-23   West finals
Won division title by 16 games, but surprised by Lakers and flashy rookie forward Elgin Baylor in West finals
303   1949-50   Anderson Packers   2.728   37-27   NBA semifinals
Only NBA franchise to drop out of the league after a season that included a playoff series victory
304   1978-79   Kansas City Kings   2.718   48-34   West semifinals
Rookie of the Year Phil Ford and Coach of the Year Cotton Fitzsimmons pushed Kings to franchise's best record of Kansas City era
305   1965-66   Los Angeles Lakers   2.713   45-35   NBA finalist
Lakers nearly made Celtics coach Red Auerbach eat victory cigar in his final game, but comeback bid fell short in 95-93 loss in Game 7 of NBA Finals
306   1978-79   Seattle Supersonics 2.696   52-30   NBA champion
Won NBA Finals rematch against defending champion Bullets to claim franchise's only title
307   1986-87   Portland Trail Blazers 2.690 49-33   West first round
First-year coach Mike Schuler named NBA's Coach of the Year for overseeing nine-win improvement
308   1947-48   Chicago Stags   2.666   28-20   BAA semifinals
Stags guard Max Zaslofsky the first Chicago professional player to win a league scoring title; Michael Jordan would be the next
309   1982-83   New Jersey Nets   2.662   49-33   East first round
Team deflated by departure of coach Larry Brown with six games left in regular season
310   1964-65   St. Louis Hawks   2.647   45-35   West first round
Leg injury limited Hall of Fame forward Bob Pettit to 50 games during his final season, but he contributed 22.5 points per game

311 1976-77   Los Angeles Lakers   2.645   53-29   West finals
Won division title and set foundation for future dynasty by allowing guard Gail Goodrich to depart in exchange for future No. 1 draft pick used to select Magic Johnson.

312 2002-03   Utah Jazz   2.635   47-35   West first round
Final season in Salt Lake City for Karl Malone and John Stockton

313 1959-60   Syracuse Nationals   2.632   45-30   East semifinals
Acquisition of talented forward George Yardley late in previous season paid off in 10-win improvement during this season

314 1962-63   Los Angeles Lakers   2.612   53-27   NBA finalist
Returned to NBA Finals even though star guard Jerry West missed 35 games with a hamstring tear

315 1997-98   New York Knickerbockers   2.609   43-39   East semifinals
No. 7 seed Knicks upset No. 2 seed Heat in first round before falling against Pacers in East semifinals

316 1984-85   Detroit Pistons   2.599   46-36   East semifinals
Isiah Thomas set then-single-season record for assist average (13.98)

317 1999-00   Minnesota Timberwolves   2.596   50-32   West first round
Franchise's first 50-win season, but team stripped of multiple first round draft picks because of salary cap violations

318 1988-89   Seattle Supersonics   2.592   47-35   West semifinals
Shooting guard Dale Ellis made more 3-pointers (162) than nine teams

319 1977-78   Los Angeles Lakers   2.587   45-37   West first round
Had seven players who made All-Star teams on roster at various times during season, but couldn't get out of the first round of the playoffs

320 1947-48   Washington Capitols   2.579   28-20
Odd team out in bizarre three-team playoff for two postseason berths

321 2002-03   Los Angeles Lakers   2.577   50-32   West semifinals
Star center Shaquille O'Neal missed first half of season with an injury and three-time defending champion Lakers never found their stride

322 1961-62   Philadelphia Warriors 2.572   49-32   East finals
Wilt Chamberlain scored 100 points in a game and averaged 50.4 points per game for the season during franchise's final year in Philadelphia

323 2000-01   Houston Rockets   2.568   45-37
Went 16-0 against Central Division, but missed postseason

324 1952-53   Rochester Royals   2.566   44-26   West semifinals
Upset in West semifinals by Pistons for second time in four years

325   1993-94   Portland Trail Blazers 2.558   47-35   West first round
Coach Rick Adelman was let go after team's record declined for third consecutive season
326   2004-05   Memphis Grizzlies   2.549   45-37   West first round
Reigning Coach of the Year Hubie Brown left team because of health reasons, but Grizzlies regrouped under replacement Mike Fratello and made the postseason
327   1966-67   San Francisco   2.546   44-37   NBA finalist
                   Warriors
Star forward Rick Barry led league in scoring, pushing Warriors to NBA Finals
328   1998-99   Phoenix Suns   2.525   27-23   West first round
Standout point guard Jason Kidd won first of three consecutive assist titles
329   2004-05   Seattle Supersonics   2.496   52-30   West semifinals
Sonics started 17-3 and went on to first division title since 1998
330   1982-83   New York   2.488   44-38   East semifinals
                   Knickerbockers
Knicks enjoyed 11-win improvement thanks to league-best defense and arrival of high-scoring forward Bernard King, coach Hubie Brown
331   2000-01   Phoenix Suns   2.487   51-31   West first round
"Backcourt 2000" of Jason Kidd and Anfernee Hardaway didn't carry over to 2001 as Hardaway played just four games because of injury
332   2005-06   Los Angeles Lakers   2.485   45-37   West first round
Reunion of star guard Kobe Bryant and coach Phil Jackson helped Bryant (35.4 points per game) win his first scoring title and boosted Lakers to 11-win improvement
333   1950-51   Rochester Royals   2.483   41-27   NBA champion
Beat division rival Lakers in West finals and held off Knicks in NBA Finals to win franchise's only NBA title
334   2004-05   Sacramento Kings   2.473   50-32   West first round
Kings hampered by injuries, deadline trade of forward Chris Webber
335   1995-96   Cleveland Cavaliers   2.471   47-35   East first round
Little offensive firepower, but reached postseason because of league-best defense
336   1998-99   Atlanta Hawks   2.451   31-19   East semifinals
Sweep loss at hands of No. 8 seed Knicks in East semifinals spelled end of the line for Hawks core group

337 1995-96   Detroit Pistons   2.434   46-36   East first round
Renewed emphasis on defense helped Pistons to 18-win improvement and playoff berth during promising forward Grant Hill's second season

338 1985-86   Atlanta Hawks   2.427   50-32   East semifinals
Hawks forward Dominique Wilkins won league scoring title; Michael Jordan would win the next seven

339 1973-74   New York   2.419   49-33   East finals
          Knickerbockers
Knicks' rapid decline began with eight-win slip during center Willis Reed's final season

340 1993-94   Miami Heat   2.416   42-40   East first round
Pushed top-seeded Hawks to five games in first round of playoffs and then blew up promising young team

341 1999-00   Charlotte Hornets   2.398   49-33   East first round
Season haunted by midseason death of guard Bobby Phills (auto accident)

342 1959-60   Philadelphia Warriors 2.390 49-26   East finals
Wilt Chamberlain averaged 37.6 points and 27.0 rebounds per game as a rookie

343 1973-74   Golden State   2.374   44-38
          Warriors
Playoff format change made Warriors the first team to finish second in a division but miss the postseason

344 1990-91   Milwaukee Bucks   2.354   48-34   East first round
Last year in string of 12 consecutive playoff appearances

345 1997-98   Charlotte Hornets   2.337   51-31   East semifinals
Departure of pint-sized point guard Muggsy Bogues left shooting guard Dell Curry as last player remaining from Hornets' expansion season

346 2002-03   Minnesota   2.333   51-31   West first round
          Timberwolves
Reward for earning home-court advantage in first round of playoffs for first time in franchise history: Six-game loss against reigning champion Lakers

347 1967-68   St. Louis Hawks   2.327   56-26   West semifinals
Won a division title and posted most wins in a season during franchise's time in St. Louis, and then moved to Atlanta

348 1980-81   San Antonio Spurs   2.317   52-30   West semifinals
Upset postseason loss against Texas rival Rockets spoiled season featuring 11-win improvement, first of three consecutive division titles

349 1975-76 Cleveland Cavaliers 2.314 49-33 East finals
Season of firsts for Cavaliers: First winning record, first playoff appearance, first playoff series win

350 1946-47 St. Louis Bombers 2.312 38-23 BAA quarterfinals
First season in franchise's four-year history was its best

351 1983-84 Philadelphia 76ers 2.303 52-30 East first round
Title defense short-circuited by loss against Nets in first round of playoffs, with all three losses at home

352 1970-71 Phoenix Suns 2.297 48-34
Dick Van Arsdale (last player remaining from Suns' expansion season) and new coach Cotton Fitzsimmons led Phoenix to its first winning record

353 1971-72 New York Knickerbockers 2.285 48-34 NBA finalist
Trade for star guard Earl Monroe provided a boost, but Knicks no match for Lakers in NBA Finals

354 1985-86 Philadelphia 76ers 2.283 54-28 East semifinals
Julius Erving missed shot at buzzer of Game 7 that would have won East semifinal series against Bucks

355 1949-50 New York Knickerbockers 2.266 40-28 East finals
Future Knicks coach Dick McGuire led league in assists as a rookie

356 1998-99 Philadelphia 76ers 2.264 28-22 East semifinals
Allen Iverson won his first scoring title and 76ers became sixth team Larry Brown would guide to the playoffs

357 1994-95 Houston Rockets 2.251 47-35 NBA champion
Became lowest seed (No. 6) to win title after late-season trade reunited center Hakeem Olajuwon with old University of Houston teammate Clyde Drexler

358 1992-93 San Antonio Spurs 2.249 49-33 West semifinals
The Jerry Tarkanian coaching experiment ended after 20 games, 9-11 record

359 1970-71 Boston Celtics 2.245 44-38
Rookie center Dave Cowens key piece in Celtics' rapid rebuilding process

360 1961-62 Syracuse Nationals 2.235 41-39 East semifinals
Standout shooting guard Hal Greer first player other than Dolph Schayes to lead team in scoring for a season as Schayes missed 24 games with a broken jaw

361 1985-86 Houston Rockets 2.235 51-31 NBA finalist
"Twin Towers" Ralph Sampson and Akeem Olajuwon boosted Rockets to the NBA Finals

362 1996-97   Cleveland Cavaliers   2.228   42-40
Home loss against Bullets on last day of the season cost Cavaliers a playoff spot

363 1975-76   Boston Celtics   2.225   54-28   NBA champion
Lucky 13th title for franchise keyed by triple-overtime victory over Suns in pivotal Game 5 of NBA Finals

364 1995-96   New York Knickerbockers   2.224   47-35   East semifinals
Coach Don Nelson lasted just 59 games as Pat Riley's successor

365 2005-06   Cleveland Cavaliers   2.217   50-32   East semifinals
Phenom forward LeBron James made his first playoff appearance a memorable one; led team to first playoff series win since 1993 and then helped Cavaliers push No. 1 seed Pistons to seven games in East semifinals

366 1953-54   Rochester Royals   2.213   44-28   West finals
Advanced to fourth West final in six years, but would not win another playoff series during the rest of franchise's time in Rochester

367 1995-96   Portland Trail Blazers 2.211   44-38   West first round
Franchise began makeover-on-the-fly after season ended with historically one-sided 102-64 Game 5 loss against Jazz in first round of playoffs

368 1957-58   Syracuse Nationals   2.182   41-31   East semifinals
Syracuse franchise icon Dolph Schayes passed George Mikan's NBA career record total of 11,764 points during season

369 1975-76   Washington Bullets   2.171   48-34   East semifinals
Added star guard Dave Bing, but failed to win division for first time in six seasons and lost in seven games against Cavaliers in East semifinals

370 1980-81   Chicago Bulls   2.166   45-37   East semifinals
Team enjoyed 15-win improvement, including 13 wins in last 15 games, as center Artis Gilmore returned from injury-plagued season to play full campaign

371 1984-85   Denver Nuggets   2.163   52-30   West finals
Improved just enough on defense (next-to-last in league instead of dead last) to improve by 14 wins

372 1947-48   New York Knickerbockers   2.161   26-22   BAA quarterfinals
Seeds of a contender in place with rookie guard Carl Braun, first-year coach Joe Lapchick

373 1993-94   New Jersey Nets   2.148   45-37   East first round
Coach Chuck Daly's patience wore out despite two playoff appearances in two seasons

374	1947-48	St. Louis Bombers	2.145	29-19	BAA semifinals

Held 3-2 series lead in BAA semifinals against Warriors, but lost last two games by combined 62 points

375	1974-75	Buffalo Braves	2.144	49-33	East semifinals

Star forward Bob McAdoo's best year (34.5 points per game) and franchise record for wins in a season

376	2004-05	Denver Nuggets	2.123	49-33	West first round

Nuggets finished season on a 28-6 tear under new coach George Karl

377	1978-79	Milwaukee Bucks	2.118	38-44	

Hard-luck season put franchise in position to draft standout guard Sidney Moncrief

378	2003-04	Houston Rockets	2.114	45-37	West first round

New coach Jeff Van Gundy helped Rockets make playoffs for first time in the Yao Ming era

379	2000-01	New York Knickerbockers	2.094	48-34	East first round

Lost decisive Game 5 of first round series against Raptors at home to conclude first season after trade of longtime center Patrick Ewing

380	1948-49	Washington Capitols	2.083	38-22	BAA finalist

Coach Red Auerbach's first league finals appearance ended in six-game loss against Lakers and George Mikan

381	2003-04	New Jersey Nets	2.029	47-35	East semifinals

Had 3-2 lead in East semifinals against eventual NBA champion Pistons

382	1996-97	Charlotte Hornets	2.020	54-28	East first round

Hornets general manager Bob Bass named NBA's Executive of the Year for directing 13-win improvement and franchise record for wins during season after departure of star forward Larry Johnson

383	1991-92	Detroit Pistons	2.019	48-34	East first round

Led league in defense for third consecutive year, but lost first round playoff series in five games against Knicks

384	1964-65	Cincinnati Royals	1.991	48-32	East semifinals

"Reward" for second place finish: East semifinals loss against 76ers and newly acquired Wilt Chamberlain

385	1982-83	Portland Trail Blazers	1.961	46-36	West semifinals

Won a playoff series for first time since 1977 championship run

386	1953-54	Boston Celtics	1.958	42-30	East finals

Second of three consecutive losses in East finals for pre-Bill Russell Celtics

387	1988-89	Chicago Bulls	1.953	47-35	East finals

Michael Jordan's game-winning shot in Game 5 of first round series against Cavaliers propelled Bulls to East finals

388	1954-55	Fort Wayne Pistons	1.944	43-29	NBA finalist

Couldn't hold 17-point lead or convert on final possession during 92-91 loss against Syracuse in Game 7 of NBA Finals

389	1984-85	Dallas Mavericks	1.914	44-38	West first round

Third year of team's five-year run of leading the NBA in fewest turnovers, but team improved by just one win

390	1978-79	Atlanta Hawks	1.912	46-36	East semifinals

Won a playoff series for the first time as an Eastern Conference team; pushed defending champion Bullets to seven games in East semifinals

391	1969-70	Baltimore Bullets	1.909	50-32	East semifinals

Highest-scoring team in franchise history pushed eventual champion Knicks to seven games in East semifinals

392	1952-53	Boston Celtics	1.899	46-25	East finals

Longest playoff game in NBA history (four overtimes) during East semifinals against Syracuse clinched franchise's first win in a playoff series

393	1960-61	Syracuse Nationals	1.886	38-41	East finals

No. 2 scorer George Yardley retired before season, contributing to seven-win decline

394	1991-92	Seattle Supersonics	1.880	47-35	West semifinals

George Karl came in as coach at midseason and led Sonics to 27-15 finish

395	2002-03	Philadelphia 76ers	1.877	48-34	East semifinals

Uneasy marriage between leading scorer Allen Iverson and coach Larry Brown ended after season as Brown left for Detroit

396	1981-82	San Antonio Spurs	1.874	48-34	West finals

Went 0-3 at home during six-game loss against Lakers in West finals

397	2000-01	Miami Heat	1.845	50-32	East first round

Onset of standout center Alonzo Mourning's kidney illness prevented a strong team from being even stronger

398	1980-81	New York Knickerbockers	1.824	50-32	East first round

Coach Red Holzman still had the magic touch at age 60, leading 11-win improvement

399	1997-98	Detroit Pistons	1.822	37-45	

Nothing went right for these Pistons, resulting in firing of coach Doug Collins after 45 games

400 2001-02   Boston Celtics   1.822   49-33   East finals
Lost East finals against Nets, but set playoff record by rallying from 21 down after three quarters to win Game 3 of series

401 1991-92   Indiana Pacers   1.819   40-42   East first round
Versatile reserve forward Detlef Schrempf joined Kevin McHale as only repeat winners of Sixth Man of the Year award

402 2000-01   Toronto Raptors   1.809   47-35   East semifinals
Leading scorer Vince Carter received college degree at North Carolina in morning; missed potential series-winning shot in Game 7 of East semifinals against 76ers in afternoon

403 1961-62   Los Angeles Lakers 1.804   54-26   NBA finalist
Lakers had a shot to win in regulation during 110-107 overtime loss in Game 7 of NBA Finals against Celtics

404 1949-50   Chicago Stags   1.797   40-28   Central semifinals
Franchise folded after season despite four winning records in four years

405 1992-93   Utah Jazz   1.786   47-35   West first round
Some incorrectly thought eight-win slip indicated John Stockton and Karl Malone had passed their primes

406 1967-68   New York   1.778   43-39   East semifinals
             Knickerbockers
Red Holzman took over as coach after 15-22 start and directed Knicks to 28-17 finish

407 2001-02   Detroit Pistons   1.766   50-32   East semifinals
Rick Carlisle named Coach of the Year after squeezing 50 wins from then-lightly regarded crew

408 2002-03   Houston Rockets   1.765   43-39
Rockets improved by 15 wins with rookie center Yao Ming and healthy guard Steve Francis, but coach Rudy Tomjanovich was pushed out after team missed playoffs for fourth consecutive year

409 1970-71   Philadelphia 76ers 1.759   47-35   East semifinals
Final season in record string of 22 consecutive playoff appearances dating back to franchise's first NBA season

410 1997-98   New Jersey Nets   1.752   43-39   East first round
Made playoffs on strength of seven players with double-digit scoring averages

411 1969-70   Los Angeles Lakers 1.735   46-36   NBA finalist
Wilt Chamberlain missed most of season, but returned for playoffs to help Lakers push eventual champion Knicks to seven games in NBA Finals

412   1978-79   Philadelphia 76ers   1.732   47-35   East semifinals
Former Philadelphia star Billy Cunningham transformed 76ers into a defense-oriented team during his first full season as coach

413   2005-06   Los Angeles Clippers   1.723   47-35   West semifinals
Career year for forward Elton Brand (24.7 points per game) boosted Clippers to best record and first playoff series win of franchise's California history

414   1993-94   Golden State Warriors   1.722   50-32   West first round
Careful what you wish for: Coach Don Nelson got the big man he always thought he needed in Rookie of the Year Chris Webber

415   1992-93   Indiana Pacers   1.718   41-41   East first round
Pacers completed first four years of the 1990s with 164-164 record and four first round playoff exits

416   1968-69   Atlanta Hawks   1.709   48-34   West finals
Traded away point guard Lenny Wilkens before the season, but still reached West finals during franchise's first season in Atlanta

417   1990-91   Golden State Warriors   1.680   44-38   West semifinals
Finest hour for "Run TMC"; Tim Hardaway, Mitch Richmond, and Chris Mullin led Warriors to first round playoff victory against No. 2 seed Spurs

418   2000-01   Minnesota Timberwolves   1.675   47-35   West first round
Team held up well after tragic offseason death of forward Malik Sealy (auto accident)

419   1964-65   Los Angeles Lakers   1.673   49-31   NBA finalist
Jerry West averaged 40.8 points during postseason after Elgin Baylor went out with a shattered kneecap, but Celtics again denied Lakers in NBA Finals

420   1998-99   Houston Rockets   1.669   31-19   West first round
Scottie Pippen-Charles Barkley-Hakeem Olajuwon combination couldn't win a playoff series

421   1959-60   St. Louis Hawks   1.666   46-29   NBA finalist
Pushed Celtics to seven games in NBA Finals, but suffered second of three Finals losses against Boston in five years

422   1996-97   Washington Bullets   1.652   44-38   East first round
Made playoffs for first time since 1988, but bounced by eventual champion Bulls in first round

423 2005-06   Indiana Pacers   1.644   41-41   East first round
Another season spoiled by internal turmoil; injury-plagued Pacers benched standout forward Ron Artest in December and traded him to Kings in January

424 2004-05   Minnesota   1.633   44-38
          Timberwolves
Missed postseason as standout guards Latrell Sprewell and Sam Cassell bickered about contract situations, ending string of eight consecutive playoff appearances

425 1995-96   Houston Rockets   1.631   48-34   West semifinals
Loss against Sonics in West semifinals ended string of eight consecutive wins in elimination games

426 2002-03   New Orleans Hornets   1.630   47-35   East first round
Coach Paul Silas led team to playoffs in all four of his full seasons, but was fired after franchise's first season in New Orleans

427 2006-07   Denver Nuggets   1.591   45-37   West first round
Acquired superstar guard Allen Iverson in blockbuster midseason trade, but still lost in the first round of the playoffs for the fourth consecutive season

428 1989-90   Houston Rockets   1.589   41-41   West first round
Star center Hakeem Olajuwon's quadruple-double game highlighted season

429 2005-06   Washington Wizards   1.587   42-40   East first round
Fell 4-2 against Cavaliers in the first round of the playoffs, with the last three losses all by one point

430 1949-50   Fort Wayne Pistons   1.583   40-28   Central finals
Realignment, solid season at guard from newcomer Fred Schaus helped Pistons to 18-win improvement

431 2005-06   Sacramento Kings   1.570   44-38   West first round
Went 26-14 after trading for forward Ron Artest to ensure eighth consecutive playoff appearance

432 2000-01   Charlotte Hornets   1.564   46-36   East semifinals
Led series 3-2 and held lead late in Game 6 of East semifinals against Bucks before succumbing

433 1956-57   Philadelphia Warriors 1.544   37-35   East semifinals
Warriors' title defense a mere sidebar during first year of the Bill Russell era in Boston

434 1980-81   Indiana Pacers   1.535   44-38   East first round
Coach of the Year Jack McKinney led Pacers to franchise's first NBA playoff appearance

435 1993-94 Denver Nuggets 1.510 42-40 West semifinals
Became first No. 8 seed to win a playoff series with first round upset of Sonics; nearly rallied from 3-0 deficit against Jazz in West semifinals

436 1988-89 Philadelphia 76ers 1.504 46-36 East first round
Star forward Charles Barkley given just enough help to get 76ers back into playoffs after one-year absence

437 1984-85 Houston Rockets 1.496 48-34 West first round
Rockets returned to postseason in first year together for centers Ralph Sampson and Akeem Olajuwon

438 1987-88 Seattle Supersonics 1.494 44-38 West first round
Posted first winning record since 1984, but couldn't repeat previous season's run to West finals

439 2003-04 Denver Nuggets 1.487 43-39 West first round
Rookie forward Carmelo Anthony propelled Nuggets to 26-win improvement, first playoff berth since 1995

440 1977-78 Seattle Supersonics 1.482 47-35 NBA finalist
Lenny Wilkens came back to franchise as coach and led Sonics to 42-18 stretch run, NBA Finals appearance

441 1995-96 Miami Heat 1.450 42-40 East first round
New coach/general manager Pat Riley quickly put stamp on team by trading for center Alonzo Mourning and point guard Tim Hardaway

442 2002-03 Phoenix Suns 1.440 44-38 West first round
Amare Stoudemire became first preps-to-pros player to win Rookie of the Year award as Suns returned to postseason

443 1989-90 Denver Nuggets 1.433 43-39 West first round
End of successful chapter in Nuggets history with departure of high-scoring forward Alex English, firing of coach Doug Moe

444 1976-77 Houston Rockets 1.428 49-33 East finals
First trip to conference finals in franchise history keyed by early season acquisition of ABA refugee Moses Malone

445 1953-54 Fort Wayne Pistons 1.406 40-32 West semifinals
Team got talent boost with arrival of 1950 draft pick George Yardley, trade for standout guard Max Zaslofsky

446 1963-64 St. Louis Hawks 1.405 46-34 West finals
Bob Pettit passed 20,000 career points mark, became NBA's then-all-time leading scorer

447 1996-97 Indiana Pacers 1.405 39-43
Injury to center Rik Smits, players' ennui with coach Larry Brown kept Pacers out of playoffs

448 1999-00 New York   1.377 50-32 East finals
              Knickerbockers
Blew double-digit lead in pivotal Game 5 of six-game East finals loss against Pacers

449 1957-58 New York   1.372 35-37
              Knickerbockers
Knicks hovered around .500 during first season after original NBA iron man Harry Gallatin's retirement

450 2001-02 Philadelphia 76ers 1.358 43-39 East first round
Star guard Allen Iverson produced better statistics than his MVP season, but 76ers couldn't recapture the magic of previous season's run to NBA Finals

451 1962-63 St. Louis Hawks 1.358 48-32 West finals
Harry Gallatin named first NBA Coach of the Year after directing 19-win improvement

452 2001-02 Orlando Magic   1.340 44-38 East first round
Versatile forward Grant Hill limited to 14 games because of ongoing foot problems, limiting team's progress

453 1992-93 Orlando Magic   1.289 41-41
Rookie of the Year Shaquille O'Neal center of 20-game improvement

454 1989-90 Seattle Supersonics 1.285 41-41
Regressed by six wins, but set foundation for future with addition of high-flying forward Shawn Kemp and drafting of point guard Gary Payton

455 1995-96 Atlanta Hawks   1.281 46-36 East semifinals
Hawks avenged two consecutive postseason defeats against Pacers with upset of Indiana in East first round

456 1985-86 Detroit Pistons 1.280 46-36 East first round
Pistons changed emphasis from offense to defense after this season; safe to say the move paid off

457 1998-99 Milwaukee Bucks 1.279 28-22 East first round
Coach George Karl directed Bucks to first playoff appearance since 1991 during his first season in Milwaukee

458 1990-91 Seattle Supersonics 1.271 41-41 West first round
Pushed top-seeded Trail Blazers to five games in first round of playoffs to conclude promising point guard Gary Payton's rookie season

459 1978-79 Denver Nuggets   1.241 47-35 West first round
Start of a trend: Coach Larry Brown departed after 53 games

460 1962-63 Cincinnati Royals 1.234 42-38 East finals
Pushed eventual champion Celtics to seven games in East finals

461 1948-49   New York   1.228   32-28   East finals
                Knickerbockers
Rookie season for franchise mainstay Harry Gallatin; start of Gallatin's then-record streak of 682 consecutive games played

462 1961-62   Cincinnati Royals   1.209   43-37   West semifinals
Star guard Oscar Robertson averaged a triple-double for the season

463 1954-55   Syracuse Nationals   1.204   43-29   NBA champion
Won title during first season for 24-second shot clock, proposed by Nationals owner Daniel Biasone

464 1999-00   Detroit Pistons   1.196   42-40   East first round
Star forward Grant Hill suffered his career-altering ankle injury during first round playoff loss against Heat

465 1973-74   Capital Bullets   1.187   47-35   East semifinals
Won a division title during franchise's only season as "Capital" Bullets

466 1983-84   New Jersey Nets   1.172   45-37   East semifinals
First round playoff upset of defending champion 76ers was team's shining moment for many years

467 1948-49   Baltimore Bullets   1.138   29-31   East semifinals
Defending league champions became first team in NBA/BAA history to be eliminated from playoffs with an overtime loss (in East semifinal against Knicks)

468 1992-93   New Jersey Nets   1.135   43-39   East first round
Rapidly improving guard Drazen Petrovic led team in scoring during Nets' first winning season since 1985, but was killed in car accident after season

469 2005-06   New Jersey Nets   1.131   49-33   East semifinals
A 14-game winning streak late in the season propelled the Nets back to the top of the Atlantic Division

470 1986-87   Chicago Bulls   1.128   40-42   East first round
Michael Jordan won first of his 10 scoring titles

471 1991-92   Los Angeles Clippers 1.124   45-37   West first round
Coach Larry Brown came in at midseason and directed team to 23-12 finish, first winning record during franchise's time in Los Angeles

472 1998-99   New York   1.119   27-23   NBA finalist
                Knickerbockers
First team to reach NBA Finals as a No. 8 seed

473 1994-95   Atlanta Hawks   1.116   42-40   East first round
Lenny Wilkens set record for most career coaching wins in NBA history, but Hawks regressed by 15 games after losing versatile forward Danny Manning via free agency

474 2001-02   Utah Jazz   1.110   44-38   West first round
Suffered nine-game slip as defense allowed 2.7 more points per game than previous season

475 1978-79   Portland Trail Blazers 1.109 45-37   West first round
Franchise parted ways with Bill Walton after center missed entire season with foot injury

476 1982-83   Kansas City Kings   1.108   45-37
Loss in regular season finale caused Kings to miss playoffs in final year of 12-team postseason format

477 1999-00   Seattle Supersonics 1.100   45-37   West first round
Gary Payton's best season (24.2 points per game), brief resurgence from forward Vin Baker helped Sonics return to postseason

478 1999-00   Philadelphia 76ers   1.080   49-33   East semifinals
Repeat of 1999 postseason; 76ers pulled an upset in the first round, then lost against Pacers in East semifinals

479 1976-77   Cleveland Cavaliers 1.080   43-39   East first round
Injuries to starters Campy Russell and Jim Cleamons enough to cause six-win decline

480 1988-89   Denver Nuggets   1.068   44-38   West first round
Defense suffered a relapse (gave up 3.6 points per game more than previous season) and team went 9-32 on the road, resulting in 10-win decline

481 1988-89   Boston Celtics   1.066   42-40   East first round
Barely squeaked into playoffs as star forward Larry Bird played just six games because of foot injury

482 1988-89   Portland Trail Blazers 1.050 39-43   West first round
Had all the pieces of a contender, but the parts didn't click until following season

483 1987-88   Houston Rockets   1.038   46-36   West first round
Broke up "Twin Towers" with midseason trade of Ralph Sampson

484 1987-88   Cleveland Cavaliers 1.027   42-40   East first round
Posted team's first winning season since 1978, but endured first of four playoff losses against Bulls in six years

485 1985-86   Denver Nuggets   1.025   47-35   West semifinals
Failed to lead league in scoring for first time since 1980, but still enjoyed successful season

486 1965-66   Cincinnati Royals   1.017   45-35   East semifinals
Oscar Robertson won fifth assist title in six seasons; Royals led Celtics 2-1 in best-of-five East semifinal, but dropped last two games

487 1997-98   Washington Wizards   1.001   42-40
Missed playoffs by one game during first year as "Wizards" and promptly disassembled promising young roster

488 1987-88   Milwaukee Bucks   0.986   42-40   East first round
Injury-depleted Bucks posted losing record in January, ending string of 52 consecutive months with winning records

489 1995-96   Washington Bullets   0.967   39-43
Team improved by 18 wins and 7-foot-7 center Gheorghe Muresan named league's Most Improved Player

490 1997-98   Portland Trail Blazers   0.961   46-36   West first round
Amassed plenty of young talent, but lost in first round of playoffs for sixth consecutive season

491 1976-77   Kansas City Kings   0.939   40-42
Team improved by nine wins despite departure of star guard Nate Archibald, but dropped nine of last 10 games to miss postseason

492 1981-82   Washington Bullets   0.938   43-39   East semifinals
Gene Shue named Coach of the Year as addition of veteran forward Spencer Haywood and bruising rookie frontliner Jeff Ruland helped Bullets post winning season

493 1976-77   Chicago Bulls   0.929   44-38   West first round
Addition of center Artis Gilmore from ABA got Bulls back into the postseason

494 1954-55   Minneapolis Lakers   0.926   40-32   West finals
Clyde Lovellette filled void at center and helped Lakers reach West finals in first season after George Mikan's retirement

495 1978-79   Houston Rockets   0.912   47-35   East first round
Moses Malone won the first of six rebound titles and first of three MVP awards

496 1971-72   Golden State Warriors   0.910   51-31   West semifinals
Ten-win improvement during franchise's first season as "Golden State" Warriors

497 1981-82   Golden State Warriors   0.907   45-37
Warriors didn't make playoffs after only winning season between 1978 and 1987, missing out on postseason by one game for second consecutive year

498 1963-64   Los Angeles Lakers   0.906   42-38   West semifinals
Brief interruption in string of four division titles in five years

499 1976-77   Washington Bullets   0.895   48-34   East semifinals
New coach (Dick Motta replaced K.C. Jones) but familiar result; Bullets lost in East semifinals for second consecutive year

500 1983-84   Utah Jazz   0.888   45-37   West semifinals
Frank Layden named Coach of the Year as surprising Jazz improved by 15 wins and captured franchise's first division title

501 1971-72   Seattle Supersonics   0.882   47-35
Achieved franchise's first winning record during high-scoring forward Spencer Haywood's first full NBA season

502 1989-90   New York Knickerbockers   0.880   45-37   East semifinals
Dramatic change in playing style resulted in seven-win decline during regular season, but Knicks salvaged season with upset win over Celtics in first round of playoffs

503 1992-93   Boston Celtics   0.876   48-34   East first round
Boston declined by just three wins during first season after star forward Larry Bird's retirement, but lost against Hornets in first round of playoffs

504 1960-61   Philadelphia Warriors   0.871   46-33   East semifinals
Wilt Chamberlain set single-season rebounds record with 27.2 per game

505 1970-71   Baltimore Bullets   0.866   42-40   NBA finalist
Stunned defending champion Knicks in East finals to reach NBA Finals for first time in franchise history

506 1994-95   Denver Nuggets   0.866   41-41   West first round
Nuggets labored (and eventually crumbled) under lofty expectations after previous season's playoff success

507 1975-76   Buffalo Braves   0.842   46-36   East semifinals
Earned franchise's first playoff series victory; next one would come 30 years later as the Los Angeles Clippers

508 1985-86   Dallas Mavericks   0.833   44-38   West semifinals
Second consecutive 44-38 season showed need for an inside presence; Dallas drafted Roy Tarpley to solve the problem

509 1974-75   Houston Rockets   0.821   41-41   East semifinals
First playoff appearance of franchise's time in Houston, along with franchise's first playoff series win

510 1977-78   Washington Bullets   0.818   44-38   NBA champion
Bullets' worst regular season record since 1972, but Washington surged through playoffs to win franchise's only NBA title

511 1973-74   Los Angeles Lakers   0.816   47-35   West semifinals
Wilt Chamberlain made surprising retirement before season; Chamberlain replacement Elmore Smith set league record with 17 blocks in one game
512 1977-78   Denver Nuggets   0.797   48-34   West finals
First ABA team to reach a conference final
513 1989-90   Atlanta Hawks   0.753   41-41
Injury to point guard Doc Rivers left talented Hawks without a floor leader, resulting in 11-win decline
514 1990-91   Atlanta Hawks   0.751   43-39   East first round
Point guard Doc Rivers returned from injury; Hawks returned to playoffs during Bob Weiss' first season as coach
515 1984-85   San Antonio Spurs   0.750   41-41   West first round
Returned to postseason during high scoring guard George Gervin's final season with franchise
516 1985-86   Portland Trail Blazers 0.746   40-42   West first round
Coach Jack Ramsay "retired" after season; accepted Pacers job a few weeks later
517 1981-82   New Jersey Nets   0.740   44-38   East first round
New coach Larry Brown, rookies Buck Williams and Albert King helped Nets to 20-win improvement
518 2004-05   Chicago Bulls   0.735   47-35   East first round
Posted winning record and returned to playoffs for first time since Michael Jordan left Chicago following 1998 championship
519 1957-58   St. Louis Hawks   0.734   41-31   NBA champion
Least dominant team to win an NBA title
520 1986-87   Houston Rockets   0.734   42-40   West semifinals
Promising center Ralph Sampson's rapid decline started with this injury-plagued season; Rockets declined by nine wins
521 1955-56   Boston Celtics   0.732   39-33   East semifinals
Celtics finished first in league on offense and last in league on defense for third consecutive year; Red Auerbach sought to change that by trading for draft rights to Bill Russell
522 1983-84   Phoenix Suns   0.732   41-41   West finals
Surprise run to West finals made up for disappointing season after trade of guard Dennis Johnson
523 1981-82   Atlanta Hawks   0.694   42-40   East first round
Returned to top of league's defensive standings; also returned to playoffs

524 1980-81   Portland Trail Blazers 0.687   45-37   West first round
Breakthrough seasons for guard Jim Paxson and center Mychal Thompson led to seven-win improvement for balanced Blazers

525 2006-07   Toronto Raptors   0.682   47-35   East first round
Improved by 20 wins and won the first division title in franchise history

526 1951-52   New York Knickerbockers   0.664   37-29   NBA finalist
Controversial overtime loss in Game 1 against Lakers eventually caused Knicks to become first team to lose consecutive NBA Finals in seven games

527 2001-02   Charlotte Hornets   0.645   44-38   East semifinals
Hornets departed for New Orleans after 10th consecutive winning season

528 1950-51   Syracuse Nationals   0.643   32-34   East finals
Suffered 19-win decline against tougher schedule during franchise's second NBA season

529 1976-77   Phoenix Suns   0.634   34-48
More dominant than 1975-1976 NBA Finals team, but couldn't catch a break in road games (8-33 record)

530 1994-95   Cleveland Cavaliers   0.627   43-39   East first round
Standout guard Mark Price played in just 48 games during his final season in Cleveland

531 1947-48   Philadelphia Warriors 0.598   27-21   BAA finalist
Defending champion Warriors blew 21-point lead in pivotal Game 2 of league finals against Bullets and never recovered

532 1975-76   Phoenix Suns   0.588   42-40   NBA finalist
"Sunderellas" stunned defending champion Warriors in West finals to earn franchise's first NBA Finals appearance

533 2004-05   Indiana Pacers   0.586   44-38   East semifinals
Franchise icon Reggie Miller's final season ruined when reigning Defensive Player of the Year Ron Artest was suspended for season after brawl in Detroit on November 19

534 1946-47   New York Knickerbockers   0.575   33-27   BAA semifinals
Knicks recorded BAA's first basket and first victory in November 1 win at Toronto

535 2003-04   Milwaukee Bucks   0.567   41-41   East first round
Made surprise playoff appearance under first-year coach Terry Porter, but late-season injury to rookie guard T.J. Ford prevented Bucks from using season as a springboard to bigger things

536 2005-06 Chicago Bulls 0.548 41-41 East first round
Won 10 of last 11 games to seal second consecutive postseason appearance

537 1958-59 New York Knickerbockers 0.532 40-32 East semifinals
Trivia answer: Ken Sears was the last player to lead the league in field goal percentage with a percentage under .500

538 1976-77 San Antonio Spurs 0.529 44-38 East first round
Injury to point guard James Silas prevented greater success for Spurs during their first season after move from ABA to NBA

539 1984-85 New Jersey Nets 0.527 42-40 East first round
Managed winning record despite myriad of injuries

540 1972-73 Detroit Pistons 0.523 40-42
Standout guard Dave Bing returned to form after injury-plagued season, resulting in 14-win improvement

541 1981-82 Portland Trail Blazers 0.500 42-40
Blazers didn't get worse, but missed postseason for first time in five seasons as the rest of the Western Conference got better

542 2000-01 Orlando Magic 0.500 43-39 East first round
Tale of two free agents: Tracy McGrady everything Magic hoped for, but Grant Hill limited to four games because of injury

543 1999-00 Orlando Magic 0.494 41-41
First-year coach Doc Rivers named NBA Coach of the Year for keeping cast of no-names in playoff contention

544 1950-51 New York Knickerbockers 0.489 36-30 NBA finalist
Only team in NBA Finals history to force a seventh game after falling behind 3-0, but lost decisive game against Royals

545 1978-79 Golden State Warriors 0.467 38-44
Warriors posted first losing record since 1969-1970 during first season after free agency departure of scoring machine Rick Barry

546 1977-78 Cleveland Cavaliers 0.437 43-39 East first round
Veteran guard Walt Frazier came aboard, but Cavaliers' window of championship opportunity closed with loss against Knicks in first round of playoffs

547 1977-78 Golden State Warriors 0.419 43-39
High-scoring forward Rick Barry's final season with Golden State marked beginning of nine-season playoff absence

548 2004-05   Boston Celtics   0.419   45-37   East first round
Won first division title since 1992, but suffered biggest Game 7 loss in franchise history (27 points) in finale of first round series against Pacers

549 2006-07   Orlando Magic   0.413   40-42   East first round
Roller coaster season (13-4 start, 6-1 finish and a 7-22 stretch in between) ended with Magic's first postseason ride since 2003

550 2000-01   Seattle Supersonics 0.410   44-38
Coaching change (Paul Westphal out; Nate McMillan in) came too late for Sonics to get into postseason

551 1955-56   Fort Wayne Pistons 0.402   37-35   NBA finalist
Pistons defended Western Division title, but no match for Warriors in NBA Finals

552 1992-93   Los Angeles Clippers 0.381 41-41   West first round
Coach Larry Brown departed after season; Clippers didn't finish above .500 again until 2006

553 1988-89   Houston Rockets   0.378   45-37   West first round
Hakeem Olajuwon became first player to record 200 steals and 200 blocks during same season and also averaged then-career best 24.8 points per game

554 1979-80   Cleveland Cavaliers 0.378 37-45
Standout forward Mike Mitchell's breakout season (22.2 points per game) resulted in seven-win improvement, but bad times just around the corner

555 1998-99   Charlotte Hornets   0.358   26-24
Hornets revamped roster during strike-shortened season, contributing to departure of coach Dave Cowens

556 2004-05   Cleveland Cavaliers 0.343 42-40
Phenom forward LeBron James led Cavaliers to first winning record since 1998, but organizational turmoil contributed to late slide and failure to make postseason

557 1982-83   Denver Nuggets   0.340   45-37   West semifinals
Alex English and Kiki Vandeweghe finished first and second in league in scoring

558 2005-06   Denver Nuggets   0.323   44-38   West first round
Won franchise's first division title since 1988, but made quick postseason exit

559 1996-97   Phoenix Suns   0.319   40-42   West first round
Opened season with 13 consecutive losses, but recovered to qualify for postseason

560 1975-76   Philadelphia 76ers   0.317   46-36   East first round
Talented frontliner George McGinnis jumped to 76ers from ABA, resulting in 12-win improvement and team's first playoff appearance since 1971

561 1989-90   Dallas Mavericks   0.311   47-35   West first round
Mavericks' key components played in enough games to get team into postseason

562 1966-67   Los Angeles Lakers   0.307   36-45   West semifinals
Top scorers Jerry West and Elgin Baylor combined to miss 26 games, enough to push Lakers below .500 mark

563 1969-70   Atlanta Hawks   0.302   48-34   West finals
Franchise's first division title of Atlanta era, but Hawks lost against Lakers in West finals

564 1997-98   Minnesota Timberwolves   0.300   45-37   West first round
Timberwolves posted franchise's first winning record during final season together for promising young trio of forwards Kevin Garnett and Tom Gugliotta, and point guard Stephon Marbury

565 1974-75   Portland Trail Blazers   0.289   38-44
Prize rookie center Bill Walton played just 35 games because of injuries, but team did escape division cellar for first time

566 1995-96   Phoenix Suns   0.286   41-41   West first round
Star forward Charles Barkley departed after Suns struggled through injury-plagued season

567 1980-81   Washington Bullets   0.264   39-43
Bullets missed playoffs for first time in 12 seasons and then bid farewell to franchise stalwarts Elvin Hayes (trade) and Wes Unseld (retired) after season

568 1957-58   Philadelphia Warriors   0.261   37-35   East finals
Aging Warriors managed a winning record, but suffered first of three East finals losses against Celtics in five years

569 2002-03   Seattle Supersonics   0.245   40-42
Traded away franchise icon Gary Payton at midseason

570 1974-75   Milwaukee Bucks   0.243   38-44
Club started 3-13 with top scorer Kareem Abdul-Jabbar sidelined with broken hand and never recovered

571 1983-84   Dallas Mavericks   0.233   43-39   West semifinals
Young Mavericks growing up fast; Dallas posted first winning season, first playoff appearance, and first playoff series win during franchise's fourth season

572 1981-82   Denver Nuggets   0.224   46-36   West first round
Set NBA records for most points scored and most points allowed during Doug Moe's first full season as coach
573 1979-80   Houston Rockets   0.220   41-41   East semifinals
Rockets no match for Celtics in East semifinals, foreshadowing 1981 NBA Finals
574 1986-87   Seattle Supersonics 0.214   39-43   West finals
First and only No. 7 seed to reach a conference final
575 1955-56   Syracuse Nationals   0.200   35-37   East finals
Key guard Paul Seymour missed 15 games during Nationals' hard-luck encore to 1954-1955 championship season
576 1952-53   Fort Wayne Pistons   0.196   36-33   West finals
Roster included baseball standout Dick Groat (11.9 points a game in 26 games)
577 1975-76   Los Angeles Lakers   0.186   40-42
Lakers debut for center Kareem Abdul-Jabbar, who won league MVP award after spearheading 10-win improvement
578 1986-87   Utah Jazz   0.180   44-38   West first round
First of two first round upset losses against Warriors in three years
579 1948-49   Philadelphia Warriors 0.178   28-32   East semifinals
Joe Fulks' single-game record of 63 points on February 10 stood as a league standard for 10 years
580 1998-99   Minnesota Timberwolves 0.168   25-25   West first round
Timberwolves made playoffs despite preseason departure of standout forward Tom Gugliotta (free agent) and midseason trade of point guard Stephon Marbury
581 2006-07   Los Angeles Lakers   0.158   42-40   West first round
Lakers needed 10 50-point games from NBA scoring champion Kobe Bryant (the most 50-point games in a season since Wilt Chamberlain) just to get into the playoffs
582 1970-71   San Diego Rockets   0.156   40-42
Most wins in franchise's four-year history, but attendance woes triggered move to Houston
583 1982-83   Washington Bullets   0.116   42-40
Bullets finished in division cellar as every team in Atlantic Division finished with a winning record

584 1954-55   New York Knickerbockers   0.116   38-34   East semifinals
Knicks' age started to show in six-win decline

585 1956-57   New York Knickerbockers   0.109   36-36
Rugged forward Harry Gallatin led Knicks in scoring during his final season to become first player other than Carl Braun to lead Knicks in scoring since 1952

586 1951-52   Indianapolis Olympians   0.082   34-32   West semifinals
Franchise staggered when stars Alex Groza and Ralph Beard were suspended for roles in college point-shaving scandal

587 1984-85   Washington Bullets   0.040   40-42   East first round
Addition of standout guard Gus Williams and forward Cliff Robinson plus breakthrough season for shooting guard Jeff Malone added up to five-win improvement for Bullets

588 1976-77   New York Knickerbockers   0.020   40-42
Acquisition of reigning scoring champion Bob McAdoo couldn't get Knicks into postseason

589 2003-04   Miami Heat   0.017   42-40   East semifinals
Rookie guard Dwyane Wade helped Heat recover from 0-9 start to reach East semifinals

590 2001-02   Indiana Pacers   0.014   42-40   East first round
Won last five games to sneak into playoffs, then pushed eventual East champion Nets to double overtime in Game 5 of first round series

591 1999-00   Milwaukee Bucks   0.007   42-40   East first round
"Most average" team in NBA history pushed top-seeded Pacers to limit in first round of playoffs

592 1954-55   Boston Celtics   -0.023   36-36   East finals
Became first team in NBA history to average 100 points per game in a season

593 1986-87   Philadelphia 76ers   -0.037   45-37   East first round
Hall of Fame forward Julius Erving retired after season after leading 76ers to 11 consecutive playoff appearances

594 1980-81   Houston Rockets   -0.045   40-42   NBA finalist
First round upset of defending champion Lakers propelled Rockets to first NBA Finals appearance

595 1989-90   Indiana Pacers   -0.060   42-40   East first round
Pacers began string of seven consecutive playoff appearances during breakout season for guard Reggie Miller (24.6 points per game)

596	1992-93	Charlotte Hornets	-0.068	44-38	East semifinals

Rookie center Alonzo Mourning pushed Hornets to first playoff appearance, first playoff series win

597	1994-95	Los Angeles Lakers	-0.081	48-34	West semifinals

Del Harris named Coach of the Year as overachieving Lakers reached West semifinals

598	2006-07	Golden State Warriors	-0.081	42-40	West semifinals

Don Nelson's triumphant return as Golden State's coach included team's first playoff berth since 1994 and an upset of the top-seeded Mavericks in first round of the playoffs

599	1987-88	New York Knickerbockers	-0.103	38-44	East first round

Star center Patrick Ewing got to make his first playoff appearance during coach Rick Pitino's first season

600	1977-78	Atlanta Hawks	-0.123	41-41	East first round

Hubie Brown named Coach of the Year for leading Hawks to 10-win improvement, playoff berth

601	2002-03	Milwaukee Bucks	-0.124	42-40	East first round

Midseason trade for guard Gary Payton got Bucks into playoffs, but Payton left to join Lakers after the season

602	1975-76	Seattle Supersonics	-0.130	43-39	West semifinals

Sonics parted ways with leading scorer Spencer Haywood, but still made second consecutive postseason appearance

603	1960-61	Los Angeles Lakers	-0.131	36-43	West finals

Rookie guard Jerry West averaged 17.6 points per game during franchise's first season in Los Angeles

604	1972-73	Atlanta Hawks	-0.131	46-36	East semifinals

Improved by 10 wins during first year in The Omni thanks to guard Lou Hudson's finest season (27.1 points per game) and a breakout year for point guard Pete Maravich (26.1 points per game)

605	1964-65	Philadelphia 76ers	-0.131	40-40	East finals

Midseason trade for star center Wilt Chamberlain immediately made Philadelphia a contender

606	2003-04	Seattle Supersonics	-0.137	37-45	

Won fewer than 40 games (lockout season excluded) for first time since 1987

607 1974-75   Kansas City/   -0.146   44-38   West semifinals
               Omaha Kings
Point guard Nate Archibald's return from injury-plagued season and presence of solid rookie forward Scott Wedman resulted in 11-win improvement, franchise's first playoff appearance of Kansas City era

608 2006-07   Los Angeles Clippers -0.148   40-42
Tiring preseason trip to Russia might have harmed the Clippers; Injuries to point guards Shaun Livingston and Sam Cassell (52 combined games missed) definitely hurt

609 1953-54   New York   -0.159   44-28   East semifinals
               Knickerbockers
Six-foot-six Harry Gallatin led league in rebounds, but Knicks missed NBA Finals for first time in three years

610 1955-56   New York   -0.159   35-37
               Knickerbockers
Knicks missed playoffs for first time after franchise's first losing season

611 1973-74   Buffalo Braves   -0.167   42-40   East semifinals
Bob McAdoo won his first scoring title and the franchise made its first postseason appearance

612 2001-02   Los Angeles Clippers -0.178   39-43
Added proven inside presence Elton Brand and improved by eight wins, but couldn't meet heightened expectations

613 1996-97   Orlando Magic   -0.183   45-37   East first round
Departure of star center Shaquille O'Neal (free agent) resulted in 15-win decline

614 1954-55   Philadelphia Warriors -0.185   33-39
Standout forward Paul Arizin returned from military service and helped team to four-win improvement

615 1993-94   Charlotte Hornets   -0.190   41-41
Star frontliners Alonzo Mourning and Larry Johnson combined to miss 53 games as Hornets missed playoffs

616 1984-85   Utah Jazz   -0.199   41-41   West semifinals
Funny to think now: Rookie John Stockton drafted to serve as backup point guard to Rickey Green

617 1967-68   Baltimore Bullets   -0.214   36-46
Rookie of the Year guard Earl Monroe led Bullets to 16-win improvement

618 1966-67   Cincinnati Royals   -0.219   39-42   East semifinals
Original owner Les Harrison sold club after team posted first losing season in five years

619 2003-04   Golden State   -0.230   37-45
                Warriors
Coach Eric Musselman produced best two-year record for Warriors since early 1990s, despite loss of top two scorers after his first year, and still got fired after this season

620 1983-84   Seattle Supersonics -0.251   42-40   West first round
Addition of gunner Tom Chambers helped Sonics manage sixth winning record in seven years

621 1982-83   Detroit Pistons   -0.260   37-45
Ironically, defensive struggles caused embryonic "Bad Boys" to regress slightly, but rapid improvement just around the corner

622 2002-03   Orlando Magic   -0.283   42-40   East first round
Magic had 3-1 lead during first round playoff series against top-seeded Pistons

623 1974-75   Cleveland Cavaliers -0.284   40-42
Revamped Cavaliers improved by 11 wins and escaped division cellar for the first time during first season in Richfield Coliseum

624 1979-80   San Antonio Spurs -0.289   41-41   East first round
Smooth guard George Gervin had his best season (33.1 points per game), but league-worst defense kept Spurs at .500

625 1956-57   St. Louis Hawks   -0.294   34-38   NBA finalist
Bob Pettit missed layup at buzzer that would have sent Game 7 of NBA Finals into triple overtime

626 1981-82   Houston Rockets   -0.296   46-36   West first round
Star center Moses Malone left the franchise after winning second MVP award

627 1986-87   Indiana Pacers   -0.300   41-41   East first round
Jack Ramsay guided team to 15-game improvement and franchise's first win in an NBA playoff game during his first season as Pacers' coach

628 1968-69   San Diego Rockets -0.321   37-45   West semifinals
No. 1 overall draft pick Elvin Hayes led league in scoring, pushed Rockets to 22-win improvement and playoff appearance

629 1985-86   Seattle Supersonics -0.328   31-51
Season memorable for NBA's first "rain delay," caused by leaky roof on Seattle Center Coliseum

630 1970-71   Detroit Pistons   -0.330   45-37
Pistons managed franchise's first winning record since 1955-1956 during big Bob Lanier's rookie year

631 1973-74   Houston Rockets   -0.332   32-50
Forward Rudy Tomjanovich and guard Calvin Murphy established themselves as individual stars, but team made little progress

632 1990-91   Indiana Pacers   -0.337   41-41   East first round
Standout forward Chuck Person's finest hour; matched Larry Bird shot for shot during five-game first round playoff loss against Celtics

633 1980-81   Kansas City Kings   -0.339   40-42   West finals
Only Kansas City Kings team to win a postseason series; upset Blazers and top-seeded Suns to reach West finals

634 1999-00   Dallas Mavericks   -0.350   40-42
Twelve-game dalliance with oddball forward Dennis Rodman probably cost team a playoff spot

635 1990-91   Philadelphia 76ers   -0.360   44-38   East semifinals
Played in an NBA record 14 overtime games

636 2001-02   Phoenix Suns   -0.387   36-46
Offseason acquisition of guard Stephon Marbury in exchange for Jason Kidd didn't turn out in Suns' favor as team saw string of 13 consecutive playoff appearances end

637 1999-00   Toronto Raptors   -0.400   45-37   East first round
Coach Butch Carter's bizarre antics got him fired despite franchise's first winning season and first playoff appearance

638 1987-88   Washington Bullets   -0.401   38-44   East first round
Former Washington star Wes Unseld took over as coach at midseason and helped Bullets qualify for playoffs for fifth consecutive year

639 1990-91   New York Knickerbockers   -0.405   39-43   East first round
Coach John MacLeod interviewed for Notre Dame job during first round playoff loss against Bulls

640 1983-84   San Antonio Spurs   -0.412   37-45
Franchise record for points in a season offset by franchise record for points allowed in a season

641 1987-88   Indiana Pacers   -0.420   38-44
Late-season collapse kept team out of playoffs during promising guard Reggie Miller's rookie season

642 1988-89   Golden State Warriors   -0.427   43-39   West semifinals
Coach Don Nelson oversaw 23-win improvement and a first round playoff series victory during his first season with Warriors

643 1950-51   Boston Celtics   -0.431   39-30   East semifinals
First season in Boston for coach Red Auerbach and guard Bob Cousy resulted in franchise's first winning record
644 1965-66   St. Louis Hawks   -0.492   36-44   West finals
Declined by nine wins during first season after retirement of franchise icon Bob Pettit, but upset Bullets in playoffs to reach West finals
645 1995-96   Charlotte Hornets   -0.494   41-41
Franchise jolted by early season trade of center Alonzo Mourning, postseason trade of forward Larry Johnson
646 1989-90   Cleveland Cavaliers   -0.495   42-40   East first round
Standout center Brad Daugherty missed half of season with an injury, triggering 15-win decline
647 1949-50   Washington Capitols   -0.523   32-36   East semifinals
Franchise began rapid disintegration during first season after departure of coach Red Auerbach
648 1985-86   Utah Jazz   -0.523   42-40   West first round
First round draft pick Karl Malone delivered 14.9 points per game as a rookie
649 1977-78   New York   -0.526   43-39   East semifinals
           Knickerbockers
New-look Knicks made brief resurgence under first-year coach Willis Reed
650 2001-02   Milwaukee Bucks   -0.542   41-41
Missed playoffs after leading division on March 1
651 1998-99   Sacramento Kings   -0.567   27-23   West first round
Trade for versatile forward Chris Webber keyed franchise's first winning season in Sacramento
652 2004-05   Los Angeles Clippers -0.569   37-45
Finished with better record than Los Angeles neighbor Lakers for first time since 1993
653 2003-04   New Orleans Hornets   -0.572   41-41   East first round
Players tuned out coach Tim Floyd by end of regular season, playoff loss against Heat
654 1979-80   Indiana Pacers   -0.583   37-45
Typical Pacer trade of the era: Traded rising star forward Alex English in exchange for aging frontliner George McGinnis
655 1977-78   Milwaukee Bucks   -0.597   44-38   West semifinals
Departure of forward Bob Dandridge (last player remaining from Bucks' 1971 NBA champions) and 14-win improvement marked beginning of new era for Milwaukee

656 2001-02   Toronto Raptors   -0.615   42-40   East first round
Nothing went as planned; acquisition of center Hakeem Olajuwon misfired, team played better down stretch without injured star Vince Carter, and team lost in first round of postseason

657 2002-03   Boston Celtics   -0.619   44-38   East semifinals
Team's biggest preseason move (guard Kenny Anderson out, forward Vin Baker in) didn't work out so well, but Celtics did manage to upset Pacers in first round of playoffs

658 1982-83   Dallas Mavericks   -0.621   38-44
Mavericks enjoyed a 10-win improvement during franchise's third season, but seven-game slide late in season kept team out of playoffs

659 1967-68   Cincinnati Royals   -0.622   39-43
New coach Ed Jucker won two NCAA titles at the University of Cincinnati, but couldn't repeat that success with Royals

660 1984-85   Chicago Bulls   -0.624   38-44   East first round
Michael Jordan averaged 28.2 points as a rookie as Bulls began a 14-year string of playoff appearances

661 1999-00   Houston Rockets   -0.629   34-48
Transition season for Rockets with arrival of guard Steve Francis, final season for forward Charles Barkley, and decline of center Hakeem Olajuwon

662 2004-05   Washington Wizards   -0.631   45-37   East semifinals
Won a playoff series for first time since 1982

663 1997-98   Orlando Magic   -0.644   41-41
Standout guard Anfernee Hardaway played just 19 games, resulting in end of four-year string of playoff appearances

664 2000-01   Indiana Pacers   -0.653   41-41   East first round
Rebuild-on-the-fly process keyed by acquisition of future star forward Jermaine O'Neal in exchange for aging frontliner Dale Davis

665 1967-68   San Francisco Warriors   -0.677   43-39   West finals
Top scorer Rick Barry departed for ABA, but Warriors declined by just one win

666 2003-04   Utah Jazz   -0.694   42-40
Jazz stayed respectable during first season after departure of Karl Malone and John Stockton

667 1992-93   Atlanta Hawks   -0.716   43-39   East first round
Star forward Dominique Wilkins returned from career-threatening injury and averaged 29.9 points per game, but Hawks no match for eventual champion Bulls in first round of playoffs

668   2002-03   Golden State   -0.717   38-44
                  Warriors
League Most Improved Player Gilbert Arenas and new coach Eric Musselman helped Warriors to 17-win improvement
669   2006-07   Washington Wizards -0.719   41-41   East first round
Late-season injuries to top players Gilbert Arenas and Caron Butler made the Wizards' chances for playoff success disappear
670   1975-76   Houston Rockets   -0.721   40-42
Balanced offense negated by league-worst defense
671   1975-76   New Orleans Jazz   -0.734   38-44
Star guard Pete Maravich sat out 20 games with a broken cheekbone, but Jazz still enjoyed 15-win improvement during franchise's second season
672   2003-04   Portland Trail Blazers -0.740   41-41
Ended string of 21 consecutive playoff appearances, then the longest active streak in the NBA
673   1981-82   Detroit Pistons   -0.748   39-43
Addition of rookies Isiah Thomas and Kelly Tripucka, trades for Bill Laimbeer and Vinnie Johnson keyed 18-win improvement
674   1977-78   Chicago Bulls   -0.787   40-42
Start of string of nine losing seasons in 10 years
675   1980-81   Denver Nuggets   -0.791   37-45
Doug Moe took over as coach at midseason and directed team to 26-25 stretch run
676   1968-69   Cincinnati Royals   -0.807   41-41
Cincinnati stars Oscar Robertson and Jerry Lucas both saw their scoring averages drop, but Royals still managed a .500 season
677   1994-95   Sacramento Kings   -0.814   39-43
Big improvement on defense (allowed 7.7 points fewer than previous season) and then-Sacramento-best 27-14 home record led to 11-win improvement
678   1979-80   Portland Trail Blazers -0.819   38-44   West first round
Blazers revamped roster during first season after Bill Walton era ended
679   1982-83   Atlanta Hawks   -0.820   43-39   East first round
Acquired future star Dominique Wilkins with shrewd trade before season, but increased win total by only one
680   1970-71   San Francisco   -0.855   41-41   West semifinals
                  Warriors
Rugged center Nate Thurmond returned from injury, helping Warriors post 11-win improvement during last season in San Francisco

681 1992-93   Golden State   -0.879   34-48
              Warriors
Top six scorers combined to miss 164 games with injuries, resulting in 21-win decline

682 1946-47   Cleveland Rebels   -0.880   30-30   BAA quarterfinals
Best of four teams to fold after BAA's first season

683 1956-57   Minneapolis Lakers -0.896   34-38   West finals
Watered-down West enabled Lakers to win last division title of franchise's Minneapolis history

684 1974-75   New York   -0.905   40-42   East first round
              Knickerbockers
Knicks posted first losing record in eight years during first season after retirement of center Willis Reed

685 1991-92   Los Angeles Lakers -0.914   43-39   West first round
Lakers rocked when star guard Magic Johnson retired early the in season after contracting HIV

686 2006-07   New Jersey Nets   -0.914   41-41   East semifinals
Vince Carter got revenge against his former team when he led the Nets to an upset win against the Raptors in the first round of the playoffs

687 1955-56   Minneapolis Lakers -0.929   33-39   West semifinals
George Mikan made an unremarkable 37-game comeback

688 1999-00   Boston Celtics   -0.934   35-47
Solid at home (26-15), but just 9-32 on the road

689 1989-90   Milwaukee Bucks   -0.942   44-38   East first round
Sixth Man of the Year Ricky Pierce averaged 23.0 points per game and led Bucks to postseason

690 1956-57   Syracuse Nationals -0.956   38-34   East finals
Franchise made its first coaching change (Al Cervi out; Paul Seymour in) after 4-8 start; recovered to post winning record

691 1992-93   Miami Heat   -0.975   36-46
Projected starting lineup played just one game together—the opener—because of injuries

692 1972-73   Phoenix Suns   -0.982   38-44
Coaching shuffle (Butch van Breda Kolff fired after seven games) and departure of center Paul Silas contributed to 11-win decline

693 2004-05   Philadelphia 76ers -0.987   43-39   East first round
Big season from guard Allen Iverson and deadline deal for forward Chris Webber got 76ers into playoffs

694 1976-77   Detroit Pistons   -0.993   44-38   West first round
Coach Herb Brown's team finished behind only brother Larry Brown's Nuggets in Midwest Division

695 1986-87   Denver Nuggets   -0.995   37-45   West first round
Absence of injured Calvin Natt (team's No. 2 scorer in 1985-1986) contributed to 10-win decline

696 1979-80   New York   -1.001   39-43
            Knickerbockers
Made eight-win improvement thanks to second-year guard Michael Ray Richardson (league leader in assists and steals) and rookie center Bill Cartwright (21.7 points per game)

697 1949-50   Tri-Cities Blackhawks -1.019   29-35   West semifinals
Red Auerbach's only sub-.500 coaching stop (28-29 over final 57 games)

698 1979-80   New Jersey Nets   -1.024   34-48
Cut ties with top two scorers from previous season's playoff team (Bernard King and John Williamson) within 28 games

699 1987-88   Philadelphia 76ers   -1.025   36-46
Missed postseason during first year after Julius Erving's retirement

700 2005-06   Milwaukee Bucks   -1.032   40-42   East first round
First team in NBA history to qualify for playoffs with four different starters from the previous season

701 1965-66   Baltimore Bullets   -1.039   38-42   West semifinals
Traded away top scorer Walt Bellamy, but still managed one-win improvement

702 1975-76   New York Knickerbockers   -1.043   38-44
Acquisition of high-scoring forward Spencer Haywood (19.9 points per game) didn't stop Knicks' slide

703 1951-52   Philadelphia Warriors -1.063   33-33   East semifinals
Had scoring champs past (Joe Fulks), present (Paul Arizin), and future (rookie Neil Johnston) on roster, but done in by defense that ranked next-to-last in league

704 1997-98   Houston Rockets   -1.092   41-41   West first round
Gave top-seeded Jazz a scare in first round of playoffs, but still declined by 16 wins during guard Clyde Drexler's final season

705 1998-99   Seattle Supersonics   -1.098   25-25
Once-promising frontliner Vin Baker's rapid decline began this season; so did mediocre era for Sonics

706 1975-76   Portland Trail Blazers -1.103   37-45
Return to division cellar, injuries to center Bill Walton spelled end of Lenny Wilkens' two-year coaching tenure in Portland

707 1999-00   New Jersey Nets   -1.108   31-51
Started slow (2-15); finished slower (lost last 11 games)
708 2006-07   Miami Heat   -1.131   44-38   East first round
Injury-plagued Heat's NBA title defense ended with sweep loss against Bulls, making Miami the first reigning champions to get swept in the first round of the postseason since 1957
709 2005-06   Golden State Warriors   -1.137   34-48
Jumped out to a 12-6 start, but decline in guard Baron Davis' production corresponded with decline in team's fortunes
710 1992-93   Detroit Pistons   -1.142   40-42
Aging Pistons missed postseason for first time since 1983 after eight-win decline
711 1992-93   Los Angeles Lakers   -1.142   39-43   West first round
Won first two games of first round playoff series against top-seeded Suns, but lost series in five games
712 1991-92   Atlanta Hawks   -1.144   38-44
Top scorer Dominique Wilkins missed half of season with Achilles injury; Hawks missed playoffs
713 1986-87   Washington Bullets   -1.169   42-40   East first round
Acquisition of veteran center Moses Malone resulted in winning record; Bullets would not finish over .500 again until 1997
714 1974-75   Detroit Pistons   -1.170   40-42   West first round
Preseason holdout led Pistons to trade away star guard Dave Bing after season
715 1974-75   Seattle Supersonics   -1.176   43-39   West semifinals
Sonics made franchise's first playoff appearance, won a playoff series
716 1983-84   Atlanta Hawks   -1.179   40-42   East first round
Dominique Wilkins led team in scoring for the first time; he would do so for the next seven seasons
717 1983-84   Denver Nuggets   -1.180   38-44   West first round
Finished first in league on offense and last in league on defense for fourth consecutive year
718 1975-76   Detroit Pistons   -1.190   36-46   West semifinals
Won a playoff series for first time since 1962
719 1998-99   Cleveland Cavaliers   -1.200   22-28
Foot injury to center Zydrunas Ilgauskas main culprit in Cavaliers' first losing season since 1991

720 1971-72   Houston Rockets   -1.214   34-48
Home sweet home? Six-win decline attributable to 15-20 home record during franchise's first season in Houston

721 1977-78   Detroit Pistons   -1.217   38-44
Injuries to big man Bob Lanier (19 games) and others enough to cause six-win decline

722 2005-06   Orlando Magic   -1.233   36-46
Won 12 of 13 games soon after trading away top scorer Steve Francis, but surge came too late to get Magic into the postseason

723 1980-81   Golden State Warriors   -1.235   39-43
Combination of gunners World B. Free and Bernard King plus rookie center Joe Barry Carroll produced a 15-win improvement, but team missed postseason by one game

724 1971-72   Baltimore Bullets   -1.241   38-44   East semifinals
Shocking trade of star guard Earl Monroe to Knicks contributed to sub-.500 record

725 1984-85   Atlanta Hawks   -1.273   34-48
Rookie Kevin Willis filled Hawks' hole at center, but the pieces still didn't fit during Mike Fratello's second season as Atlanta coach

726 2006-07   New Orleans/Oklahoma City Hornets   -1.274   39-43
Tied a league record with a 7-0 mark in overtime games, but injury-riddled Hornets couldn't crack the postseason

727 1974-75   Atlanta Hawks   -1.307   31-51
Trading away point guard Pete Maravich and elbow injury to shooting guard Lou Hudson hurt in the short term, but helped Hawks rebuild quickly

728 2005-06   Houston Rockets   -1.331   34-48
Top scorer Tracy McGrady and center Yao Ming combined to miss 60 games with injuries, resulting in a 17-win decline despite a breakthrough season for Yao (22.3 points per game)

729 1959-60   New York Knickerbockers   -1.336   27-48
Tradition of patience in New York: Coach Andrew Levane fired after 8-19 start one year after directing Knicks to then-rare playoff appearance

730 1970-71   Atlanta Hawks   -1.338   36-46   East semifinals
Rookie guard Pete Maravich not enough to offset center Joe Caldwell's jump to ABA; team declined by 12 wins

731 2002-03 Washington Wizards -1.353 37-45
Michael Jordan retired for good after disappointing season

732 1991-92 Philadelphia 76ers -1.376 35-47
Star forward Charles Barkley traded away after season following second consecutive nine-win decline

733 1978-79 Indiana Pacers -1.393 38-44
Garnered more headlines after season (sale of franchise, signing of women's star Ann Meyers) than during season

734 1954-55 Rochester Royals -1.400 29-43 West semifinals
Worst record of franchise's time in Rochester during final Royal seasons for center Arnie Risen, guard Bob Davies

735 1995-96 Golden State Warriors -1.408 36-46
Despite injuries and trade of guard Tim Hardaway, Warriors did manage 10-win improvement

736 1985-86 Washington Bullets -1.414 39-43 East first round
League blocks leader Manute Bol averaged more blocks (5.0) than points (3.7) during his first NBA season

737 1955-56 St. Louis Hawks -1.415 33-39 West finals
Bob Pettit won first of two MVP awards, first of two scoring titles

738 2006-07 Sacramento Kings -1.419 33-49
Eric Musselman was hired as coach to take the Kings to a new level and was fired after one season when he took Sacramento down to the lottery level, ending a string of eight consecutive playoff appearances

739 1976-77 Seattle Supersonics -1.424 40-42
Coach/general manager Bill Russell left the franchise after putting pieces in place for NBA Finals runs during next two seasons

740 1966-67 St. Louis Hawks -1.427 39-42 West finals
Rookie guard Lou Hudson led team in scoring, contributed to three-win improvement

741 1958-59 Minneapolis Lakers -1.435 33-39 NBA finalist
Became least dominant team to reach NBA Finals during Elgin Baylor's rookie season

742 1997-98 Milwaukee Bucks -1.442 36-46
Injuries to starters Glenn Robinson (missed 26 games) and Terrell Brandon (32 games) ensured seventh consecutive losing season

743 1973-74 Atlanta Hawks -1.443 35-47
Pete Maravich took more shots than anyone in the league, but didn't make enough as Hawks missed playoffs for first time in 11 seasons

744   1991-92   Milwaukee Bucks   -1.456   31-51
Tried to bolster roster with veterans (center Moses Malone and guard Dale Ellis), but instead suffered 17-win decline

745   1963-64   Baltimore Bullets   -1.466   31-49
Franchise played a Western Division schedule during its first three seasons in Baltimore

746   2002-03   New York   -1.469   37-45
             Knickerbockers
Improved by seven wins, but injury to newly acquired forward Antonio McDyess hampered Knicks' chances of returning to postseason

747   1996-97   Milwaukee Bucks   -1.473   33-49
Addition of rookie guard Ray Allen big part of eight-win improvement

748   2001-02   Washington Wizards -1.480   37-45
Michael Jordan sparked Wizards to 18-win improvement during first year of his final comeback

749   1957-58   Cincinnati Royals   -1.499   33-39   West semifinals
Pall cast over franchise's first year in Cincinnati when forward Maurice Stokes was incapacitated by head injury during final game of regular season

750   1946-47   Providence   -1.510   28-32
             Steamrollers
Mediocre first season would be short-lived franchise's best

751   1985-86   New Jersey Nets   -1.514   39-43   East first round
Started 23-14, but unraveled after guard Michael Ray Richardson received NBA's first lifetime ban for substance abuse; Nets eliminated from playoffs in first round sweep for fourth time in five years

752   1970-71   Seattle Supersonics -1.518   38-44
Arrival of high-scoring forward Spencer Haywood gave Sonics a talent boost, but just a two-win improvement

753   1968-69   San Francisco   -1.522   41-41   West semifinals
             Warriors
Won first two games of playoff series against Lakers, but then lost last four by an average of 19.3 points per game

754   1983-84   Kansas City Kings   -1.531   38-44   West first round
Reached playoffs thanks to expanded postseason format, but coach Cotton Fitzsimmons departed after season

755   1991-92   New Jersey Nets   -1.550   40-42   East first round
Nets hoped combination of second-year forward Derrick Coleman and rookie point guard Kenny Anderson would become "Stockton and Malone East"

756 2005-06 Boston Celtics -1.551 33-49
Standout forward Paul Pierce (26.8 points per game) enjoyed one of his most productive seasons, but turnover-plagued young Celtics regressed by 12 wins

757 1975-76 Milwaukee Bucks -1.558 38-44 West first round
Bucks struggled through season after trading away center Kareem Abdul-Jabbar, but still won weak Midwest Division

758 1969-70 Boston Celtics -1.566 34-48
First season without retired Bill Russell meant 19-season string of playoff appearances came to an end

759 1981-82 Indiana Pacers -1.594 35-47
Couldn't sustain momentum from previous season's playoff appearance

760 1980-81 San Diego Clippers -1.608 36-46
Donald Sterling purchased team after season and Clippers' era of futility kicked into high gear

761 1958-59 Detroit Pistons -1.609 28-44 West semifinals
Reigning NBA scoring champion George Yardley traded after dispute with owner Fred Zollner

762 1988-89 Dallas Mavericks -1.622 38-44
Trade of top scorer Mark Aguirre and suspension of center Roy Tarpley contributed to 15-win decline

763 1998-99 Toronto Raptors -1.628 23-27
Raptors began to take flight during Rookie of the Year Vince Carter's first season

764 1969-70 Phoenix Suns -1.659 39-43 West semifinals
Eventual team owner Jerry Colangelo coached last 44 games and led second-year franchise to a playoff berth

765 1967-68 Detroit Pistons -1.667 40-42 East semifinals
Dave Bing's only scoring title (27.2 points per game) sparked Pistons to 10-win improvement and playoff appearance

766 1981-82 Chicago Bulls -1.670 34-48
Eleven-win decline one season after playoff appearance resulted in departure of center Artis Gilmore, coach Jerry Sloan

767 1976-77 Indiana Pacers -1.672 36-46
Rough initial NBA season for franchise that won three ABA titles

768 1980-81 Seattle Supersonics -1.688 34-48
Acquisition of shooting guard Paul Westphal in exchange for point guard Dennis Johnson fizzled when Westphal played just 36 games; Gus Williams sat out season because of a contract dispute

769   2004-05   Toronto Raptors   -1.708   33-49
Air Canada era ended when Raptors traded away top scorer Vince Carter in midst of second consecutive 33-49 season

770   1996-97   Minnesota   -1.711   40-42   West first round
              Timberwolves
Promising trio of forwards Kevin Garnett and Tom Gugliotta and point guard Stephon Marbury led Timberwolves to franchise's first playoff appearance

771   1969-70   Chicago Bulls   -1.712   39-43   West semifinals
Newly acquired forward Chet Walker helped Bulls set team record for highest scoring average and team returned to playoffs

772   1961-62   Detroit Pistons   -1.713   37-43   West finals
Center Walter Dukes led league in fouling out for record fourth consecutive year

773   2004-05   New Jersey Nets   -1.733   42-40   East first round
Midseason trade for high-scoring forward Vince Carter helped Nets reach playoffs despite injury-plagued season

774   1977-78   Kansas City Kings   -1.751   31-51
Departure of No. 2 scorer Brian Taylor contributed to nine-win decline

775   2001-02   Miami Heat   -1.762   36-46
Veteran center Alonzo Mourning (15.7 points per game) made a courageous comeback from kidney illness, but Heat got old in a hurry

776   1978-79   San Diego Clippers   -1.766   43-39
Franchise's first season in San Diego was its best in San Diego

777   1972-73   Houston Rockets   -1.771   33-49
Rockets traded away leading scorer and hometown hero Elvin Hayes before season

778   2005-06   Minnesota   -1.785   33-49
              Timberwolves
Star forward Kevin Garnett ended a streak of 351 consecutive games started once Timberwolves officially were eliminated from playoff contention for second consecutive season

779   1951-52   Fort Wayne Pistons   -1.789   29-37   West semifinals
Larry Foust beat out George Mikan to win league rebounding title, but Pistons couldn't keep up in league standings

780   1994-95   Miami Heat   -1.794   32-50
Curious early season trade (acquired aging center Kevin Willis for in-prime guard Steve Smith and forward Grant Long) contributed to 10-win decline

781 1977-78   New Orleans Jazz   -1.800   39-43
Best record of franchise's time in New Orleans
782 1950-51   Fort Wayne Pistons   -1.806   32-36   West semifinals
Season "remembered" for 19-18 win at Minneapolis on November 22
783 1946-47   Detroit Falcons   -1.810   20-40
Folded after one unremarkable season
784 2003-04   New York   -1.812   39-43   East first round
            Knickerbockers
New general manager Isiah Thomas made a splash with midseason acquisition of guard Stephon Marbury
785 1999-00   Denver Nuggets   -1.824   35-47
Nuggets responded favorably to return of Dan Issel as coach
786 2004-05   Golden State   -1.829   34-48
            Warriors
Acquisition of standout guard Baron Davis provided spark to otherwise dreary season
787 2003-04   Boston Celtics   -1.841   36-46   East first round
Managed to sneak into playoffs after new general manager Danny Ainge revamped roster
788 1994-95   Boston Celtics   -1.845   35-47   East first round
High-scoring forward Dominique Wilkins got the Celtics into the postseason during team's final season in Boston Garden, but no further
789 1977-78   Boston Celtics   -1.858   32-50
Celtics wisely drafted Larry Bird after season, even though he would not join team until 1979
790 1950-51   Baltimore Bullets   -1.885   24-42
Player/coach Buddy Jeannette was glue that held franchise together, but he was ousted after 14-23 start
791 1976-77   Boston Celtics   -1.891   44-38   East semifinals
Shooting guard Charlie Scott (broken arm) and center Dave Cowens (leave of absence) combined to miss 71 games, contributing to 10-win decline
792 1985-86   San Antonio Spurs   -1.902   35-47   West first round
Made playoffs despite franchise's first last-place finish
793 1953-54   Philadelphia Warriors -1.905   29-43
Final season for franchise icon Joe Fulks
794 1962-63   San Francisco   -1.925   31-49
            Warriors
Retirement of longtime forward Paul Arizin contributed to 18-win decline during franchise's first season on West Coast

795 1991-92   Houston Rockets   -1.926   42-40
Rockets icon Rudy Tomjanovich began his coaching tenure with team over last 30 games, but losses in last three games cost team playoff spot

796 1950-51   Indianapolis   -1.929   31-37   West semifinals
              Olympians
Olympians struggled against tougher schedule during second NBA season, but did win longest game (six overtimes) in NBA history

797 1988-89   Washington Bullets -1.935   40-42
Beginning of string of eight consecutive seasons without postseason play

798 1964-65   Baltimore Bullets -1.936   37-43   West finals
Qualified for playoffs and won a postseason series for first time in franchise history under direction of coach Buddy Jeannette, coach of previous Baltimore Bullets franchise

799 1949-50   Boston Celtics   -1.944   22-46
Celtics hired Red Auerbach as coach after last-place finish; Boston would not finish below .500 again until 1970

800 1971-72   Atlanta Hawks   -1.944   36-46   East semifinals
Sophomore slump for guard Pete Maravich kept team in status quo

801 2000-01   Detroit Pistons   -1.950   32-50
Franchise initially staggered by star forward Grant Hill's decision to leave as a free agent

802 2000-01   Denver Nuggets   -1.956   40-42
Respectable record, but only 11th-best in Western Conference

803 1968-69   Chicago Bulls   -1.980   33-49
Missed playoffs for first time in franchise's three-year history (drawing a "crowd" of just 891 for one game), but shrewdly traded for future star forward Bob Love

804 1997-98   Philadelphia 76ers -2.012   31-51
Coach Larry Brown spent first season in Philly assembling supporting cast of rebounders and defenders around high-scoring guard Allen Iverson

805 1998-99   Washington Wizards -2.036   18-32
Trading away star forward Chris Webber for aging guard Mitch Richmond sent franchise into a tailspin

806 1956-57   Rochester Royals   -2.053   31-41
Took Sihugo Green with No. 1 overall draft pick, ahead of No. 2 selection Bill Russell, before final season in Rochester

807 1997-98   Boston Celtics   -2.068   36-46
Rick Pitino's coaching tenure not viewed favorably in Boston, but he did direct a 21-win improvement during his first season

808 1960-61   Detroit Pistons   -2.077   34-45   West semifinals
Respectable at home (20-11), but league-worst 3-19 in true road games
809 2005-06   Philadelphia 76ers   -2.077   38-44
Star guard Allen Iverson (33.0 points per game) and veteran forward Chris Webber (20.2 points per game) scored big in their only full season together, but 76ers' defense regressed and kept team out of postseason
810 1998-99   Boston Celtics   -2.089   19-31
Lockout-shortened season put coach Rick Pitino's rebuilding drive in neutral
811 1992-93   Denver Nuggets   -2.108   36-46
Breakthrough season for guard Mahmoud Abdul-Rauf and contributions from rookie forward LaPhonso Ellis resulted in 12-win improvement
812 1996-97   Sacramento Kings   -2.117   34-48
Couldn't build on momentum from previous season's playoff appearance
813 1998-99   Dallas Mavericks   -2.142   19-31
End of rebuilding process in sight as forward Dirk Nowitzki and point guard Steve Nash arrived in Dallas
814 1956-57   Fort Wayne Pistons   -2.146   34-38   West semifinals
Franchise won third consecutive division title and then departed for Detroit
815 1958-59   Philadelphia Warriors -2.176 32-40
Neil Johnston's career cut short by a knee injury, but Warriors had another center—Wilt Chamberlain—on the way
816 1984-85   Phoenix Suns   -2.213   36-46   West first round
Top scorers Larry Nance and Walter Davis combined to miss 80 games with injuries, dooming Suns to first losing season since 1977
817 1949-50   St. Louis Bombers   -2.239   26-42
Franchise folded after missing postseason for first time in four-year history, despite presence of hometown hero Ed Macauley
818 1981-82   New York Knickerbockers -2.248 33-49
Trade of No. 2 scorer Ray Williams, subpar season for center Bill Cartwright contributed to 17-win slide
819 2000-01   Boston Celtics   -2.254   36-46
Celtics went 12-22 with Rick Pitino as coach; 24-24 after he resigned
820 1952-53   Indianapolis Olympians -2.274 28-43 West semifinals
Franchise folded after making playoffs in all four of its seasons

821	1965-66	New York Knickerbockers	-2.275	30-50	

First round draft pick and future star Bill Bradley spent next two seasons completing Rhodes Scholar studies

822	1998-99	Golden State Warriors	-2.280	21-29	

Stayed competitive by leading the league in rebounding

823	1990-91	Cleveland Cavaliers	-2.284	33-49	

Standout guard Mark Price played just 16 games because of an injury, resulting in team's only losing record during an 11-year span

824	1973-74	Seattle Supersonics	-2.293	36-46	

Bill Russell helped Sonics to 10-win improvement during first season of three-year run as team's coach

825	1989-90	Washington Bullets	-2.296	31-51	

Highlight of season: Three former Bullets (Elvin Hayes, Earl Monroe, and Dave Bing) were inducted into the Basketball Hall of Fame on the same day in fall of 1989

826	1979-80	Washington Bullets	-2.301	39-43	East first round

Injuries, improvement of division rivals led to 15-win decline

827	1985-86	Cleveland Cavaliers	-2.306	29-53	

Seven-win decline one season after a postseason appearance cost coach George Karl his job

828	1965-66	San Francisco Warriors	-2.319	35-45	

Added No. 1 overall draft pick Fred Hetzel; another Warriors rookie by the name of Rick Barry would make a much bigger impact

829	1957-58	Detroit Pistons	-2.321	33-39	West finals

Franchise moved to Detroit and endured 13 consecutive losing seasons

830	1974-75	Phoenix Suns	-2.324	32-50	

Suns began defense-oriented makeover that would lead to NBA Finals appearance during following season

831	1977-78	Indiana Pacers	-2.360	31-51	

Acquired reigning Rookie of the Year Adrian Dantley, then traded him away after 23 games

832	2000-01	Los Angeles Clippers	-2.362	31-51	

Exciting young team made 16-win improvement

833	1952-53	Milwaukee Hawks	-2.381	27-44	

Frontcourt newcomer Jack Nichols led team in scoring, helping player-coach Andrew Levane lead team to 10-win improvement

834 1972-73   Kansas City/   -2.382   36-46
              Omaha Kings
Nate "Tiny" Archibald became only player in NBA history to lead league in points and assists

835 1984-85   Cleveland Cavaliers   -2.385   36-46   East first round
Reached playoffs for first time since 1978 despite 2-19 start during George Karl's first season as an NBA coach

836 1986-87   Golden State   -2.385   42-40   West semifinals
              Warriors
Least dominant team to finish with a winning record

837 2004-05   Los Angeles Lakers   -2.395   34-48
Decision to trade center Shaquille O'Neal and build around guard Kobe Bryant initially resulted in 22-win decline, first postseason absence since 1994

838 1983-84   Washington Bullets   -2.422   35-47   East first round
Made playoffs despite finishing last in division

839 2004-05   Orlando Magic   -2.426   36-46
Improved by 15 wins as versatile forward Grant Hill stayed healthy for most of season and frontliner Dwight Howard enjoyed a solid rookie year

840 1969-70   Seattle Supersonics   -2.431   36-46
Player-coach Lenny Wilkens led league in assists, helped Sonics to six-win improvement

841 1994-95   Dallas Mavericks   -2.443   36-46
Co-Rookie of the Year Jason Kidd sparked 23-win improvement

842 1986-87   Phoenix Suns   -2.476   36-46
Coach John MacLeod stepped down after 13-plus seasons

843 1949-50   Philadelphia Warriors -2.494   26-42   East semifinals
Mysterious dip in top scorer Joe Fulks' production (14.2 points per game) corresponded with dip in team's fortunes

844 1969-70   Cincinnati Royals   -2.501   36-46
Royals guard Oscar Robertson and first-year coach Bob Cousy often clashed during Robertson's final season in Cincinnati

845 1980-81   Atlanta Hawks   -2.519   31-51
Injuries, collapse of defense (allowed 6.4 more points per game than previous season) led to 19-win decline

846 2006-07   Seattle Supersonics   -2.519   31-51
Bad travel report: Sonics set a franchise record with 15 consecutive road losses amidst talk of possible franchise relocation

847 2005-06   Utah Jazz   -2.529   41-41
Versatile forward Andrei Kirilenko made strong comeback from injury-plagued season, helping young Jazz improve by 15 wins

848 2005-06   New Orleans/   -2.535   38-44
            Oklahoma City Hornets
Arrival of Rookie of the Year guard Chris Paul inspired 20-win improvement, optimism after Hurricane Katrina forced franchise to play majority of games in Oklahoma City

849 2006-07   Indiana Pacers   -2.539   35-47
Worst shooting team in the NBA lost 23 of last 29 games to end a string of nine consecutive playoff appearances

850 1996-97   Los Angeles Clippers   -2.546   36-46   West first round
Snuck into playoffs behind workmanlike effort from forward Loy Vaught; team wouldn't return to postseason until 2006

851 1979-80   Chicago Bulls   -2.570   30-52
Bulls center Artis Gilmore missed 34 games with injuries, ensuring one-win decline during Jerry Sloan's first season as an NBA coach

852 1955-56   Rochester Royals   -2.572   31-41
Talented forward Maurice Stokes (one of seven rookies on roster) named Rookie of the Year, but franchise missed playoffs for first time

853 1984-85   Kansas City Kings   -2.573   31-51
New coach Jack McKinney became former coach Jack McKinney after 1-8 start; franchise departed for Sacramento after second of 15 consecutive losing seasons

854 1974-75   Philadelphia 76ers   -2.577   34-48
High-scoring forward Billy Cunningham returned after two-year stint in ABA, contributing to nine-win improvement

855 1954-55   Milwaukee Hawks   -2.581   26-46
Hawks made five-game improvement as forward Bob Pettit earned Rookie of the Year honors, but team finished last in division for fourth consecutive season

856 1972-73   Cleveland Cavaliers   -2.590   32-50
Newly acquired guard Lenny Wilkens averaged 20.5 points per game at age 35, contributing to nine-win improvement

857 1978-79   Detroit Pistons   -2.601   30-52
Big man Bob Lanier's injury troubles continued, resulting in eight-win decline during Dick Vitale's first season as coach

#	Season	Team	Rating	Record	Playoffs
858	1995-96	Denver Nuggets	-2.603	35-47	

Controversy over guard Mahmoud Abdul-Rauf's refusal to stand for national anthem deflected attention away from team's struggles

#	Season	Team	Rating	Record	Playoffs
859	1995-96	Sacramento Kings	-2.603	39-43	West first round

Made franchise's first playoff appearance since 1986

#	Season	Team	Rating	Record
860	2004-05	New York Knickerbockers	-2.633	33-49

Sad end to Lenny Wilkens' coaching career; season fell apart soon after Stephon Marbury proclaimed himself league's best point guard

#	Season	Team	Rating	Record
861	1996-97	Toronto Raptors	-2.645	30-52

Finished in cellar, but improved by nine wins during franchise's second season

#	Season	Team	Rating	Record
862	1989-90	Golden State Warriors	-2.646	37-45

Warriors led league in scoring, but only expansion Magic gave up more points

#	Season	Team	Rating	Record
863	1975-76	Atlanta Hawks	-2.648	29-53

Second-year forward John Drew emerged as team's leading scorer, but Hawks finished in cellar for first time since 1955 after top two draft picks spurned team and joined the ABA

#	Season	Team	Rating	Record
864	1976-77	New Orleans Jazz	-2.675	35-47

Pete Maravich (31.1 points per game) won only scoring title by whopping 4.5 points per game over runner-up

#	Season	Team	Rating	Record	Playoffs
865	1966-67	New York Knickerbockers	-2.711	36-45	East semifinals

Knicks qualified for playoffs for first time since 1959

#	Season	Team	Rating	Record
866	2002-03	Memphis Grizzlies	-2.713	28-54

Team started to turn around when new general manager Jerry West replaced coach Sidney Lowe with Hubie Brown

#	Season	Team	Rating	Record
867	1948-49	Boston Celtics	-2.732	25-35

Boston Garden mystique begins: First Celtics team to finish with winning record at home

#	Season	Team	Rating	Record
868	1968-69	Detroit Pistons	-2.758	32-50

Pistons traded standout forward Dave DeBusschere to Knicks as part of franchise makeover

#	Season	Team	Rating	Record
869	1985-86	Indiana Pacers	-2.786	26-56

Knee injury wrecked career of standout forward Clark Kellogg

870 2003-04   Philadelphia 76ers   -2.789   33-49
Injury-plagued season for top scorer Allen Iverson resulted in 15-win decline
871 1948-49   Fort Wayne Pistons   -2.803   22-38
Team switched coaches after 0-6 start to first BAA season
872 1975-76   Kansas City Kings   -2.830   31-51
Team dropped its Omaha affiliation; also dropped by 13 wins when defense allowed 4.6 more points per game than previous season
873 1961-62   St. Louis Hawks   -2.871   29-51
Departure of point guard Lenny Wilkens (military service) contributed to 22-win decline
874 1975-76   Chicago Bulls   -2.885   24-58
Age, injuries quickly took a toll after team's playoff heartbreak of previous season
875 1989-90   Los Angeles Clippers   -2.899   30-52
First round draft pick Danny Ferry refused to play with Clippers, but team still managed a nine-win improvement
876 1969-70   Detroit Pistons   -2.904   31-51
First of three consecutive last-place finishes did put franchise in position to draft big man Bob Lanier
877 2003-04   Cleveland Cavaliers   -2.905   35-47
Rookie of the Year LeBron James lived up to expectations, propelled Cavaliers to 18-win improvement
878 2005-06   Seattle Supersonics   -2.920   35-47
League-worst defense resulted in 17-win decline despite career-best season for guard Ray Allen (25.1 points per game)
879 1992-93   Sacramento Kings   -2.928   25-57
Kings' fourth consecutive last-place finish
880 1969-70   San Diego Rockets   -2.943   27-55
Injury to No. 2 scorer Don Kojis resulted in 10-win decline under new coach Alex Hannum
881 1960-61   Cincinnati Royals   -2.975   33-46
Rookie of the Year guard Oscar Robertson directed Royals to a 14-win improvement
882 2006-07   New York Knickerbockers   -2.981   33-49
General manager/coach Isiah Thomas got to keep his jobs thanks to a 10-win improvement, but the Knicks lost 15 of 19 after Thomas got his contract extension

883 2004-05   Milwaukee Bucks   -2.982   30-52
Bucks hampered by absence of injured point guard T.J. Ford; suffered 11-win decline

884 1970-71   Cincinnati Royals   -2.982   33-49
Franchise icon Oscar Robertson traded to Bucks before the season

885 1976-77   Milwaukee Bucks   -2.983   30-52
Don Nelson assumed coaching reins after 3-15 start

886 1964-65   Detroit Pistons   -2.986   31-49
Dave DeBusschere, 24, became youngest coach in NBA history when named player-coach after 2-9 start

887 2005-06   Toronto Raptors   -2.994   27-55
Lost 15 of first 16 games and 12 of last 13 games, but All-Star forward Chris Bosh kept the Raptors competitive in between

888 1985-86   Phoenix Suns   -3.007   32-50
Aging Suns missed postseason for first time since 1977

889 1983-84   Houston Rockets   -3.023   29-53
Best of both worlds: Rookie center Ralph Sampson sparked 15-game improvement and team still received No. 1 overall draft pick and rights to Akeem Olajuwon

890 1985-86   Sacramento Kings   -3.032   37-45   West first round
Snuck into playoffs during franchise's first season in Sacramento

891 2003-04   Phoenix Suns   -3.095   29-53
Suns dealt away point guard Stephon Marbury at midseason to prepare to make a run at free agent guard Steve Nash in the offseason

892 1983-84   San Diego Clippers   -3.111   30-52
Five-win improvement, but finished last in division for third consecutive time during franchise's final season in San Diego

893 1988-89   Indiana Pacers   -3.128   28-54
Coach Jack Ramsay quit after 0-7 start; team later tied franchise record with 12-game losing streak spanning January and February

894 1981-82   Kansas City Kings   -3.133   30-52
Injuries, roster turnover prevented Kings from building on previous season's run to West finals

895 1950-51   Tri-Cities Blackhawks -3.150   25-43
Relinquished rights to coach Red Auerbach and Bob Cousy before final season in "Tri-Cities"

896 1948-49   St. Louis Bombers   -3.163   29-31   West semifinals
Addition of powerful Lakers and Royals to Bombers' Western Division sent St. Louis franchise reeling

897   1986-87   Sacramento Kings   -3.177   29-53
Sank eight wins and back to reality during second year in Sacramento after previous season's surprise playoff appearance

898   2006-07   Philadelphia 76ers   -3.181   35-47
Sixers were 5-18 and losers of 11 in a row before they traded star guard Allen Iverson; Philly went 30-29 after the big deal

899   1990-91   Los Angeles Clippers   -3.188   31-51
Another year, another injury to a key Clipper; Shooting guard Ron Harper missed first 41 games with knee injury

900   1973-74   Phoenix Suns   -3.198   30-52
First season of John MacLeod's lengthy coaching tenure in Phoenix also was his worst

901   1964-65   New York Knickerbockers   -3.205   31-49
Franchise's revival started with arrival of rookie center Willis Reed

902   1973-74   Kansas City/Omaha Kings   -3.218   33-49
Coach Bob Cousy departed after 6-16 start; reigning scoring champion Nate "Tiny" Archibald missed most of season with Achilles injury

903   1994-95   New Jersey Nets   -3.221   30-52
Nets declined by 15 wins during last full season in New Jersey for forward Derrick Coleman and guard Kenny Anderson

904   2006-07   Minnesota Timberwolves   -3.228   32-50
Timberwolves were 20-20 and in playoff contention when coach Dwayne Casey was fired for no apparent reason; Minnesota staggered to a 12-30 mark the rest of the way

905   1985-86   Chicago Bulls   -3.239   30-52   East first round
Michael Jordan missed 54 games with an injury during the regular season, but set playoff record with 63 points during Game 2 of first round series against eventual champion Celtics

906   1983-84   Golden State Warriors   -3.247   37-45
Warriors cut ties with top scorers World B. Free and Bernard King, but still managed seven-win improvement

907   2003-04   Toronto Raptors   -3.252   33-49
League-worst offense too much for Raptors to overcome

908 1978-79   New York Knickerbockers   -3.286   31-51
Traded away high-scoring forwards Bob McAdoo and Spencer Haywood in midst of 12-win decline

909 1992-93   Milwaukee Bucks   -3.290   28-54
Brought in seven new players and new coach Mike Dunleavy, but finished alone in cellar for first time since 1977

910 1986-87   Cleveland Cavaliers   -3.309   31-51
Rookie class of Brad Daugherty, Ron Harper, and Mark Price produced just a two-win improvement this year, but would get better in a hurry

911 1966-67   Chicago Bulls   -3.336   33-48   West semifinals
No other post-1961 expansion team has won as many games or qualified for postseason during inaugural campaign

912 1962-63   Detroit Pistons   -3.338   34-46   West semifinals
Last year in string of 14 consecutive playoff appearances, the last seven despite losing records

913 1982-83   Golden State Warriors   -3.374   30-52
Al Attles ended distinguished coaching tenure after Warriors' injury-plagued season

914 1995-96   Boston Celtics   -3.389   33-49
Signs of franchise in flux: New coach (M.L. Carr), new home (Fleet Center), and forward Dino Radja fourth player in four years to lead Celtics in scoring

915 1959-60   Detroit Pistons   -3.404   30-45   West semifinals
Player Dick McGuire assumed coaching duties at midseason, but Pistons still finished well under .500

916 1971-72   Philadelphia 76ers   -3.404   30-52
Leading scorer Billy Cunningham would jump to ABA after season

917 1999-00   Washington Wizards   -3.404   29-53
Top players Mitch Richmond, Juwan Howard, and Rod Strickland all saw their production decline, guaranteeing similar fate for team

918 2001-02   Cleveland Cavaliers   -3.432   29-53
Andre Miller's assist title only highlight in a tough season

919 1985-86   Golden State Warriors   -3.436   30-52
Eight-win improvement as center Joe Barry Carroll rejoined franchise and rookie forward Chris Mullin came aboard

920   1995-96   Los Angeles Clippers -3.450   29-53
      Brought in aggressive rebounders Brian Williams (later Bison Dele) and Rodney Rogers, resulting in 12-win improvement
921   1962-63   Chicago Zephyrs   -3.467   25-55
      Second-year franchise had second nickname and second Rookie of the Year (Terry Dischinger), but left for Baltimore after season
922   1998-99   New Jersey Nets   -3.490   16-34
      Nets literally and figuratively failed to rebound from lockout, injury to top rebounder Jayson Williams
923   2004-05   Portland Trail Blazers -3.530   27-55
      Blazers avoided negative off-court headlines, but ended 15-year run of on-court winning records
924   1977-78   Buffalo Braves   -3.542   27-55
      Braves moved to San Diego after season following bizarre "franchise swap" between Buffalo owner John Y. Brown and Celtics owner Irv Levin
925   1978-79   Cleveland Cavaliers   -3.558   30-52
      Bill Fitch, Cavaliers' original coach, departed after 13-win decline and beginning of string of nine consecutive losing seasons
926   2002-03   Los Angeles Clippers -3.559   27-55
      Took 12-loss step backwards after showing promise during previous season
927   1963-64   Philadelphia 76ers   -3.567   34-46   East semifinals
      Curse of Syracuse? 76ers had inexplicable 14-win decline during first season after franchise moved to Philadelphia from Syracuse
928   1999-00   Cleveland Cavaliers   -3.570   32-50
      As top scorer Shawn Kemp's weight ballooned, Cavaliers' fortunes went bust
929   1991-92   Charlotte Hornets   -3.578   31-51
      No. 1 overall draft pick Larry Johnson named Rookie of the Year as Hornets enjoyed five-win improvement
930   2006-07   Boston Celtics   -3.632   24-58
      Celtics endured a gloomy year on the court (franchise record 17-game losing streak) and off (Boston icons Red Auerbach and Dennis Johnson died during the season)
931   1989-90   Minnesota   -3.691   22-60
                   Timberwolves
      Best first-year record of late-1980s expansion teams
932   1947-48   Boston Celtics   -3.725   20-28   BAA quarterfinals
      First sub-.500 team in league history to qualify for the postseason

The NBA From Top to Bottom

933 2002-03   Atlanta Hawks   -3.746   35-47
Unfulfilled playoffs "guarantee" cost franchise money in ticket refunds; cost coach Lon Krueger his job

934 1967-68   Chicago Bulls   -3.747   29-53   West semifinals
Presence of two expansion teams in same division helped Bulls qualify for playoffs

935 1978-79   Chicago Bulls   -3.772   31-51
Solid defense, but last in the league on offense despite midseason coaching change

936 1983-84   Cleveland Cavaliers   -3.776   28-54
Rebuilding process began with five-win improvement under new owners George and Gordon Gund

937 1990-91   Minnesota Timberwolves   -3.778   29-53
Coach Bill Musselman fired after directing seven-win improvement during franchise's second season

938 1977-78   Houston Rockets   -3.819   28-54
Loss of starting forward Rudy Tomjanovich (punched out by Lakers' Kermit Washington) cast dark cloud over season

939 2004-05   Utah Jazz   -3.824   26-56
Injury-plagued season for versatile forward Andrei Kirilenko doomed Jazz to losing season, marking end of 21-season string without a sub-.500 record

940 1990-91   Orlando Magic   -3.825   31-51
Scott Skiles' single-game assist record of 30 on December 30 highlighted season

941 2005-06   Charlotte Bobcats -3.850   26-56
Improved by eight wins during franchise's second year despite injury-plagued season

942 2006-07   Portland Trail Blazers -3.854   32-50
Roy for ROY: Rookie of the Year Brandon Roy helped the young Blazers to an 11-win improvement

943 1976-77   Atlanta Hawks   -3.855   31-51
Hubie Brown's first season as Atlanta coach; standout guard Lou Hudson's final season as a Hawks player

944 1961-62   New York Knickerbockers   -3.875   29-51
Respectable at home (19-14), but just 2-23 on the road

945 2006-07   Charlotte Bobcats   -3.889   33-49
Young core continued to progress, resulting in a seven-win improvement during the franchise's third season
946 2003-04   Los Angeles Clippers -3.895   28-54
Clippers set a new precedent by retaining free agent forward Elton Brand, but kept with old precedent with subpar season
947 1979-80   San Diego Clippers   -3.904   35-47
Good news: Clippers acquired center Bill Walton. Bad news: Walton played just 14 games because of injury and team endured eight-win decline
948 1974-75   Los Angeles Lakers   -3.907   30-52
Lakers suffered 17-win decline during first season after Hall of Fame guard Jerry West retired
949 1991-92   Miami Heat   -3.940   38-44   East first round
First of late-1980s expansion teams to qualify for postseason
950 1993-94   Los Angeles Lakers   -3.947   33-49
Former Lakers star Magic Johnson couldn't revive team as coach for last 16 games during standout forward James Worthy's final season
951 1959-60   Minneapolis Lakers   -3.955   25-50   West finals
Least dominant team to win a playoff series and to reach conference finals
952 1996-97   New Jersey Nets   -3.970   26-56
New coach John Calipari went through 23 players, but did finish season with respectable talent
953 1946-47   Toronto Huskies   -3.970   22-38
First BAA game took place in Toronto, but Huskies folded after inaugural season
954 1978-79   New Jersey Nets   -3.993   37-45   East first round
Made franchise's first NBA playoff appearance
955 2001-02   New York Knickerbockers -4.054   30-52
Coach Jeff Van Gundy resigned after 10-9 start; team missed him more than it realized
956 1971-72   Cincinnati Royals   -4.108   30-52
Franchise went out with a whimper during final season in Cincinnati
957 1973-74   Cleveland Cavaliers   -4.118   29-53
Cavaliers' fourth last-place finish in four years of existence
958 1982-83   Utah Jazz   -4.125   30-52
Traded away first round draft pick Dominique Wilkins to Hawks in exchange for John Drew before season; Drew promptly entered drug rehabilitation program and Wilkins promptly became a star

959   1979-80   Golden State   -4.130   24-58
                Warriors
Warriors fans still rue after-season trade that sent Robert Parish and draft pick used to select Kevin McHale to Boston for draft rights to Joe Barry Carroll

960   1969-70   San Francisco   -4.131   30-52
                Warriors
Injury-plagued season for center Nate Thurmond resulted in 11-win decline

961   1948-49   Indianapolis Jets   -4.138   18-42
Folded after one season to make way for new Indianapolis franchise

962   1979-80   Denver Nuggets   -4.153   30-52
Good news: Nuggets acquired high-scoring forward Alex English; Bad news: High-flying forward David Thompson's downward spiral began

963   1995-96   New Jersey Nets   -4.154   30-52
Center Yinka Dare's season: 58 games, 626 minutes, 0 assists

964   1984-85   New York   -4.206   24-58
                Knickerbockers
Season fell apart quickly after knee injury to NBA scoring leader Bernard King

965   1994-95   Milwaukee Bucks   -4.222   34-48
Top rookie scorer Glenn Robinson (21.9 points per game) led Bucks to 14-win improvement

966   1993-94   Boston Celtics   -4.249   32-50
Tragic offseason death of leading scorer Reggie Lewis and retirement of star forward Kevin McHale contributed to 16-win decline

967   1976-77   Buffalo Braves   -4.272   30-52
Traded away reigning scoring champion Bob McAdoo for financial reasons early in the season, triggering a 16-win decline

968   1973-74   Portland Trail Blazers -4.286 27-55
Fourth consecutive last-place finish put Trail Blazers in position to draft center Bill Walton

969   1990-91   Dallas Mavericks -4.288   28-54
Injury to guard Fat Lever and lifetime suspension of center Roy Tarpley resulted in first of 10 consecutive losing seasons for Mavericks

970   1983-84   Indiana Pacers   -4.310   26-56
Stable local ownership only positive to emerge during third of five consecutive losing seasons

971 1980-81   Cleveland Cavaliers   -4.311   28-54
Owner Ted Stepien's "reign of error" began with nine-win decline
972 2001-02   Atlanta Hawks   -4.322   33-49
Addition of hometown hero and new go-to scorer Shareef Abdur-Rahim paid off in modest eight-win improvement
973 1968-69   Seattle Supersonics   -4.330   30-52
Lenny Wilkens provided veteran presence at point guard, leading to seven-win improvement during franchise's second season
974 2000-01   Cleveland Cavaliers   -4.336   30-52
Cavaliers cut ties with forward Shawn Kemp; Standout center Zydrunas Ilgauskas again missed time because of foot injury
975 2006-07   Milwaukee Bucks   -4.343   28-54
Bucks were 6-23 when top scorer Michael Redd sat out with a knee injury; Milwaukee fell out of playoff contention with a 3-22 skid to start the New Year
976 1981-82   Dallas Mavericks   -4.365   28-54
Addition of rookies Mark Aguirre and Rolando Blackman contributed to 13-win improvement during franchise's second season
977 1991-92   Washington Bullets   -4.377   25-57
Pervis Ellison (20.0) was league's Most Improved Player, but Bullets got worse by five games
978 2001-02   Houston Rockets   -4.389   28-54
Season after departure of center Hakeem Olajuwon; season before arrival of center Yao Ming
979 1946-47   Boston Celtics   -4.405   22-38
Chuck Connors of *The Rifleman* fame played for first Celtics team; broke wooden backboard with warm-up dunk before first Celtics home game
980 1984-85   Los Angeles Clippers -4.417   31-51
Typical Clipper campaign during franchise's first year in Los Angeles: two coaches, poor record, and the team drafted underachieving center Benoit Benjamin after the season
981 1982-83   Chicago Bulls   -4.482   28-54
Team declined by six wins after trading away center Artis Gilmore
982 1982-83   San Diego Clippers   -4.493   25-57
Rookie of the Year Terry Cummings (23.7 points per game) and partial season from center Bill Walton helped Clippers to modest eight-win improvement
983 2006-07   Memphis Grizzlies   -4.494   22-60
Top scorer Pau Gasol missed the first 22 games with a foot injury sustained during the offseason, leading to a 6-24 start that got coach Mike Fratello fired

984 1990-91   New Jersey Nets   -4.495   26-56
High-scoring forward Derrick Coleman named Rookie of the Year and franchise still was able to add point guard Kenny Anderson with No. 2 overall pick in the draft

985 1989-90   Sacramento Kings   -4.509   23-59
Posted franchise's worst record of Sacramento era after adding No. 1 overall draft pick Pervis Ellison

986 1986-87   New Jersey Nets   -4.545   24-58
Decline of 15 wins started string of five consecutive seasons without a playoff berth

987 1987-88   Phoenix Suns   -4.564   28-54
Midseason makeover, including trade for guard Kevin Johnson, would pay dividends next season

988 1950-51   Washington Capitols -4.597   10-25
Folded after 35 games despite presence of high-scoring guard Bill Sharman

989 2005-06   Atlanta Hawks   -4.644   26-56
Hawks started 2-16, but went on to double previous season's win total as offense scored 4.7 more points per game

990 1953-54   Milwaukee Hawks   -4.688   21-51
Traded away leading scorer Jack Nichols and brought in Red Holzman as coach at midseason; finished season as most inept offensive team (70.0 points per game) in post-1950 NBA history

991 1995-96   Dallas Mavericks   -4.691   26-56
Combination of young standouts Jason Kidd, Jamal Mashburn and Jimmy Jackson produced another "J": jealousy, along with a 10-win decline

992 1978-79   Boston Celtics   -4.759   29-53
Franchise's first last-place finish since 1950

993 1949-50   Baltimore Bullets   -4.760   25-43
Lost previous season's leading scorer for second consecutive year, a pattern that took a toll on the franchise

994 1983-84   Chicago Bulls   -4.764   27-55
Third consecutive decline in record did put Bulls in position to draft Michael Jordan

995 2006-07   Atlanta Hawks   -4.771   30-52
Scored fewer points than any team in the league, but still managed a four-win improvement

996 1987-88   San Antonio Spurs   -4.772   31-51   West first round
Managed to earn playoff berth without services of No. 1 overall draft pick David Robinson (fulfilling military obligations)

997 1996-97   Golden State   -4.785   30-52
                 Warriors
Warriors played home games in San Jose during arena renovation; declined by six wins during forward Chris Mullin's final season with team
998 1990-91   Washington Bullets   -4.787   30-52
One last blaze of glory for Bernard King (28.4 points per game) before knee injuries wrecked his career for good.
999 2003-04   Atlanta Hawks   -4.838   28-54
Hawks acknowledged beginning of rebuilding process by going through 23 players, trading top frontcourt players Shareef Abdur-Rahim and Theo Ratliff
1000 2001-02   Golden State   -4.876   21-61
                 Warriors
Rookie Jason Richardson's Slam Dunk title highlight of another dreary season
1001 1990-91   Charlotte Hornets   -4.895   26-56
Newly acquired guard Johnny Newman led team in scoring and franchise made seven-win improvement
1002 1995-96   Milwaukee Bucks   -4.914   25-57
Team-record 15-game losing streak lowlight of season
1003 1966-67   Detroit Pistons   -4.916   30-51
Rookie of the Year guard Dave Bing (20.0 points per game) keyed eight-win improvement
1004 1986-87   San Antonio Spurs   -4.917   28-54
Defensive whiz Alvin Robertson (NBA steals leader for second consecutive year) couldn't stop Spurs' slide
1005 1985-86   New York   -4.938   23-59
                 Knickerbockers
Patrick Ewing named Rookie of the Year, but injuries to Ewing and reigning NBA scoring champ Bernard King prevented progress
1006 1994-95   Golden State   -4.959   26-56
                 Warriors
Franchise sent reeling by preseason trade of forward Chris Webber, ensuing resignation of coach Don Nelson after 45 games
1007 2002-03   Miami Heat   -4.984   25-57
Heat coach Pat Riley's last season before brief "retirement" was his worst
1008 1994-95   Philadelphia 76ers   -4.990   24-58
League Most Improved Player Dana Barros started record string of 89 consecutive games with a 3-pointer, but 76ers still struggled

1009 2000-01   Vancouver Grizzlies -5.065   23-59
Franchise's last season in Canada was its best season in Canada

1010 1968-69   Milwaukee Bucks   -5.070   27-55
Put together respectable showing during expansion season and still received No. 1 overall draft pick and rights to center Lew Alcindor (later Kareem Abdul-Jabbar)

1011 1995-96   Minnesota Timberwolves   -5.120   26-56
Promising forward Kevin Garnett arrived straight out of high school and averaged 10.4 points per game

1012 1988-89   Sacramento Kings   -5.143   27-55
Belated switch from Midwest Division to Pacific Division didn't help Kings' fortunes

1013 1999-00   Vancouver Grizzlies   -5.153   22-60
Top draft pick Steve Francis refused to join team, so Grizzlies shipped him to Houston in roster-revamping trade; changes didn't help much

1014 2000-01   New Jersey Nets   -5.165   26-56
Added No. 1 overall draft pick Kenyon Martin, but victory total still declined by five

1015 2002-03   Chicago Bulls   -5.167   30-52
Climbed out of division cellar for first time in post-Jordan rebuilding process, but true turnaround still two years down the road

1016 2001-02   Denver Nuggets   -5.270   27-55
Coach Dan Issel triggered his own departure by shouting insults at a fan

1017 1960-61   New York Knickerbockers   -5.273   21-58
Franchise mainstay Carl Braun concluded his career with Knicks as a player-coach

1018 1992-93   Philadelphia 76ers   -5.275   26-56
76ers suffered third consecutive nine-win decline during first season after trading away star forward Charles Barkley

1019 1993-94   Los Angeles Clippers -5.287   27-55
Departure of coach Larry Brown and midseason trade of versatile forward Danny Manning triggered 14-win decline

1020 1980-81   New Jersey Nets   -5.291   24-58
Defense allowed 3.5 more points per game than previous season, resulting in 10-win decline and departure of longtime coach Kevin Loughery

1021 1984-85   Seattle Supersonics   -5.298   31-51
Lenny Wilkens ended his second run as Sonics' coach after 11-win decline, including 12 losses in last 13 games

1022 1972-73   Seattle Supersonics   -5.332   26-56
First season after departure of player/coach Lenny Wilkens resulted in 21-win decline

1023 1993-94   Sacramento Kings   -5.333   28-54
Season remembered for rookie point guard Bobby Hurley's near-fatal auto accident

1024 1999-00   Atlanta Hawks   -5.337   28-54
Decision to acquire Isaiah Rider as team's go-to scorer sent franchise reeling during first season in Phillips Arena

1025 1964-65   San Francisco Warriors   -5.414   17-63
Season collapsed after midseason trade of center Wilt Chamberlain

1026 1949-50   Sheboygan Redskins   -5.420   22-40   West semifinals
Made playoffs in weak division, but franchise dropped out of the NBA after season

1027 2000-01   Atlanta Hawks   -5.420   25-57
Midseason trade of center Dikembe Mutombo signaled beginning of ongoing rebuilding process

1028 1982-83   Indiana Pacers   -5.439   20-62
Most losses in franchise history

1029 1959-60   Cincinnati Royals   -5.443   19-56
Royals posted worst record in franchise history during season spent waiting for arrival of University of Cincinnati guard Oscar Robertson

1030 1994-95   Washington Bullets   -5.483   21-61
Win total declined, but team had hope with combination of former University of Michigan teammates Chris Webber and Juwan Howard

1031 1981-82   Utah Jazz   -5.506   25-57
Endured franchise-worst 18-game losing streak late in season

1032 1986-87   New York Knickerbockers   -5.522   24-58
High-scoring forward Bernard King returned from knee injury late in season, but too late to help much

1033 1949-50   Waterloo Hawks   -5.535   19-43
Hawks' 1-22 road record would be franchise's Waterloo; team dropped out of the NBA after only one season

1034 1984-85 Indiana Pacers -5.550 22-60
Coaching change (Jack McKinney out, George Irvine in) couldn't change team's fortunes

1035 1991-92 Sacramento Kings -5.575 29-53
Acquisition of skilled shooting guard Mitch Richmond resulted in four-win improvement

1036 1987-88 Sacramento Kings -5.585 24-58
Bill Russell stepped down as coach after 17-41 start

1037 1977-78 New Jersey Nets -5.597 24-58
High-scoring rookie Bernard King the lone bright spot

1038 1979-80 Utah Jazz -5.634 24-58
Trading away flashy guard Pete Maravich part of makeover during franchise's first season in Utah

1039 1957-58 Minneapolis Lakers -5.678 19-53
Former Lakers star George Mikan gave up coaching reins after 9-30 start

1040 1997-98 Sacramento Kings -5.686 27-55
Franchise bid farewell to top scorer Mitch Richmond after season and promptly got better

1041 1972-73 Portland Trail Blazers -5.687 21-61
No. 1 overall draft pick LaRue Martin (4.4 points per game during rookie season) on short list of worst No. 1 picks ever

1042 1952-53 Baltimore Bullets -5.696 16-54 East semifinals
Least dominant team to qualify for the postseason

1043 1980-81 Detroit Pistons -5.743 21-61
Talent-challenged Pistons slowed the pace and managed a five-win improvement

1044 1946-47 Pittsburgh Ironmen -5.755 15-45
Had future NBA star Pete Maravich's father, Press, on roster, but finished in cellar and folded after first BAA season

1045 1966-67 Baltimore Bullets -5.794 20-61
Last in league in offense, last in league on defense, last in standings during first season in Eastern Division

1046 1980-81 Utah Jazz -5.833 28-54
Adrian Dantley's scoring title highlight of team's second season in Utah

1047 1988-89 New Jersey Nets -5.834 26-56
Veteran frontliner Buck Williams departed after the season as franchise's career leader in points and rebounds

1048 1990-91   Miami Heat   -5.863   24-58
Improved by six wins, but coach Ron Rothstein departed after franchise's third season
1049 1973-74   Philadelphia 76ers   -5.875   25-57
First-year coach Gene Shue led respectable 16-win improvement after historically bad 1972-1973 season
1050 1953-54   Baltimore Bullets   -5.899   16-56
Franchise's final full season; became most recent NBA team to fold 14 games into 1954-55 campaign
1051 1978-79   New Orleans Jazz   -5.953   26-56
Franchise departed for Utah after 13-win decline
1052 1967-68   Seattle Supersonics -5.960   23-59
Strong year for guard Walt Hazzard (24.0 points per game) resulted in respectable expansion season
1053 2002-03   Toronto Raptors   -5.964   24-58
Raptors needed star forward Vince Carter after all; Toronto took a 12-game tumble as Carter missed 39 games with injuries
1054 2003-04   Washington Wizards   -5.967   25-57
Wizards would see belated payoff in acquisition of high-scoring Gilbert Arenas and Antawn Jamison
1055 1996-97   Philadelphia 76ers   -5.970   22-60
Rookie of the Year Allen Iverson scored bunches of points, but 76ers won just four more games
1056 1965-66   Detroit Pistons   -5.972   22-58
Absence of previous season's leading scorer Terry Dischinger (military duty) and 4-19 finish resulted in nine-win slide
1057 1962-63   New York   -6.037   21-59
             Knickerbockers
Worst record in franchise history, in midst of seven-year string of last-place finishes
1058 1971-72   Detroit Pistons   -6.046   26-56
Veteran guard Dave Bing missed 37 games with detached retina, contributing to 19-win decline
1059 2004-05   Charlotte Bobcats   -6.057   18-64
Boasted Rookie of the Year forward Emeka Okafor, but otherwise endured typical expansion struggles
1060 1970-71   Portland Trail Blazers -6.076 29-53
Best of season's three expansion teams

1061 1997-98   Dallas Mavericks   -6.185   20-62
Forward Michael Finley established himself as first cornerstone in franchise's rebuilding process; Don Nelson took over as head coach after 4-12 start

1062 1993-94   Milwaukee Bucks   -6.197   20-62
Worst season in franchise history resulted in No. 1 overall draft pick and selection of high-scoring forward Glenn Robinson

1063 1963-64   New York Knickerbockers   -6.225   22-58
Tried to shake things up with multiple trades, but league-worst defense hampered progress

1064 2005-06   New York Knickerbockers   -6.251   23-59
A $128.8 million payroll bought the least dominant team in franchise history

1065 1996-97   Denver Nuggets   -6.282   21-61
Departure of guard Mahmoud Abdul-Rauf and center Dikembe Mutombo resulted in 14-win decline, including 18 losses by four points or less

1066 1998-99   Denver Nuggets   -6.285   14-36
Talented forward Antonio McDyess returned to Denver, but couldn't help much during lockout-shortened season

1067 1990-91   Sacramento Kings   -6.289   25-57
Set NBA record with 1-40 road mark

1068 1996-97   Dallas Mavericks   -6.351   24-58
Went through 27 players; traded away top scorers Jason Kidd, Jamal Mashburn and Jimmy Jackson by midseason

1069 2004-05   New Orleans Hornets-6.363   18-64
Moved to Western Conference and set franchise record for fewest wins in a season

1070 1951-52   Baltimore Bullets   -6.455   20-46
Tried its luck with another player-coach (Freddie Scolari lasted 39 games) but doomed to further decline by league-worst defense

1071 1992-93   Washington Bullets   -6.511   22-60
Injuries, decline in defense (allowed 2.1 more points per game than previous season) made bad team even worse

1072 1991-92   Orlando Magic   -6.515   21-61
Top eight scorers missed an average of 32 games apiece, leading to 10-win decline during franchise's third season

1073　2003-04　　Chicago Bulls　　　-6.523　　23-59
Aging star forward Scottie Pippen returned to Chicago for his final season, but Bulls regressed by seven wins

1074　1976-77　　New York Nets　　-6.529　　22-60
Nets sold ABA icon Julius Erving to 76ers before first NBA season to stay afloat financially, but took big hit on court

1075　1993-94　　Minnesota　　　　-6.561　　20-62
　　　　　　　　Timberwolves
Michael Williams completed record string of 97 consecutive made free throws early in season

1076　1963-64　　Detroit Pistons　　-6.574　　23-57
Injury to standout forward Dave DeBusschere contributed to 11-win decline

1077　2000-01　　Washington Wizards　-6.601　　19-63
General manager Michael Jordan watched his team produce the franchise's worst record of its time in Washington

1078　1985-86　　Los Angeles Clippers　-6.657　　32-50
Stayed reasonably competitive despite injury to leading scorer Derek Smith

1079　1996-97　　Boston Celtics　　　-6.699　　15-67
Established franchise record for fewest wins in a season

1080　1991-92　　Minnesota　　　　-6.797　　15-67
　　　　　　　　Timberwolves
Unlucky three: Franchise posted its worst record during its third season

1081　2001-02　　Memphis Grizzlies　-6.813　　23-59
Pau Gasol won Rookie of the Year honors, starting franchise on road to respectability

1082　1982-83　　Cleveland Cavaliers　-6.841　　23-59
Midseason acquisition World B. Free averaged 24.2 points a game for Cleveland, contributing to eight-win improvement

1083　1951-52　　Milwaukee Hawks　-6.879　　17-49
Relocated from Tri-Cities to Milwaukee, but forgot to bring offense; Hawks averaged 73.2 points, 4.8 less than any other team

1084　1981-82　　San Diego Clippers　-6.903　　17-65
Standout forward Tom Chambers had solid rookie season, but Clippers posted worst record of their stay in San Diego

1085　1994-95　　Detroit Pistons　　-7.000　　28-54
Co-Rookie of the Year Grant Hill didn't have much help during his first season

1086 1984-85   Golden State   -7.062   22-60
                 Warriors
Starting center Joe Barry Carroll left the franchise to play in Italy and Warriors declined by 15 wins
1087 2003-04   Orlando Magic   -7.079   21-61
Magic lost 19 in a row after winning season opener, paving way for departure of NBA scoring champion Tracy McGrady
1088 1993-94   Washington Bullets -7.084   24-58
NBA Most Improved Player Don MacLean (improved from 6.6 points per game to 20.0 points per game) lone bright spot in another dismal season
1089 1989-90   Charlotte Hornets   -7.084   19-63
Western Conference schedule for a North Carolina team contributed to one-win decline during franchise's second season
1090 1987-88   New Jersey Nets   -7.186   19-63
Started 2-13 and went through three coaches before Willis Reed took over as coach and brought some sense of stability
1091 1995-96   Toronto Raptors   -7.203   21-61
Rookie of the Year guard Damon Stoudamire highlight of franchise's expansion season
1092 1974-75   New Orleans Jazz   -7.236   23-59
Traded to acquire former LSU star Pete Maravich for expansion season, but team still started 1-14 and got coach Scotty Robertson fired
1093 1988-89   San Antonio Spurs   -7.251   21-61
Even first-year coach Larry Brown couldn't win with this crew while future star David Robinson completed military obligations
1094 1997-98   Vancouver Grizzlies -7.322   19-63
Only time Grizzlies avoided last place during their time in Canada
1095 1993-94   Philadelphia 76ers -7.328   25-57
Prize rookie center Shawn Bradley missed 33 games with a knee injury as 76ers continued to struggle
1096 1997-98   Los Angeles Clippers -7.380   17-65
Veteran forward Loy Vaught's career-derailing back injury another setback for franchise
1097 1993-94   Detroit Pistons   -7.404   20-62
Final season for franchise icon Isiah Thomas
1098 1961-62   Chicago Packers   -7.416   18-62
Play of Rookie of the Year Walt Bellamy highlight of expansion season
1099 1991-92   Dallas Mavericks   -7.420   22-60
Call it the storm before the storm

1100 1958-59   Cincinnati Royals   -7.488   19-53
Royals last in league on offense and defense, and posted 2-25 record on the road
1101 2002-03   Denver Nuggets   -7.515   17-65
Season actually considered a success considering lack of name talent
1102 1991-92   Denver Nuggets   -7.527   24-58
Switched from run-and-gun team to defense-oriented squad during center Dikembe Mutombo's rookie season
1103 1992-93   Minnesota Timberwolves   -7.540   19-63
Tumbled to bottom of league's defensive standings after trading away top player Tony Campbell
1104 1979-80   Detroit Pistons   -7.579   16-66
Coach Dick Vitale free to begin his TV career after 4-8 start
1105 1989-90   New Jersey Nets   -7.667   17-65
Finished with worst record in franchise's NBA history
1106 1999-00   Golden State Warriors   -7.670   19-63
Worst defense in the league and not much offense to go with it
1107 1952-53   Philadelphia Warriors -7.671   12-57
Neil Johnston became third Warrior in seven-year BAA/NBA history to win scoring title, but team took a tumble when forward Paul Arizin began two-year stint in military
1108 1970-71   Buffalo Braves   -7.847   22-60
Ominous sign for franchise: Expansion team sold one day before its first game
1109 1981-82   Cleveland Cavaliers   -7.857   15-67
Cavaliers went through four coaches and 23 players, all to match franchise-worst record posted during team's expansion season
1110 1988-89   Charlotte Hornets   -7.873   20-62
Fashionable teal uniforms got more attention than team during franchise's expansion season
1111 1967-68   San Diego Rockets   -7.885   15-67
Expansion team's top rookie (Pat Riley) would prove better coach than player
1112 1971-72   Cleveland Cavaliers   -7.906   23-59
Overall No. 1 draft pick Austin Carr (21.2 points per game) led Cavaliers to eight-win improvement during franchise's second season

1113 1987-88 Golden State -8.124 20-62
Warriors
Traded for Ralph Sampson at midseason, but endured 22-win decline with two injury-plagued centers on roster (Joe Barry Carroll was the other)

1114 1980-81 Dallas Mavericks -8.138 15-67
Mavericks struggled during expansion season, but would improve quickly

1115 1993-94 Dallas Mavericks -8.200 13-69
Young stars Jimmy Jackson and Jamal Mashburn chafed under one-year-and-done coach Quinn Buckner

1116 2000-01 Golden State -8.220 17-65
Warriors
Worst record in franchise history

1117 1968-69 Phoenix Suns -8.222 16-66
Posted franchise's worst record during expansion season and also lost coin flip for No. 1 overall draft pick and rights to Lew Alcindor (later Kareem Abdul-Jabbar)

1118 1994-95 Minnesota -8.256 21-61
Timberwolves
Good news: Talk of moving team to New Orleans squelched. Bad news: Timberwolves made little upward movement in standings

1119 1948-49 Providence -8.327 12-48
Steamrollers
Franchise mercifully folded after posting league's worst record in two consecutive seasons

1120 1997-98 Toronto Raptors -8.418 16-66
Third-year franchise's progress derailed by squabbles among management and ownership

1121 2001-02 Chicago Bulls -8.422 21-61
Coach Tim Floyd departed after 4-21 start; ended Chicago tenure with .205 winning percentage

1122 1994-95 Los Angeles Clippers -8.475 17-65
Starters Dominique Wilkins, Ron Harper, and Mark Jackson all left before season as free agents, resulting in 0-16 start, 10-win decline in overall record

1123 1998-99 Los Angeles Clippers -8.569 9-41
Lost first 17 games of strike-shortened 50-game season

1124 1989-90 Orlando Magic -8.580 18-64
Franchise posted its worst record during its expansion season

1125 1998-99   Vancouver Grizzlies -8.582   8-42
On a 13-69 pace for a full regular season
1126 1971-72   Portland Trail Blazers -8.769   18-64
Worst record in franchise history, but forward Sidney Wicks did give Blazers two consecutive Rookie of the Year winners
1127 1972-73   Buffalo Braves   -8.788   21-61
Bob McAdoo named Rookie of the Year, but team declined by one win
1128 1998-99   Chicago Bulls   -8.835   13-37
Bulls set modern NBA record for fewest points per game during first season after mass exodus of Michael Jordan, Scottie Pippen, Dennis Rodman, and coach Phil Jackson
1129 2005-06   Portland Trail Blazers -8.926   21-61
Skidded to a 4-33 finish to conclude the least-dominant season in franchise history
1130 2000-01   Chicago Bulls   -8.933   15-67
Had three future All-Stars on roster (Elton Brand, Ron Artest, Brad Miller), but posted worst record in franchise history and ended consecutive sellouts streak at 610 games
1131 1997-98   Golden State   -9.050   19-63
              Warriors
Top scorer Latrell Sprewell suspended for last 68 games after choking coach P.J. Carlesimo
1132 1999-00   Chicago Bulls   -9.144   17-65
Elton Brand shared Rookie of the Year award, but he had little help
1133 1996-97   San Antonio Spurs   -9.205   20-62
Star center David Robinson played just six games, but franchise's worst season put Spurs in position to draft future star Tim Duncan
1134 1988-89   Los Angeles Clippers -9.282   21-61
No. 1 overall draft pick Danny Manning missed 56 games with injuries
1135 1995-96   Philadelphia 76ers   -9.435   18-64
76ers finished in last place for first time since 1975, but did wind up in position to draft future star Allen Iverson
1136 2002-03   Cleveland Cavaliers -9.436   17-65
Disastrous season put franchise in position to draft Ohio prep legend LeBron James
1137 1989-90   Miami Heat   -9.439   18-64
Improved by three wins and escaped division cellar during franchise's second season, all with a young roster

1138 1971-72   Buffalo Braves   -9.467   22-60
Randy Smith started consecutive games streak of 906 during Braves' second season

1139 2004-05   Atlanta Hawks   -9.503   13-69
Rookie Josh Smith's Slam Dunk title only highlight of worst season in franchise history

1140 1995-96   Vancouver Grizzlies -9.517   15-67
NBA single-season record 23-game losing streak lowlight of expansion season

1141 1987-88   Los Angeles Clippers -9.978   17-65
Only team in the league to average less than 100 points per game

1142 1996-97   Vancouver Grizzlies -10.040   14-68
Added rookie scoring machine Shareef Abdur-Rahim, but regressed by one win during franchise's second season

1143 1947-48   Providence Steamrollers -10.096   6-42
NBA/BAA record low for wins in a season

1144 1990-91   Denver Nuggets   -10.318   20-62
Gave up more points than any team in NBA history

1145 1999-00   Los Angeles Clippers -10.767   15-67
Assembled roster of young talent, but finished next-to-last in league on offense and defense, and last in league in wins

1146 1949-50   Denver Nuggets   -10.771   11-51
Mercifully left the league after one disastrous NBA season

1147 1986-87   Los Angeles Clippers -10.806   12-70
Least-dominant season in franchise's undistinguished history

1148 1988-89   Miami Heat   -10.913   15-67
Set NBA record with 17 consecutive losses to start expansion season

1149 1982-83   Houston Rockets   -10.986   14-68
Season after departure of star center Moses Malone; season before arrival of promising center Ralph Sampson

1150 1972-73   Philadelphia 76ers   -11.418   9-73
76ers' 9-73 record is mark all not-so-dominant teams seek to avoid

1151 1997-98   Denver Nuggets   -11.579   11-71
Matched NBA single-season record with 23 consecutive losses

1152 1970-71   Cleveland Cavaliers -11.790   15-67
Only soft expansion schedule saved Cavaliers from historically bad record

1153 1992-93   Dallas Mavericks   -14.575   11-71
Produced average point differential almost three points per game worse than any other team in league history

Conclusion

Discussing dominance: The POST formula's results

It was Benjamin Disraeli who dismissed statistics as one of the three forms of lies.

The thought here: Disraeli had some lingering bitterness over a bad grade in a math class.

Statistics in the wrong hands can prove dangerous. Statistics used properly can unveil truths about the answers to challenging questions.

The POST formula offers unbiased and accurate opinions about the NBA's best and worst teams.

The formula has no agenda. If it did, the author would have found a way to get some Indiana Pacer teams into the top 10.

The formula digests rational information and reaches reasoned conclusions. More than a few "experts" work in reverse. They come to unreasonable conclusions first and then get irrational when they seek supporting information.

The formula seeks the truths behind the answers to the NBA's most compelling questions. That's no lie.

Let the arguments continue.

Most dominant teams

1. 1970-1971 Milwaukee Bucks
2. 1995-1996 Chicago Bulls
3. 1971-1972 Los Angeles Lakers
4. 1985-1986 Boston Celtics
5. 1986-1987 Los Angeles Lakers
6. 1966-1967 Philadelphia 76ers
7. 1969-1970 New York Knickerbockers
8. 1999-2000 Los Angeles Lakers
9. 2006-2007 San Antonio Spurs
10. 1961-1962 Boston Celtics

The POST formula ranks the 1970-1971 Milwaukee Bucks, 1995-1996 Chicago Bulls, and 1971-1972 Los Angeles Lakers head and shoulders above every other team in NBA history.

All three teams enjoyed an average point differential of more than +12.0 points per game. No other team in league history has an average point differential greater than +11.1 points per game.

The 1970-1971 Milwaukee Bucks get the nod as the most dominant team in NBA history by a slim margin over the 1995-1996 Chicago Bulls because Milwaukee played a tougher schedule.

On a representative night, the 1995-1996 Bulls would win by 12.2 points against a team that would finish with a 41-41 record. On a representative night, the 1970-1971 Bucks also would win by 12.2 points, but they would do it against a team with a 45-37 record.

Most dominant teams not to win a championship

1. 1946-1947 Washington Capitols
2. 1993-1994 Seattle Supersonics
3. 1985-1986 Milwaukee Bucks
4. 1990-1991 Portland Trail Blazers
5. 1996-1997 Utah Jazz

The 1946-1947 Washington Capitols should have won the championship in the first season for the league now known as the NBA. The Capitols still stand as the most dominant team not to win a league title, according to the POST formula.

Washington set records for best single-season winning percentage (a 49-11 record) and best single-season average point differential (+9.9 points per game) that stood for two decades.

The Capitols fell short of the championship, in part because of a quirky playoff format that pitted Washington against the Western Division champion Chicago Stags in the first round of the postseason. The Stags matched up well against the Capitols and eliminated Washington in six games.

Least dominant teams to win a championship

1. 1957-1958 St. Louis Hawks
2. 1977-1978 Washington Bullets
3. 1954-1955 Syracuse Nationals
4. 1975-1976 Boston Celtics
5. 1994-1995 Houston Rockets

The 1957-1958 St. Louis Hawks hold a respected place in NBA history because they were one of just two non-Boston Celtic teams to win a championship during Boston's run of 11 titles in 13 years during the Bill Russell era.

The POST formula exposes the 1957-1958 Hawks as the least dominant team to claim an NBA championship.

St. Louis went 41-31 during the regular season, a pace that would yield a 47-35 record over a modern 82-game schedule. No other team in the Hawks' division finished with a winning record. St. Louis did defeat Boston in six games in the NBA Finals, but the Hawks needed a stellar effort from star forward Bob Pettit and injuries to key Celtic players to eke out a victory in the championship series.

Least dominant teams

1,153. 1992-1993 Dallas Mavericks
1,152. 1970-1971 Cleveland Cavaliers
1,151. 1997-1998 Denver Nuggets
1,150. 1972-1973 Philadelphia 76ers
1,149. 1982-1983 Houston Rockets
1,148. 1988-1989 Miami Heat
1,147. 1986-1987 Los Angeles Clippers
1,146. 1949-1950 Denver Nuggets
1,145. 1999-2000 Los Angeles Clippers
1,144. 1990-1991 Denver Nuggets

Last and least, the POST formula identifies the 1992-1993 Dallas Mavericks as the least dominant team in NBA history.

The 1992-1993 Mavericks went 11-71. They produced an average point differential of -15.2 points per game, more than three points worse than any team in NBA history.

The 1970-1971 Cleveland Cavaliers rank as the second-worst team in league history because they managed just 15 wins against the soft schedule drawn up for the team's expansion season.

The 1972-1973 Philadelphia 76ers went 9-73 and hold the record for fewest wins in a modern NBA season. Yet the POST formula rates the 1972-1973 76ers as just the fourth-worst team of all time because they played a reasonably difficult schedule.

Selected bibliography

www.basketball-reference.com

www.basketballreference.com

www.nba.com

Bjarkman, Peter C. *The Biographical History of Basketball.* Lincolnwood, Ill.: Masters Press, 2000.

Bjarkman, Peter C. *The Encyclopedia of Pro Basketball Team Histories.* New York: Carroll & Graf, 1994.

Carter, Craig, and Rob Reheuser. *The Sporting News Official NBA Guide.* St. Louis, Mo.: The Sporting News, 2002.

Devaney, John. *Alcindor and the Big O.* New York: Lancer Books, 1971.

Gould, Todd. *Pioneers of the Hardwood: Indiana and the Birth of Professional Basketball.* Bloomington, Ind.: University Press, 1998.

Hubbard, Jan. *The Official NBA Encyclopedia.* New York: Doubleday, 2000.

Lazenby, Roland. *Chicago Bulls: The Authorized Pictorial.* Arlington, Texas: Summit Publishing Group, 1997.

Lazenby, Roland. *The Lakers: A Basketball Journey.* New York: St. Martin's Press, 1993.

Lynch, Wayne. *Season of the 76ers: The Story of Wilt Chamberlain and the 1967 NBA Champion Philadelphia 76ers.* New York: Thomas Dunne/St. Martin's Press, 2002.

May, Peter. *The Last Banner: The Story of the 1985-86 Celtics, the NBA's Greatest Team of All Time.* New York: Simon & Schuster, 1996.

Pluto, Terry. *Tall Tales: The Glory Years of the NBA*. New York: Simon & Schuster, 1992.

Sachare, Alex. *The Chicago Bulls Encyclopedia*. Lincolnwood, Ill.: Contemporary Books, 1999.

Smith, Ron. *The Ultimate Encyclopedia of Basketball*. Italy: Carlton Books, 1996.

Vancil, Mark. *NBA at 50*. New York: Random House, Inc., 1996.

978-0-595-45959-9
0-595-45959-5

Lightning Source UK Ltd.
Milton Keynes UK
23 February 2010

150514UK00002B/84/A